Table of Contents

World History

Four Great Revolutions in Thought and Religion

From Chapter 2 of *The Heritage of World Civilizations*, Ninth Edition. Albert M. Craig, William A. Graham, Donald Kagan, Steven Ozment, Frank M. Turner. Copyright © 2011 by Pearson Education, Inc. Published by Pearson Prentice Hall.

Four Great Revolutions in Thought and Religion

The Way. Detail from a twelfth-century Daoist scroll, showing the feats of the "Eight Immortals," the most famous characters in Daoist folklore. The landscape evokes the ineffability and mystery of Dao, or "the way."

ALL HUMAN CULTURES DEVELOP religious or philosophical systems. Some scientists have even debated whether humans are somehow "hard-wired" biologically to tend toward religious beliefs. Regardless of the outcome of that debate, clearly religion and philosophy meet profound human psychological needs. They offer people explanations of where they and their societies came from, why they exist, and what the future holds for them, in this life and beyond. ■

Comparing the Four Great Revolutions

The most straightforward case is that of China. Both geographically and culturally, its philosophical breakthrough grew directly out of the earlier river valley civilization. No such continuity existed elsewhere in the world. The natural barriers of the Central Asian steppes, mountain ranges, and deserts allowed China to develop its own unique culture relatively undisturbed and uninfluenced by outside forces.

The sharpest contrast with China is the Indian subcontinent, which lacked geographic and cultural continuity. By the middle of the second millennium B.C.E., the Indus civilization had collapsed. It had been replaced by the culture of the Indo-Aryan warriors who swept in from the northwest. Absorbing many particulars from the earlier tradition, they built a new civilization on the plains farther east along the mighty Ganges River. From this latter civilization there emerged the great traditions of Indian thought and religion.

In southwest Asia and along the shores of the Mediterranean, the transition was more complex than that in either China or India. No direct line of development can be traced from the Nile civilization of ancient Egypt or the civilization of the Tigris-Euphrates river valley to Greek philosophy or to Judaic monotheism. Rather, the ancient river valley civilizations evolved into a complex amalgam that we call ancient Near Eastern civilization. This cosmopolitan culture included diverse older religious, mythical, and cosmological traditions, as well as newer mystery cults. The Greeks and the ancient Hebrews were two among many outside peoples who invaded this region, settled down, and both absorbed and contributed to the composite civilization.

Judaic monotheism and Greek philosophy—representing different outgrowths of this amalgam—were each important in their own right. They have continued as vital elements in Western and Near Eastern civilizations. But their greatest influence occurred centuries later when they helped shape first Christianity and then Islam. The major cultural zones in world history since the mid–first millennium C.E. are the Chinese, the Indian, the Western Christian, and the Islamic. But the latter two were formed much later than the Chinese and the Indian. They represent a second-stage formation of which the first stage comprised the Judaic and the Greek.

Philosophy in China

The beauty of ancient Shang bronzes is breathtaking, but they also have an archaic strangeness. Like the Olmec stone sculpture of prehistoric America, they are products of a culture so far removed from our own as to be almost incomprehensible. By contrast, the humanism of the Confucian writings and the poetry of the Eastern Zhou (771–256 B.C.E.) speak to us directly. However much the philosophies of these centuries grew out of the earlier matrix of archaic culture, they mark a break with it and the beginning of what we think of today as the Chinese tradition.

The background of the philosophical revolution in China was the disintegration of the old Zhou society. New territorial states replaced the many Zhou city-states. Ruthless, upstart, peasant armies, augmented by an Early Iron Age cavalry armed with crossbows, began to replace the old nobility, who had gone to war in chariots. A rising merchant class disrupted the formerly stable agricultural economy. As the old etiquette crumbled and old rituals lost their force, a search began for new principles by which to re-create a peaceful society and new rules by which to live.

Read the Document
Origins of the Chinese Civilization – Confucianism, Daoism or Legalism? at **MyHistoryLab.com**

Of the four great revolutions in thought of the first millennium B.C.E., the Chinese revolution was more akin, perhaps, to the Greek than to the Indian religious transformations or to Judaic monotheism. Just as Greece had a gamut of philosophies, so in China there were the "one hundred schools." (When Mao Zedong said in 1956, "Let the one hundred flowers bloom"—encouraging a momentary easing of intellectual repression—he was referring to the creative era of Zhou philosophy.) Whereas Greek thought was speculative and more concerned with the world of nature, Chinese thought was sociopolitical and more practical. Even the Daoist sages, who were inherently apolitical, found it necessary to offer a political philosophy. Chinese thought also had far greater staying power than Greek thought, which only a few centuries after the glory of Athens was submerged by Christianity. Greek thought became the handmaiden of theology and did not reemerge as an independent force until the Renaissance. In contrast, Chinese philosophy, though challenged by Buddhism, remained dominant until the early twentieth century. How were these early philosophies able to maintain such a grip on China when the cultures of every other part of the world fell under the sway of religions?

Part of the answer is that most Chinese philosophy had a religious dimension. But it was another kind of religion, with assumptions different from those derived from Judaic roots. In the Christian or Islamic worldview, there is a God who, however concerned with humankind, is not of this world. This worldview leads to dualism, the distinction between an otherworld, which is supernatural, and this world, which is natural.

In the Chinese worldview, the two spheres are not separate: The cosmos is single, continuous, and nondualistic. It includes heaven, earth, and humans. Heaven is above. Earth is below. Humans, ideally guided by a wise

Philosophy and Religion

Greece
Near East
India *China*

Between 800 and 200 B.C.E., four philosophical or religious revolutions occurred that shaped the subsequent history of the world. The names of many involved in these revolutions are world-famous—Socrates, Plato, Aristotle, the Buddha, Isaiah, and Confucius. All the revolutions occurred in or near the four heartland areas in which the river valley civilizations had appeared 1,500 or more years earlier. The transition from the early river valley civilizations to the intellectual and spiritual breakthroughs of the middle of the first millennium B.C.E. is schematized in Figure 1.

Before considering each of the original breakthroughs that occurred during this time period, we might ask whether they have anything in common. Five points are worth noting.

1. All the philosophical or religious revolutions occurred in or near the original river valley civilizations. These areas contained the most advanced cultures of the ancient world. They had sophisticated agriculture, cities with many literate inhabitants, and specialized trades and professions. In short, they had the material preconditions for breakthroughs in religion and thought.

2. Each of the revolutions in thought and ethos was born of a crisis in the ancient world. The appearance of iron meant better tools and weapons and, by extension, greater riches and more powerful armies. Old societies began to change and then to disintegrate. Old aristocratic and priestly codes of behavior broke down, producing a demand for more universalized rules of behavior—in other words, for ethics. The very relation of humans to nature or to the universe seemed to be changing. This predicament led to new visions of social and political order. The similarities between the Jewish Messiah, the Chinese sage-king, the Indian model of the *Chakravartin*, or Universal Ruler, and Plato's philosopher-king are more

and virtuous ruler, stand in between and regulate or harmonize the cosmological forces of heaven and earth by the power of their virtue and by performing the sacrifices. The forms that this cosmology took under the last Manchu Dynasty (1644–1912) can be seen today in the city of Beijing: The Temple of Heaven is in the south; the Temple of Earth is in the northeast; and the Imperial Palace is—symbolically, at least—in between. To say that the emperor's sacrifices at the Temple of Heaven were secular (and, therefore, not religious) or religious (and not secular) misses the point. It projects our own dualistic assumptions onto China. Similarly, when we speak of the Daoist sage becoming one with nature, it is not the nature of a twenty-first-century natural scientist; it is a nature that contains metaphysical and cosmological forces that our worldview might label as religious.

Most of the one hundred schools—if, in fact, there were that many—are unknown today. Many works disappeared in the book burning of the Qin Dynasty (256–221 B.C.E.). But apart from the three major schools of Confucianism, Daoism, and Legalism, texts of enough other schools have survived to convey a sense of the range and vitality of Zhou thought:

1. *Rhetoricians.* This school taught the arts of persuasion to be used in diplomatic negotiations. Its principal work instructed the rulers of territorial states by using the historical anecdote. A practical work, it was popular for its humor and lively style.

2. *Logicians.* This school taught logic and relativity. For example, one proposition was "The south has no limit and has a limit." Another was "A white horse is not a horse": The concept of *horse* is not the same as the concept of *white horse*.

3. *Strategists.* *The Art of War* by Sunzi became the classic of military science in China and is studied today by guerrillas and in military academies around the world. It praises the general who wins victories without battles but it also talks of organizing states for war, of supply, of spies, and of propaganda.

4. *Cosmologists.* This school described the functions of the cosmos in terms of *yin* and *yang*, the complementary negative and positive forces of nature, and in terms of the five elements (metal, wood, earth, fire, and water). Its ideas were later absorbed by Confucian thinkers.

5. *Mohists.* Mozi (470–391 B.C.E.) was an early critic of Confucius. His goals were peace, wealth, and the

than accidental. Each responded to a crisis in a society of the ancient world. Each would reconnect ethics to history and restore order to a troubled society.

3. The number of philosophical and religious revolutions can be counted on the fingers of one hand. The reason is not that humans' creativity dried up after 200 B.C.E., but that subsequent breakthroughs and advances tended to occur within the original traditions, which, absorbing new energies, continued to evolve.

4. After the first- and second-stage transformations, much of the cultural history of the world involves the spread of cultures derived from these original heartlands to ever-wider spheres. Christianity spread to northern and eastern Europe, the Americas, and parts of Asia and Africa; Buddhism to central, southeastern, and eastern Asia; Confucianism to Korea, Vietnam, and Japan; and Islam to Africa, southeastern Europe, and southern, central, and southeastern Asia. Sometimes the spread was the result of movements of people; other areas were like dry grasslands needing only the spark of the new ideas to be ignited. Typically, the process spread out over centuries.

5. Once a cultural pattern was set, it usually endured. Each major culture was resistant to the others and was only rarely displaced. Even in modern times, although the culture of modern science and the learning associated with it, have penetrated every cultural zone, have reshaped—and are reshaping, not displacing—the major cultures. Only Confucianism, the most secular of the traditional cultures, crumbled at the touch of science, and even its ethos remains a potent force in East Asian societies. These major cultures endured because they were not only responses to particular crises, but also attempts to answer universal questions concerning the human condition: What are human beings? What is our relation to the universe? How should we relate to others?

Focus Questions

■ Why do you think so many revolutionary philosophical and religious ideas emerged at about the same time in many different regions? Do these ideas share any fundamental concerns?

■ Why is this period in Eurasian history sometimes referred to by the philosopher Karl Jaspen's term "axial age"?

increase of population. He taught an ethic of universal love—to overcome a selfish human nature. He preached discipline and austerity and was critical of whatever lacked utility, including music and the other arts, elaborate funerals, wasteful rites, and, above all, war. To achieve his goals, Mozi argued for a strong state: Subjects must obey their rulers, who in turn must obey Heaven. Heaven would punish evil and reward good. To promote peace, Mozi organized his followers into military units to aid states that were attacked.

Confucianism

Confucius was born in 551 B.C.E. in a minor state in northeastern China. He probably belonged to the lower nobility or the knightly class, because he received an education in writing, music, and rituals. His father died when Confucius was young, so he may have known privation. He made his living by teaching. He traveled with his disciples from state to state, seeking a ruler who would put his ideas into practice. Although he may once have held a minor position, his ideas were rejected as impractical. He died in 479 B.C.E.,

Confucius, depicted wearing the robes of a scholar of a later age.
Collection of the National Palace Museum, Taipei, Taiwan.

National Palace Museum, Taipei, Taiwan, Republic of China

honored as a teacher and scholar but having failed to find a ruler to advise. The name Confucius is the Latinized form of Kong Fuzi, or Master Kong, as he is known in China.

We know of Confucius only through the *Analects*, his sayings collected by his disciples, or perhaps by their disciples. They are mostly in the form of "The Master said," followed by his words. (See Document, "Confucius Defines the Gentleman.") The picture that emerges is that of a man of moderation, propriety, optimism, good sense, and wisdom. In an age of cruelty and superstition, he was humane, rational, and upright, demanding much of others and more of himself. Asked about death, he replied, "You do not understand even life. How can you understand death?"[1] Asked about how to serve the spirits and the gods, in which he did not disbelieve, he answered, "You are not able even to serve man. How can you serve the spirits?"

Confucius described himself as a transmitter and a conservator of tradition, not an innovator. He idealized the early Shang and Zhou kings as paragons of virtue and saw early Zhou society as a golden age. He sought the secrets of this golden age in its writings. Some of these writings, along with later texts, became the Confucian classics, which through most of Chinese history had an authority not unlike Scripture in the West.

•●─ Read the Document
Confucous, selections from the
Analects at **MyHistoryLab.com**

Five of the thirteen classics were the following:

1. *The Book of Changes* (also known as the *Classic of Divination*). A handbook for diviners, this book was later seen as containing metaphysical truths about the universe.

2. *The Book of History.* This book contains documents and speeches from the early Zhou, some of which are authentic. Chinese tradition holds that it was edited by Confucius. It was interpreted as the record of sage-kings.

3. *The Book of Poetry.* This book contains some 300 poems from the early Zhou. Representing a sophisticated literary tradition, it includes love songs as well as poems of friendship, ritual, and politics. Many were given political and moral interpretations in later times.

4. *The Book of Rites.* This book includes both rituals and rules of etiquette. Rites were important to Confucians, both because they were a support for proper behavior and because they were seen as corresponding to the forces of nature.

5. *The Spring and Autumn Annals.* A brief record of the major occurrences from 722 to 481 B.C.E. in the state where Confucius was born, this book, according to Chinese tradition, was edited by Confucius and reflected his moral judgments on past historical figures.

Basing his teachings on these writings, Confucius proposed to resolve the turmoil of his own age by a return to the good old ways of the early Zhou. When asked about government, he said, "Let the ruler be a ruler, the subject a subject, the father a father, the son a son." (The five Confucian relationships were ruler–subject, father–son, husband–wife, older brother–younger brother, and friend–friend.) If everyone fulfilled the duties of his or her status, then harmony would prevail. Confucius understood the fundamental truth that the well-being of a society depends on the morality of its members. His vision was that of an unbroken social harmony extending from the individual family member to the monarch.

•●─ Read the Document
Confucianism: Government and
the Superior (551-479 B.C.E.) at
MyHistoryLab.com

But a return to the early Zhou was impossible. China was undergoing a dynamic transition from hundreds of small city-states to a few large territorial states. Specialized classes were appearing. Old rituals no longer worked. It was thus not enough to stress basic human relationships. The genius of Confucius was to transform the old aristocratic code into a new ethic that any educated Chinese could practice. His reinterpretation of the early Zhou tradition can be seen in the concept of the junzi. This term literally meant "the son of the ruler" (or the aristocrat). Confucius redefined it to mean one of noble behavior, a person with the inner virtues of humanity, integrity, righteousness, altruism, and loyalty, and an outward demeanor and propriety to match.

This redefinition was not unlike the change in the meaning of *gentleman* in England from "one who is gentle-born" to "one who is gentle-behaved." But whereas *gentleman* remained a fairly superficial category in the West, in China *junzi* went deeper. Confucius saw ethics as grounded in nature. The true gentleman was in touch with his own basic nature, which in turn was a part of the cosmic order. Confucius expressed this saying: "Heaven is the author of the virtue that is in me." Confucius's description of his own passage through life goes far beyond good manners: "At fifteen I set my heart on learning; at thirty I took my stand; at forty I came to be free from doubts; at fifty I understood the Decree of Heaven; at sixty my ear was attuned; at seventy I followed my heart's desire without overstepping the line."

Confucius often contrasted the gentleman with the small or common person. The gentleman, educated in the classics and cultivating the Way, understands moral

---

[1] This quotation and all quotations from Confucius in this passage are from Confucius, *The Analects*, trans. by D. C. Lau (New York: Penguin Books, 1979).

Document   Confucius Defines the Gentleman

For more than 2,000 years in China, the cultural ideal was the gentleman, who combined knowledge of the ancient sages with an inner morality and outer propriety.

■ *How does the injunction "to repay an injury with straightness" compare to the Christian injunction to turn the other cheek? Which do you think is more appropriate?*

The Master said, "I never enlighten anyone who has not been driven to distraction by trying to understand a difficulty or who has not got into a frenzy trying to put his ideas into words.

"When I have pointed out one corner of a square to anyone and he does not come back with the other three, I will not point it out to him a second time."

The Master said, "Yu, shall I tell you what it is to know? To say you know when you know, and to say you do not when you do not, that is knowledge."

The Master said, "Is it not a pleasure, having learned something, to try it out at due intervals? Is it not a joy to have friends come from afar? Is it not gentlemanly not to take offence when others fail to appreciate your abilities?"

Someone said, "Repay an injury with a good turn. What do you think of this saying?" The Master said, "What, then, do you repay a good turn with? You repay an injury with straightness, but you repay a good turn with a good turn."

Lin Fang asked about the basis of the rites. The Master said, "A noble question indeed! With the rites, it is better to err on the side of frugality than on the side of extravagance; in mourning, it is better to err on the side of grief than on the side of formality."

The Master said, "I suppose I should give up hope. I have yet to meet the man who is as fond of virtue as he is of beauty in women."

The Master said, "The gentleman agrees with others without being an echo. The small man echoes without being in agreement."

The Master said, "The gentleman is at ease without being arrogant; the small man is arrogant without being at ease."

The Master said, "There is no point in seeking the views of a gentleman who, though he sets his heart on the Way, is ashamed of poor food and poor clothes."

Source: Confucius, *The Analects,* trans. by D. C. Lau (New York: Penguin Classics, 1979). © D. C. Lau, 1979.

---

action. The common people, in contrast, "can be made to follow a path but not to understand it." Good government for Confucius depended on the appointment to office of good men, who would serve as examples for the multitude: "Just desire the good yourself and the common people will be good. The virtue of the gentleman is like wind; the virtue of the small man is like grass. Let the wind blow over the grass and it is sure to bend." Beyond the gentleman was the sage-king, who possessed an almost mystical virtue and power. For Confucius, the early Zhou kings were clearly sages. But he wrote, "I have no hopes of meeting a sage. I would be content if I met someone who is a gentleman." Confucianism was not adopted as the official philosophy of China until the second century B.C.E., during the Han Dynasty (202 B.C.E.–9 C.E.). But two other important Confucian philosophers had appeared in the meantime. Mencius (370–290 B.C.E.) represents the idealistic

extension of Confucius's thought. His interpretation was accepted during most of history. He is famous for his argument that humans tend toward the good just as water runs downward. The role of education, therefore, is to uncover and cultivate that innate goodness. Moreover, just as humans tend toward the good, so does Heaven possess a moral will. The will of Heaven is that a government should see to the education and well-being of its people. The rebellion of people against a government is the primary evidence that Heaven has withdrawn its mandate. At times in Chinese history, concern for the people was given only lip service. In fact, rebellions occurred more often against weak governments than against harsh ones. But

◆◆◆ Read the Document
Confucian Political Philosophy: An Excerpt from Mencius at
MyHistoryLab.com

the idea that government ought to care for the people became a permanent part of the Confucian tradition.

Chronology

China

551–479 B.C.E.	Confucius
370–290 B.C.E.	Mencius
Fourth century B.C.E.	Laozi
221 B.C.E.	Qin unifies China

The other influential Confucian philosopher was Xunzi (300–237 B.C.E.), who represents a tough-minded extension of Confucius's thought. Xunzi felt Heaven was amoral, indifferent to whether China was ruled by a tyrant or a sage. He believed human nature was bad or at least that desires and emotions, if unchecked and unrefined, led to social conflict. So he emphasized etiquette and education as restraints on an unruly human nature, and good institutions, including punishments and rewards, as a means of shaping behavior. These ideas influenced the thinkers of the Legalist school.

Daoism

It is often said that the Chinese have been Confucian while in office and Daoist in their private lives. **Daoism** offered a refuge from the burden of social responsibilities. The classics of the school are the *Laozi*, dating from the fourth century B.C.E., and the *Zhuangzi*, dating from about a century later.

The central concept of Daoism is the *Dao*, or Way. It is mysterious, ineffable, and cannot be named. It is the creator of the universe, the sustainer of the universe, and the process or flux of the universe. The *Dao* functions on a cosmic, not a human, scale. As the *Laozi* put it, "Heaven and Earth are ruthless, and treat the myriad creatures as straw dogs; the sage (in accord with the *Dao*) is ruthless, and treats the people as straw dogs."[2]

What does it mean to be a sage? How does a human join the rhythms of nature? The answer given by the *Laozi* is by regaining or returning to an original simplicity. Various similes describe this state: "to return to the infinite," "to return to being a babe," or "to return to being the uncarved block." To attain this state, one must "learn to be without learning." Knowledge is bad because it creates distinctions and because it leads to the succession of ideas and images that interfere with participation in the *Dao*. One must also learn to

Laozi, the founder of Daoism, as imagined by a later artist. *Courtesy of the Freer Gallery of Art, Smithsonian Institution, Washington, DC (72.1).*

Courtesy of the Freer Gallery of Art, Smithsonian Institution, Washington, D.C. (72.1)

be without desires beyond the immediate and simple needs of nature: "The nameless uncarved block is but freedom from desire."

If the sage treats the people as straw dogs, it would appear that he is beyond good and evil. But elsewhere in the *Laozi*, the sage is described as one who "excels in saving people." If not a contradiction, this is at least a paradox. The resolution is that the sage is clearly beyond morality but is not immoral or even amoral. On the contrary, by being in harmony with the *Dao*, the sage is impeccably moral—as one who clings to the forms of morality or makes morality a goal could never be. So in the *Laozi* it is written, "Exterminate benevolence, discard rectitude, and the people will again be filial; exterminate ingenuity, discard profit, and there will be no more thieves and bandits." In this formulation we also see the basis for the political philosophy of Daoism, which can be summed up as "not doing" (*wuwei*). This means something between "doing nothing" and "being, but not acting." In this concept, there is some overlap with Confucianism. The Confucian sage-king exerts a moral force by dint of his internal accord with nature. A perfect Confucian sage could rule without doing. Confucius said, "If there was a ruler who achieved order without taking any action, it was, perhaps, Shun [the sage-emperor]. There was nothing for him to do but to hold himself in a respectful posture and to face due

> ◆•━ Read the Document
> Laozi, excerpt from Tao Te Ching, "The Unvarying Way" at **MyHistoryLab.com**

---

[2] All quotations from the *Laozi* are from *Tao Te Ching*, trans. by D. C. Lau (New York: Penguin Books, 1963).

Document Daoism

Can inner, transformative, religious experience take people beyond everyday worldly concerns and imbue them with moral charisma or moral authority? What other religions might call "supernatural," Daoism sees as truly natural.

■ *How does the Way in Daoism compare with Confucius's use of the same term?*

LAOZI TELLS OF THE WAY OF THE SAGE

*The way that can be spoken of
Is not the constant way;
The name that can be named
Is not the constant name.
The nameless was the beginning of heaven and earth;
The named was the mother of the myriad creatures.
The spirit of the valley never dies
This is called the mysterious female.
The gateway of the mysterious female
Is called the root of heaven and earth.
Dimly visible, it seems as if it were there,
Yet use will never drain it.
There is a thing confusedly formed,
Born before heaven and earth.
Silent and void
It stands alone and does not change,
Goes round and does not weary.
It is capable of being the mother of the world.
I know not its name
So I style it "the way."*

When the way prevails in the empire, fleetfooted horses are relegated to ploughing the fields; when the way does not prevail in the empire, war-horses breed on the border.

One who knows does not speak; one who speaks does not know.

*Therefore the sage puts his person last and it comes first,
Treats it as extraneous to himself and it is preserved.*

Is it not because he is without thought of self that he is able to accomplish his private ends?

ZHUANGZI COMPARES GOVERNMENTAL OFFICE TO A DEAD RAT

When Hui Tzu was prime minister of Liang, Chuang Tzu (Zhuangzi) set off to visit him. Someone said to Hui Tzu, "Chuang Tzu is coming because he wants to replace you as prime minister!" With this Hui Tzu was filled with alarm and searched all over the state for three days and three nights trying to find Chuang Tzu. Chuang Tzu then came to see him and said, "In the south there is a bird called the Yuan-ch'u— I wonder if you've ever heard of it? The Yuan-ch'u rises up from the South Sea and flies to the North Sea, and it will rest on nothing but the Wu-t'ung tree, eat nothing but the fruit of the Lien, and drink only from springs of sweet water. Once there was an owl who had gotten hold of a half-rotten old rat, and as the Yuan-ch'u passed by, it raised its head, looked up at the Yuan-ch'u, and said, 'Shoo!' Now that you have this Liang state of yours, are you trying to shoo me?"

Source: From *The Analects*, translated by D.C. Lau, © 1979 (Penguin Classics) Reprinted by permission.

south." In Daoism, all true sages had this Shun-like power to rule without action: "The Way never acts yet nothing is left undone. Should lords and princes be able to hold fast to it, the myriad creatures will be transformed of their own accord." Or, says the *Laozi*, "I am free from desire and the people of themselves become simple like the uncarved block." The sage acts without acting, and "when his task is accomplished and his work is done, the people will say, 'It happened to us naturally.'" (See Document, "Daoism.")

Along with the basic Daoist prescription of becoming one with the *Dao* are two other assumptions or principles. One is that any action pushed to an extreme will initiate a counter-vailing reaction in the direction of the opposite extreme. The other is that too much government, even good government, can become oppressive by its very weight. As the *Laozi* put it, "The people are hungry; it is because those in authority eat up too much in taxes that the people are hungry. The people are difficult to govern; it is because those in authority are too fond of action that the people are difficult to govern." Elsewhere, the same idea was expressed in even homelier terms: "Govern a large state as you would cook small fish," that is, without too much stirring.

●●[Read the Document
Daoism: The Classic of the Way and Virtue (500s-400s B.C.E.)" at **MyHistoryLab.com**

Document Legalism

According to Legalism, the state can only regulate behavior; it cannot affect the inner dimensions of human life. Furthermore, rewards and punishments are far more efficient in controlling behavior than moral appeals.

■ *Do the tenets of Legalism have any modern parallels? What do you think of Legalism as a philosophy of government? As an approach to the problem of crime? How does Legalism compare with other approaches to law, leadership, and government?*

HAN FEIZI ARGUES FOR THE EFFICACY OF PUNISHMENTS

Now take a young fellow who is a bad character. His parents may get angry at him, but he never makes any change. The villagers may reprove him, but he is not moved. His teachers and elders may admonish him, but he never reforms. The love of his parents, the efforts of the villagers, and the wisdom of his teachers and elders—all the three excellent disciplines are applied to him, and yet not even a hair on his shins is altered. It is only after the district magistrate sends out his soldiers and in the name of the law searches for wicked individuals that the young man becomes afraid and changes his ways and alters his deeds. So while the love of parents is not sufficient to discipline the children, the severe penalties of the district magistrate are. This is because men became naturally spoiled by love, but are submissive to authority. . . .

That being so, rewards should be rich and certain so that the people will be attracted by them; punishments should be severe and definite so that the people will fear them; and laws should be uniform and steadfast so that the people will be familiar with them. Consequently, the sovereign should show no wavering in bestowing rewards and grant no pardon in administering punishments, and he should add honor to rewards and disgrace to punishments—when this is done, then both the worthy and the unworthy will want to exert themselves. . . .

●—[Read the Document
The Way of the State
(475-221 B.C.E.) Legalism at
MyHistoryLab.com

HAN FEIZI ATTACKS CONFUCIANISM

There was once a man of Sung who tilled his field. In the midst of his field stood the stump of a tree, and one day a hare, running at full speed, bumped into the stump, broke its neck, and died. Thereupon the man left his plow and kept watch at the stump, hoping that he would get another hare. But he never caught another hare, and was only ridiculed by the people of Sung. Now those who try to rule the people of the present age with the conduct of government of the early kings are all doing exactly the same thing as that fellow who kept watch by the stump. . . .

Those who are ignorant about government insistently say: "Win the hearts of the people." If order could be procured by winning the hearts of the people, then even the wise ministers Yi Yin and Kuan Chung would be of no use. For all that the ruler would need to do would be just to listen to the people. Actually, the intelligence of the people is not to be relied upon any more than the mind of a baby. If the baby does not have his head shaved, his sores will recur; if he does not have his boil cut open, his illness will go from bad to worse. However, in order to shave his head or open the boil someone has to hold the baby while the affectionate mother is performing the work, and yet he keeps crying and yelling incessantly. The baby does not understand that suffering a small pain is the way to obtain a great benefit.

Now, the sovereign urges the tillage of land and the cultivation of pastures for the purpose of increasing production for the people, but they think the sovereign is cruel. The sovereign regulates penalties and increases punishments for the purpose of repressing the wicked, but the people think the sovereign is severe. Again he levies taxes in cash and in grain to fill up the granaries and treasuries in order to relieve famine and provide for the army, but they think the sovereign is greedy. Finally, he insists upon universal military training without personal favoritism, and urges his forces to fight hard in order to take the enemy captive, but the people think the sovereign is violent. These four measures are methods for attaining order and maintaining peace, but the people are too ignorant to appreciate them.

Source: From *Sources of Chinese Tradition,* trans. by William Theodore de Bary. © 1960 by Columbia University Press. Reprinted by permission of the publisher.

Legalism

A third great current in classical Chinese thought, and by far the most influential in its own age, was **Legalism**. Like the philosophers of other schools, the Legalists were concerned with ending the wars that plagued China. True peace, they believed, required a united country and a strong state. They favored conscription and considered war a means of extending state power.

The Legalists did not seek a model in the distant past. In ancient times, said one, there were fewer people and more food, so it was easier to rule; different conditions require new principles of government. Nor did the Legalists model their state on a heavenly order of values. Human nature is selfish, argued both of the leading Legalists, Han Feizi (d. 233 B.C.E.) and Li Si (d. 208 B.C.E.). It is human to like rewards or pleasure and to dislike punishments or pain. If laws are severe and impartial, if what strengthens the state is rewarded and what weakens the state is punished, then a strong state and a good society will ensue.

Laws, therefore, should contain incentives for loyalty and bravery in battle, and for obedience, diligence, and frugality in everyday life. The Legalists despised merchants as parasites and approved of productive farmers. They particularly despised purveyors of doctrines different from their own and were critical of rulers who honored philosophers while ignoring their philosophies.

Legalism was the philosophy of the state of Qin, which destroyed the Zhou in 256 B.C.E. and unified China in 221 B.C.E. Because Qin laws were cruel and severe, and because Legalism put human laws above an ethic modeled on Heaven, later generations of Chinese have denounced its doctrines. They saw it, not without justification, as a philosophy that consumed its founders: Han Feizi became an official of the Qin state but was eventually poisoned in a prison cell by Li Si, who was jealous of his growing influence. Li Si, although he became prime minister of Qin, was killed in 208 B.C.E. in a political struggle with a court eunuch. Yet for all the abuse heaped on Legalist doctrines, its legacy of administrative and criminal laws became a vital part of subsequent dynastic China. Even Confucian statesmen could not do without them.

Read the Document
Li Si and the Legalist Policies of Qin Shihuang (280-208 B.C.E.) at **MyHistoryLab.com**

Religion in India

By 400 B.C.E., new social and religious forms took shape on the Indian subcontinent that drew both on the older traditions of the Aryan noble and priestly elites and on non-Aryan ideas and practices. This tradition took its classical "Indian" shape in the early first millennium C.E. when its fundamental institutions and ideas came to prevail virtually throughout the subcontinent. Despite staggering internal diversity and divisions, and long periods of foreign rule, this Indian culture has survived for over 2,000 years as a coherent tradition of cultural heritage, social organization, and religious worldview.

"Hindu" and "Indian"

Indian culture and tradition include more than what the word **Hindu** commonly implies today. Earlier, *Hindu* simply meant "Indian." Taken from the Indo-Iranian name for the Indus, it was the term outsiders, like the Persians and the Greeks, used for the people or land of the subcontinent. Later, first invading Muslims and then Europeans used *Hindu* to characterize the most prominent religious and social institutions of India as a whole. Heading the list of such "Hindu" institutions were the concept of transmigration, the sacredness of the Vedas and the cow, worship of Shiva and Vishnu, and caste distinctions. Most Indians in the past 2,500 years have accepted these institutions, but Indian Buddhists, Jains, Muslims, Sikhs, and Christians have rejected some or all of them.

Hindu is not a term for any single or uniform religious community. "Hindu" religion and culture lump together an immense diversity of social, racial, linguistic, and religious groups.

Indian, on the other hand, commonly refers today to all native inhabitants of the subcontinent, whatever their beliefs. In this book we shall generally use the term *Indian* in this inclusive sense when referring to the subcontinent or its peoples. However, for the period before the arrival of Muslim culture (ca. 1000 C.E.), we will use *Indian* also to refer to the distinctively Indian tradition of thought and culture that began around the middle of the first millennium B.C.E. and achieved its classical formulation in the Hindu society and religion of the first millennium C.E.

Historical Background

In the late Vedic or Brahmanic period, a priest-centered cult dominated the upper classes of Aryanized northern Indian society. By the sixth century B.C.E., this had become an elite, esoteric cult to which most people had little or no access. Elaborate animal sacrifices on behalf of Aryan rulers were an economic burden on the peasants, whose livestock provided the victims. Such sacrifices were also largely irrelevant to the religious concerns of both peasants and town dwellers. New, ascetic tendencies questioned the basic values and practices of the older Aryan religion. During the seventh and sixth centuries B.C.E., skepticism in religious matters accompanied social and political upheavals.

The latest Vedic texts themselves reflected a reaction against excessive emphasis on the power of sacrifice and ritual, accumulation of worldly wealth and power, and hope for an afterlife in a paradise. The treatises of the **Brahmanas** (ca. 1000–800 B.C.E.) dealt with the ritual application of the old Vedic texts, the explanation of Vedic rites and mythology, and the theory of the sacrifice. Early on, they focused on controlling the sacred power (*Brahman*) of the sacrificial ritual, but they gradually stressed acquiring this power through knowledge instead of ritual.

●●●[Read the Document
Selections from the *Rig Veda* at
MyHistoryLab.com

This tendency became central in the Upanishads (ca. 800–500 B.C.E.). The Upanishadic sages and the early Jains and Buddhists (fifth century B.C.E.) shared certain revolutionary ideas and concerns. Their thinking and piety influenced not only all later Indian intellectual thought but also, through the spread of the Buddhist tradition, much of the intellectual and religious life of East and Southeast Asia as well. Thus, the middle centuries of the first millennium B.C.E. in India began a religious and philosophical revolution that ranks alongside those of Chinese philosophy and religion, Judaic monotheism, and Greek philosophy as a turning point in the history of civilization.

The Upanishadic Worldview

In the Upanishads two new emphases emerge: knowledge is elevated over ritual and immortality is defined in terms of escape from existence itself. These were already evident in two sentences from the prayer of an early Upanishadic thinker who said, "From the unreal lead me to the Real. . . . From death lead me to immortality." The first sentence points to the Upanishadic focus on speculation about the nature of things, the quest for ultimate truth. Here knowledge, not the sacred word or act, has become the ultimate source of power. The second sentence reflects a new kind of concern with life after death. The old Vedic ideal of living a full and upright life so as to attain an afterlife among the gods no longer appears adequate. Immortality is now interpreted in terms of escape from mundane existence in any form. These two Upanishadic emphases gave birth to ideas that were to change the shape of Indian thought forever. They also provide the key to its basic worldview.

The Nature of Reality The quest for knowledge by the Upanishadic sages focused on the nature of the individual self (*atman*) and its relation to ultimate reality (*Brahman*). The gods are now merely part of the total scheme of things, subject to the laws of existence, and not to be put on the same plane with the transcendent Absolute. Prayer and sacrifice to particular gods for their help continue; but the higher goal is realization of *Brahman* through mental action alone, not ritual performance.

The culmination of Upanishadic speculation is the recognition that the way to the Absolute is through the self. Through contemplation, **atman-Brahman** is recognized not as a deity, but as the principle of reality itself: the unborn, unmade, unitary, unchanging infinite. Of this reality, all that can be said is that it is "neither this nor that," because the ultimate cannot be conceptualized or described in finite terms. Beneath the impermanence of ordinary reality is the changeless *Brahman*, to which every being's immortal self belongs and of which it partakes. The difficulty is recognizing this self, and with it the Absolute, while one is enmeshed in mortal existence. (See Document, "Discussions of Brahman and Atman from the *Upanishads*.")

A second, related focus of Upanishadic inquiry was the nature of "normal" existence. The realm of life is seen to be ultimately impermanent, ever changing. What seem to be "solid" things—the physical world, our bodies and personalities, worldly success—are revealed in the *Upanishads* as insubstantial and, impermanent. Even happiness is transient. Existence is neither satisfying nor lasting. Only *Brahman* is eternal, unchanging. This perception already shows a marked tendency toward the eventual Buddhist emphasis on impermanence and suffering as the fundamental facts of existence.

Life after Death The new understanding of immortality that emerges in the Upanishads is related to these basic perceptions about the self, the Absolute, and the world of existence. The Upanishadic sages conceived of existence as a ceaseless cycle, a never-ending alternation between life and death. This idea became the basic assumption of all Indian thought and religious life.

The idea of the endless cycle of existence, or *samsara*, is only superficially similar to our idea of "transmigration" of souls. For Indians, it is the key to understanding reality. Furthermore, it is not a liberating, but a burdensome reality: the terrifying prospect of endless "re-death" as the normal lot of all beings in this world, whether animals, plants, humans, or gods. This is the fundamental problem for all later Indian thought.

Karma The key to resolving the dilemma of *samsara* lies in the concept of **karma**, which in Sanskrit literally means "work" or "action." At base, it is the concept that every action has its inevitable effects, sooner or later; as long as there is action of mind or body, there are continued effects and hence continued existence. Good deeds bring good results, perhaps even rebirth in a heaven or as a god, and evil deeds bring evil consequences, whether in this life or by rebirth in the next, whether in the everyday world or in the lower worlds of hell. Because of the fundamental impermanence of

Document

Discussions of Brahman and Atman from the Upanishads

Much of the *Upanishads* is couched in the form of teacher–student dialogue. The following two selections are responses of teachers to the questions of their disciples.

■ *Does either of these passages provide a guide to salvation? If so, why, and what is the suggested path to salvation? In what sense and degree are the passages concerned with ignorance and enlightenment?*

A REPORT OF THE SAGE SANDILYA'S STATEMENT ABOUT THE IDENTITY OF ATMAN AND BRAHMAN

Verily, this whole world is Brahman. Tranquil, let one worship it as that from which he came forth, as that into which he will be dissolved, as that in which he breathes. Now, verily, a person consists of purpose. According to the purpose which a person has in this world, thus does he become on departing hence. So let him form for himself a purpose. He who consists of mind, whose body is life, whose form is light, whose conception is truth, whose soul *atman* is space, containing all odors, containing all tastes, encompassing this whole world, the unspeaking, the unconcerned—this Soul of mine within the heart is smaller than a grain of rice, or a barley-corn, or a mustard-seed, or a grain of millet; or the kernel of a grain of millet; this Soul of mine within the heart is greater than the earth, greater than the atmosphere, greater than the sky, greater than these worlds. Containing all works, containing all desires, containing all odors, containing all tastes, encompassing this whole world, the unspeaking, the unconcerned—this Soul of mine within the heart, this is Brahman. Into him I shall enter on departing hence. If one would believe this, he would have no more doubt."—Thus used Sandilya to say. . . .

Chandogya Upanishad 3.14

THE YOUNG BRAHMAN, SHVETAKETU, IS INSTRUCTED IN THE IDENTITY OF ATMAN AND BRAHMAN BY HIS FATHER

"These rivers, my dear, flow, the eastern toward the east, the western toward the west. They go just from the ocean to the ocean. They become the ocean itself. As there they know not 'I am this one,' 'I am that one'—even so, indeed, my dear, all creatures here, though they have come forth from Being, know not 'We have come forth from Being.' Whatever they are in this world, whether tiger, or lion, or wolf, or boar, or worm, or fly, or gnat, or mosquito, that they become. That which is the finest essence—this whole world has that as its soul. That is Reality. That is Atman. That art thou, Shvetaketu."

Chandogya Upanishad 6.10

Source: Selections taken with minor changes from *The Thirteen Principal Upanishads*, 2nd ed., Robert Ernest Hume, trans. Copyright © 1931, Oxford University Press, pp. 209–210, 246–247. Reprinted by permission of Oxford University Press, New Delhi.

everything in existence (heavens and hells included), good as well as evil is temporary. The flux of existence knows only movement, change, endless cause and effect far transcending a mere human life span, or even a mere world eon.

Solutions The Indian tradition developed two kinds of solutions to the problem of *samsara*. The first involves a strategy of maximizing good actions and minimizing bad actions to achieve the best possible rebirth in one's next round of existence. The second, and more radical, solution seeks "liberation" (*moksha*) from existence: escaping all karmic effects by escaping action itself.

The first strategy has been followed by the great masses of Hindus, Buddhists, and Jains over the centuries. It has been characterized by Franklin Edgerton as the "ordinary norm," as opposed to the "extraordinary norm," the path of only the select elite, the greatest seekers of Upanishadic truth, Jain asceticism, or the Buddhist Middle Path. Essentially, the ordinary norm aims at living according to a code of social and moral responsibility. The most significant such codes in Indian history are those of the masses of Hindus, Buddhists, and Jains over the centuries. On the other hand, the seekers of the extraordinary norm usually follow an ascetic discipline aimed at transcending action, at withdrawal from the karmic cycle altogether and consequent release (*moksha*) from cause and effect, good and evil, birth and rebirth. These two characteristic Indian responses to the problem posed by *samsara* underlie the fundamental forms of Indian thought and piety that took shape in the mid- to late first millennium B.C.E.

Social Responsibility: Dharma as Ideal

The "ordinary norm" of life in the various traditions of Indian religiousness can be summarized as life lived according to **dharma**. Although *dharma* has many meanings, its most common meaning is similar to that of the Vedic Aryan concept of *Rta*. In this sense, it means "the right (order of things)," "moral law," "right conduct," or even "duty." It includes the cosmic order (compare the Chinese *Dao*) as well as the right conduct of political, commercial, social, and religious affairs and individual moral responsibility. For most people—those we might call the laity, as distinguished from monks and ascetics—life according to *dharma* is the life of moral action that will lead to a better birth in the next round of existence. The ideal of leadership that developed out of this view of moral duty (likely stimulated by the model of the Indian Buddhist ruler Ashoka) is that of the *Chakravartin*, or Universal Ruler ("one whose wheels are turning in all directions"), the emperor who sees to the good of all of society.

Life according to *dharma* has several implications. First, it accepts action in the world of *samsara* as necessary and legitimate. Second, it demands acceptance of the responsibilities appropriate to one's sex, class and caste group, stage in life, and other life circumstances. Third, it allows for legitimate self-interest: One's duty is to do things that acquire merit for one's eternal *atman* and to avoid those things that bring evil consequences. Fourth, rebirth in heaven, in paradise, is the highest goal attainable through the life of *dharma*. However (fifth), all achievement in the world of *dharma* (which is also the world of *samsara*), even the attainment of heaven, is ultimately subject to change.

Ascetic Discipline: Moksha as Ideal

For those who abandon the world of ordinary life to gain freedom from *samsara*, the implications for living are in direct contrast to those of the ordinary norm. First, any action, good or bad, is at least counterproductive, for action produces only more action, more *karma*, more rebirth. Second, nonaction is achieved only by withdrawal from "normal" existence. The person seeking release from *samsara* has to move beyond the usual responsibilities of family and society. Most often, this involves becoming a "renouncer" (*sannyasi*)—whether a Hindu hermit, yogi, or wanderer, or a Jain or Buddhist monk. Third, this renunciation of the world and its goals demands selflessness, absence of ego. One must give up the desires and attachments that the self normally needs to function in the world. Fourth, the highest goal is not rebirth

in heaven, but liberation (*moksha*) from all rebirth and redeath. Finally, this *moksha* is permanent. Its realization means no more becoming, no more suffering in the realm of *samsara*. Permanence, eternity, transcendence, and freedom from suffering are its attributes.

Seekers of the Extraordinary Norm

The ideas that led individuals to seek the extraordinary norm were first fully elaborated in the Upanishads. These ideas appealed to an increasing number of persons who abandoned both the ritualistic religious practices and the society of class distinctions and material concerns around them. Many of these seekers were of warrior-noble (*Kshatriya*), not Brahman, birth. They took up the wandering or hermitic existence of the ascetic, seeking spiritual powers in yogic meditation and self-denial or even self-torture. Such seekers wanted to transcend bodily existence to realize the Absolute.

In the sixth century B.C.E., teachers of new ideas appeared, especially in the lower Ganges basin, in the area of Magadha (modern Bihar). Most of them rejected traditional religious practices as well as the authority of the Vedas in favor of ascetic discipline as the true spiritual path. The ideas and practices of two of these teachers became the foundations of new and lasting traditions of piety and faith, those of the Jains and the Buddhists.

Mahavira and the Jain Tradition

The **Jains** are an Indian community that traces its tradition to Vardhamana, known as Mahavira ("the great hero"), who is traditionally believed to have lived from about 540 to 468 B.C.E. The Jains consider Mahavira as the final *Jina* ("victor" over *samsara*) or *Tirthankara* ("ford maker," one who finds a way across the waters of existence), in a line of twenty-four great teachers who have appeared in the latter, degenerative half of the time cycle in which the world currently finds itself. The Jains (or *Jainas*, "adherents of the *Jina*") see in Mahavira not a god, but a human teacher who found and taught the way to extricate the self, or soul, from the bonds of the material world and its karmic accretions.

Chronology

India	
ca. 800–500 B.C.E.	The Upanishads
540–ca. 468 B.C.E.	Mahavira, the Jina/Vardamana
ca. 566–ca. 486 B.C.E.	Siddhartha Gautama, the Buddha

Document

The "Turning of the Wheel of the Dharma": Basic Teachings of the Buddha

Following are selections from the sermon said to have been the first preached by the Buddha. It was directed at five former companions with whom he had practiced extreme austerities. When he abandoned asceticism to meditate under the Bodh tree, they had become disillusioned and left him. This sermon is said to have made them the first to follow him. Because it set in motion the Buddha's teaching, or *Dharma*, on earth, it is usually described as "setting in motion the wheel of Dharma." The text is from the *Dhammacakkappavattanasutta*.

■ *What extremes does the Middle Path try to avoid? What emotion drives the chain of suffering? How does the "knowledge" that brings salvation compare to the knowledge sought in the Hindu tradition?*

Thus have I heard. The Blessed One was once living in the Deer Park at Isipatana (the Resort of Seers) near Baranasi (Benares). There he addressed the group of five *bhikkhus*.

"Bhikkhus, these two extremes ought not to be practiced by one who has gone forth from the household life. What are the two? There is devotion to the indulgence of sense-pleasures, which is low, common, the way of ordinary people, unworthy and unprofitable; and there is devotion to self-mortification, which is painful, unworthy and unprofitable.

"Avoiding both these extremes, the Tathagata has realized the Middle Path: it gives vision, it gives knowledge, and it leads to calm, to insight, to enlightenment, to Nibbana. And what is that Middle Path? It is simply the Noble Eightfold Path, namely, right view, right thought, right speech, right action, right livelihood, right effort, right mindfulness, right concentration. This is the Middle Path realized by the Tathagata, which gives vision, which gives knowledge, and which leads to calm, to insight, to enlightenment, to Nibbana. . . .

"The Noble Truth of suffering (*Dukkha*) is this: Birth is suffering; aging is suffering; sickness is suffering; death is suffering; sorrow and lamentation, pain, grief and despair are suffering; association with the unpleasant is suffering; dissociation from the pleasant is suffering; not to get what one wants is suffering—in brief, the five aggregates of attachment are suffering.

"The Noble Truth of the origin of suffering is this: It is this thirst (craving) which produces re-existence and re-becoming, bound up with passionate greed. It finds fresh delight now here and now there, namely, thirst for nonexistence (self-annihilation).

"The Noble Truth of the Cessation of suffering is this: It is the complete cessation of that very thirst, giving it up, renouncing it, emancipating oneself from it, detaching oneself from it.

"The Noble Truth of the Path leading to the Cessation of suffering is this: It is simply the Noble Eightfold Path. . . .

"'This is the Noble Truth of Suffering (*Dukkha*)': such was the vision, the knowledge, the wisdom, the science, the light, that arose in me with regard to things not heard before. 'This suffering, as a noble truth, should be fully understood.'

"'This is the Noble Truth of the Cessation of suffering': such was the vision, 'This Cessation of suffering, as a noble truth, should be realized.'

"'This is the Noble Truth of the Path leading to the Cessation of suffering': such was the vision, 'This Path leading to the Cessation of suffering, as a noble truth, has been followed (cultivated).'

"As long as my vision of true knowledge was not fully clear regarding the Four Noble Truths, I did not claim to have realized the perfect Enlightenment that is supreme in the world with its gods, in this world with its recluses and brahmanas, with its princes and men. But when my vision of true knowledge was fully clear regarding the Four Noble Truths, then I claimed to have realized the perfect Enlightenment that is supreme in the world with its gods, in this world with its recluses and brahmanas, with its princes and men. And a vision of true knowledge arose in me thus: My heart's deliverance is unassailable. This is the last birth. Now there is no more re-becoming (rebirth)."

This the Blessed One said. The group of five bhikkhus was glad, and they rejoiced at his words.

Samyutta-nikaya, LVI, II

Source 1: Excerpt from What the Buddha Taught, second and enlarged edition, copyright © 1974 by Walpola Rahula. Used by permission of Grove/Atlantic, Inc.
Source 2: Excerpt from What the Buddha Taught, second and enlarged edition, copyright © 1974 by Walpola Rahula. Used by permission of Oneworld Publications, Inc.

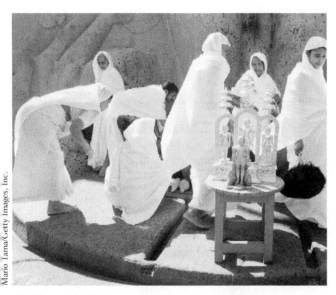

Jain Nuns, Jain pilgrims attend the Mahamastak Abhisheka ceremony in Shravanabelagola, India. During this ceremony, which takes place once every twelve years, the statue of Jain sage Gomateswara is bathed with milk, yogurt, saffron, gold coins, and religious items. This statue is thought to be the world's largest monolith.

In the Jain view, there is no beginning or end to phenomenal existence, only innumerable, ceaseless cycles of generation and degeneration. The universe is alive from end to end with an infinite number of souls, all immortal, omniscient, and pure in their essence. But all are trapped in *samsara*, whether as animals, gods, humans, plants, or even inanimate stones or fire. *Karma* here takes on a quasi-material form: Any thought, word, or deed attracts karmic matter that clings to and encumbers the soul. The greatest amounts come from evil acts, especially those done out of hate, greed, or cruelty to any other being.

Read the Document
Jainism: Selections from The Book of Sermons and The Book of Good Conduct 6th century B.C.E.-5th century C.E. at **MyHistoryLab.com**

Mahavira's path to release focused on eliminating evil thoughts and acts, especially those harmful to others. His radical ascetic practice aimed at destroying karmic defilements and, ultimately, all actions leading to further karmic bondage. At the age of thirty, Mahavira began practicing the radical self-denial of a wandering ascetic, eventually even giving up clothing altogether. After twelve years of self-deprivation and yogic meditation, he attained enlightenment. Then, for some thirty years, he went about teaching his discipline to others. At the age of seventy-two he chose to fast to death to burn out the last karmic residues, an action that some of the most advanced Jain ascetics have emulated down to the present day.

Read the Document
Vardhamana Mahariva, selections from Akaranga-sutra, "Jain Doctrines and Practices of Nonviolence" at **MyHistoryLab.com**

It would, however, be wrong to think of the Jain tradition in terms only of the extreme ascetic practices of some Jain mendicants. Jain monks are bound basically by the five great vows they share with other monastic traditions like the Buddhist and the Christian: not to kill, steal, lie, engage in sexual activity, or own anything.

Most Jains are not monks. Today there is a thriving lay community of perhaps 3 million Jains, most in western India (Gujarat and Rajasthan). Laypersons have close ties to the monks and nuns, whom they support with gifts and food. Many Jain laypersons spend periods of their lives in retreat with monks or nuns. They are vegetarians and regard *ahimsa* ("non-injury") to any being as paramount. Compassion is the great virtue for them, as for Buddhists. The merit of serving the extraordinary-norm seekers who adopt the mendicant life and of living a life according to the high standards of the community provides a goal even for those who as laypersons are following the ordinary norm.

The Buddha's Middle Path

It can be argued that India's greatest contribution to world civilization was the Buddhist tradition, which ultimately faded out in India. Yet there it was born, developed its basic contours, and left its mark on Hindu and Jain religion and culture. Like the two other great universalist traditions, Christianity and Islam, it traces its origins to a single figure who for centuries has loomed larger than life for the faithful.

This figure is Siddhartha Gautama, known as the "sage of the Shakya tribe (Shakyamuni)" and, above all, as the Buddha, or "Enlightened/Awakened One." A contemporary of Mahavira, Gautama was also born (ca. 566 B.C.E.) of a *Kshatriya* family in comfortable—if not, as legend has it, royal—circumstances. His people lived near the modern Nepalese border in the Himalayan foothills. The traditional story of how Gautama came to teach the Middle Path to liberation from *samsara* begins with his sheltered life of ease as a young married prince.

Watch the Video
Siddhartha Gautama at **MyHistoryLab.com**

At the age of twenty-nine, Gautama first perceived the reality of aging, sickness, and death as the human lot. Revolted at his previous delight in sensual pleasures and even in his wife and child, he abandoned his home and family to seek an answer to the dilemma of the endless cycle of mortal existence. After this Great Renunciation, he studied first with renowned teachers and then took up extreme ascetic disciplines of penance and self-mortification. Still unsatisfied, Gautama turned finally to intense yogic meditation under a pipal tree in the place near Varanasi (Banaras) known as Gaya. In one historic night, he moved through different levels of trance, during which he realized all of his past lives,

Read the Document
Buddha's Sermon at Benares - The Edicts of Ashoka (530 B.C.E., 268-233 B.C.E.) at **MyHistoryLab.com**

A Closer Look

Statue of Siddhartha Gotama as Fasting Ascetic (2nd century C.E.)

THIS GANDHARAN STATUE represents Siddhartha Gotama before his enlightenment and achievement of Buddhahood, when he spent six years practicing ascetic austerities of extreme fasting and self-denial—an experience that he abandoned for what became his "Middle Path" teaching and practice. The Kushan dynasty (1st to 7th century C.E.) of NW India and modern Pakistan and Afghanistan patronized art and architecture that seem to have had their formative patronage from the Buddhist Kushan king, Kanishka, in the early second century C.E. in the region of Gandhara (in present-day Pakistan). Gandharan art developed from the Kushana's employment of foreign artisans trained in Roman styles, leading to an art that fused Greco-Roman with Indian and Central Asian styles to produce one of the great cross-cultural traditions of art history. In its heyday, down to roughly the early 3rd century C.E., Gandhara produced some of the most remarkable Buddhist art ever, influencing not only Buddhist but also Indian art long after.

Note the highly realistic depiction of bone structure and sinew on the emaciated ascetic figure. Not only is the Gandharan School credited with the first anthropomorphic depictions of the Buddha, these depictions were done in highly realistic style, likely influenced by Roman realism.

Borromeo, EPA/Art Resource, New York.

The proportions of the body have a 1:5 relation of head-to-body height (more evident in standing statues), which is exactly that of late Roman and early Christian sculptures. Note the nimbus behind the realistic head; this motif may have originated in Central Asia and diffused east to China and west to the Mediterranean, but the earliest evidence for Buddhist use is in Kushan sculpture from the late 1st and 2nd centuries.

The drapery style of the Gandharan figures is clearly derived from Roman style of the Imperial Period, which derives in turn from Greek styles.

Questions

1. What might the various indications of Greco-Roman influence in this south-central Asian Buddhist sculpture suggest about the permeability of political and cultural boundaries from the Mediterranean to South and Central Asia in the early centuries C.E.?

2. The nimbus or halo of light behind the head here is widely attested in various forms across Asia as well as in the Mediterranean, in Hellenistic, Greek, Roman, Christian, Buddhist, and Hindu art. Why might this be so attractive, and what particular purposes would you think it serves in this or other figures in various traditions?

3. Most religious traditions have strands of piety within them that emphasize ascetic renunciation of worldly things, often involving extreme renunciation involving fasting (even to death in a few cases), sexual and other kinds of abstinence, and refusal to have any "possessions". In the Buddha's teaching, why is extreme renunciation and asceticism rejected? Can you compare these ideas to those in another tradition with which you are familiar?

the reality of the cycle of existence of all beings, and how to stop the karmic outflows that fuel suffering. Thus he became the Buddha; that is, he achieved full enlightenment—the omniscient consciousness of reality as it truly is. Having realized the truth of suffering existence, he pledged himself to achieving release for all beings.

From the time of the experience under the Bodh tree, or "Enlightenment Tree," Gautama devoted the last of his earthly lives before his final release to teaching others his Middle Path between asceticism and indulgence. This path has been the core of Buddhist faith and practice ever since. It begins with realizing the Four Noble Truths: (1) all life is *dukkha*, or suffering; (2) the source of suffering is desiring; (3) the cessation of desiring is the way to end suffering; and (4) the path to this end is eightfold: Right Understanding, Right Thought, Right Speech, Right Action, Right Livelihood, Right Effort, Right Mindfulness, and Right Concentration. The key idea of the Buddha's teaching, or *dharma*, is that everything in the world of existence is causally linked. The essential fact of existence is *dukkha*: For no pleasure—however great—is permanent (here we see the Buddhist variation on the central Indian theme of *samsara*).

Thus, Buddhist discipline focuses on the moral Eightfold Path, and the cardinal virtue of compassion for all beings, as the way to eliminate the selfish desiring that is the root of *samsara* and its unavoidable suffering. The Buddha himself had attained this goal; when he died (ca. 486 B.C.E.) after a life of teaching others how to master desiring, he passed from the round of existence forever. In Buddhist terminology, he attained *nirvana*, the extinguishing of karmic bondage. This attainment became the starting point for the growth and eventual spread of the Buddhist *dharma*, which was to assume new and diverse forms in its long history.

View the Image
Buddhist Religious Site at
MyHistoryLab.com

The Buddhist movement, like the Jain, included not only those who were willing to renounce marriage and normal occupations to become part of the Buddha's communities of monks or nuns, but also laypersons who would strive to live by the high moral standards of the tradition and support those who became mendicants in attaining full release.

Read the Document
Rise of Buddhism—Forces for Social
Change? at MyHistoryLab.com

Buddhist tradition, again like that of the Jains, from the outset encompassed seekers of both the extraordinary and the ordinary norms in their present lives. This dual community has remained characteristic of all forms of Buddhism wherever it is practiced. Later we shall see how varied these forms have been historically. But however much the essentially a-theistic, a-ritualistic, and pragmatic tradition was later modified and expanded (so that popular Buddhism would cultivate even theistic devotion to a divinized Buddha and other enlightened beings), the fundamental vision persisted of a humanly attainable wisdom that leads to compassion and release.

The varying visions of Upanishadic, Jain, and Buddhist thought proved durable, albeit in different ways and degrees in India itself, as we have noted. The later emergence of "Hindu" tradition drew on all three of these revolutionary strands in Indian thought and integrated parts of their fundamental ideas about the universe, human life, morality, and society into the cultic and mythic strands of both Brahmanic and popular Indian practice.

The Religion of the Israelites

The ancient Near East was a **polytheistic** world; its people worshiped many gods. They worshiped local or regional gods and goddesses. Some of these deities were associated with natural phenomena such as mountains or animals, the sky, or the earth. For example, Shamash in Mesopotamia and Re in Egypt were both sun gods. Others were tribal or local deities, such as Marduk in Babylonia or Atum, the patron god of the Egyptian city of On (Heliopolis). Still others represented elemental powers of this world or the next, as with Baal, the fertility god of the Canaanites, and Ishtar, whom the Assyrians worshiped as goddess of love and of war. Furthermore, from our perspective, the gods were represented largely as capricious, amoral beings who were no more affected by the actions of humans than were the natural forces that some of them represented.

If the gods were many and diverse, so too were the religious traditions of the ancient Near Eastern world. Even the major traditions of religious thought in Egypt and Mesopotamia did not offer comprehensive interpretations of human life that linked history and human destiny to a transcendent or eternal realm of meaning beyond this world—or at least no one interpretation was able to predominate in this pluralistic, religiously fragmented region.

Out of this polytheistic and pluralistic world came the great tradition of monotheistic faith represented historically in the Jewish, Christian, and Islamic communities. This tradition traces its origin not to any of the great imperial cultures of the ancient world, but to the small nation of the Israelites, or Hebrews. Although they were people from a tiny tribe, people whose external fortunes were at the mercy of the ebb and flow of the great dynasties and empires of the second and first millennia B.C.E., their impact on world civilization was far greater than that of their giant neighbors. For all the glories of the major civilizations of the Fertile Crescent and Nile valley, it was the Israelites, not the Babylonians or Egyptians, who generated a tradition that significantly affected later history. This tradition was ethical monotheism.

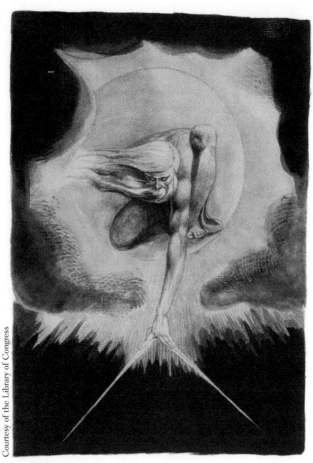

God the Sole Creator, as painted by the British poet and artist William Blake (1757–1827).

Courtesy of the Library of Congress

Monotheism, faith in a single, all-powerful God as the sole Creator, Sustainer, and Ruler of the universe, may be older than the Hebrews, but its first clear historical manifestation was with them. It was among the Hebrew tribes that

((•─Hear the Audio
at **MyHistoryLab.com**

emphasis on the moral demands and responsibilities that the one God placed on individual and community was first definitively linked to human history itself, and that history to a divine plan. This historically based ethical and monotheistic tradition culminated in the Jewish, Christian, and Islamic religions, but its direction was set among the ancient Hebrews.

The path from the appearance of the Hebrews as a nomadic people in the northern Arabian Peninsula, sometime after 2000 B.C.E., to the full flowering of Judaic monotheism in the mid–first millennium B.C.E. was a long one. Before we turn to the monotheistic revolution itself, we need to look briefly at this history.

From Hebrew Nomads to the Israelite Nation

The history of the Hebrews, later known as Israelites, must be pieced together from various sources. The records of their ancient Near Eastern neighbors mention the Hebrews only rarely, so historians must rely on their own accounts as compiled in the Hebrew Bible (the Old Testament in Christian terminology). It was not intended as a history in the contemporary sense; rather, it is a complicated collection of historical narrative, wisdom literature, poetry, law, and religious witness. Scholars once tended to discard the Bible as a source for historians, but the trend today is to take it seriously while using it cautiously and critically. Although its earliest writings go back at most to the ninth century B.C.E. (it was fixed in its present form only in the second century C.E.), it contains much older oral materials that allow us at least some glimpses of the earliest history of the Hebrew people.

We need not reject the core reality of the tradition that the Hebrew Abraham came from Ur in southern Mesopotamia and wandered west with his Hebrew clan to tend his flocks in the land later known as Palestine. Such a movement would be in accord with what we know of a general westward migration of seminomadic tribes from Mesopotamia after about 1950 B.C.E. Any precise dating of the arrival of the Hebrews in Palestine is impossible, but it was likely between 1900 and 1600 B.C.E.

It is with Moses, at about the beginning of the thirteenth century B.C.E., that the Hebrews tread clearly upon the stage of history. Some of Abraham's people had settled in the Palestinian region, but others apparently wandered farther, into Egypt, perhaps with the Hyksos invaders. By about 1400 B.C.E., as the biblical narrative tells it, they had become a settled but subjected, even enslaved, people there. Under Moses, some of the Egyptian Israelites fled Egypt to find a new homeland to the east, from which Abraham's descendants had come. They may then have wandered in the Sinai Desert and elsewhere for several decades before reaching Canaan, the province of Palestine that is described in the Bible as their promised homeland. The Bible presents this experience as the key event in Israel's history: the forging of the covenant, or mutual pact, between God, or Yahweh, and his people. We interpret this Exodus as the time when the Israelites emerged as a nation, a people with a sense of community and common faith.

By about 1200 B.C.E., they had displaced the Canaanite inhabitants of ancient Palestine. After perhaps two centuries of consolidation as a loose federation of tribes, the now settled nation reached its peak as a kingdom under David (r. ca. 1000–961 B.C.E.) and Solomon (r. ca. 961–922 B.C.E.). But in the ninth century B.C.E., the kingdom split

Map Exploration

To explore this map further, go to
http://www.myhistorylab.com

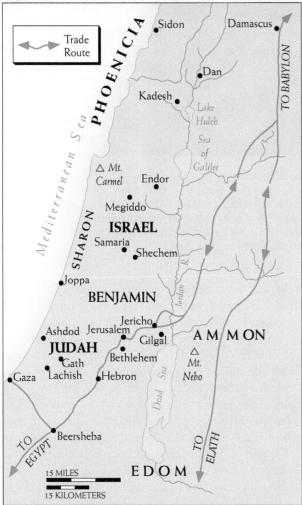

Map 1. Ancient Palestine. The Hebrews established a unified kingdom under Kings David and Solomon in the 10th century B.C.E. After Solomon, the kingdom was divided into Israel in the north and Judah, with its capital, Jerusalem, in the south. North of Israel were the great commercial cities of Phoenicia.

into two parts: Israel in the north and Judah, with its capital at Jerusalem, in the south (see Map 1).

The rise of great empires around them brought disaster to the Israelites. The Northern Kingdom fell to the Assyrians in 722 B.C.E.; its people were scattered and, according to tradition, lost forever—the so-called ten lost tribes. Only the Kingdom of Judah, with its seat at Jerusalem, remained, and after that we may call the Israelites Jews. In 586 B.C.E., Judah was defeated by the Neo-Babylonian king Nebuchadnezzar II (d. 562 B.C.E.). He destroyed the Jewish cult center, the great

Temple built by Solomon, and carried off the cream of the Jewish nation as exiles to be resettled in Babylon. There, in the "Babylonian captivity" of the Exile, without a temple, the Jews clung to their traditions and faith. After the new Persian dynasty of the Achaemenids defeated the Babylonians in 539 B.C.E., the Jews were allowed to return and resettle in their homeland. Many, but not all, of the exiles did return, and by about 516 B.C.E., they erected a second temple in a restored Jerusalem.

See the Map
Israel and Judah, Eighth Century B.C.E. at
MyHistoryLab.com

The new Judaic state continued for centuries to be dominated by foreign peoples but was able to maintain its religious and national identity and occasionally to assert itself. However, it was again destroyed and its people dispersed after the Romans' destruction of Jerusalem, in 70 C.E. and again in 132 C.E. By this era, however, the Jews had developed a religious worldview that would long outlive any Judaic national state.

Watch the Video
The Old City of Jerusalem at
MyHistoryLab.com

The Monotheistic Revolution

The fate of this small nation would be of little interest were it not for its unique religious achievement. It developed a tradition of faith that amounted to a revolution in ways of thinking about the human condition, the meaning of life and history, and the nature of the Divine. It was not the overt history of the Judaic state down to its catastrophic end in 132 C.E. that was to have lasting historical importance, but what the Jews made of that history—how they interpreted it and built upon it a lasting Jewish culture and identity. The revolutionary character of this interpretation lay in its uniquely moralistic understanding of human life and history and the uncompromising monotheism on which it was based.

At the root of this monotheistic tradition stands the figure of Abraham. Not only Jews but also Christians and Muslims look to him as the symbolic founder of their monotheistic faith. The Hebrews in Abraham's time were probably much like other primitive tribal peoples in their religious attitudes. For them, the world must have been alive with supernatural powers: ancestral spirits, personifications of the forces of nature, and deities of local places. Abraham probably conceived of his Lord simply as his chosen deity among the many divinities who might be worshiped. Yet for the strength of his faith in his God, the biblical account recognizes him as the "Father of the Faithful," the first of the Hebrew patriarchs to make a **covenant** with the God who would become unique and supreme. In this, Abraham promised to serve only him, and his God promised to bless his descendants and guide them as his special people.

After Abraham, the next major step came with Moses. As with Abraham's faith, it is difficult to say how much the

Mosaic covenant at Sinai actually marked the achievement of an exclusively monotheistic faith. A notion of the supremacy of Yahweh is reflected in the biblical emphasis on the Israelites' rejection of all other gods after Sinai—and on their subsequent victory, through Yahweh's might, over the Canaanites. Certainly, the covenant event was decisive in uniting the Israelites as a people with a special relationship to God. At Sinai, they received both God's holy Law (the Torah) and his promise of protection and guidance as long as they kept the Law. This was the pivotal moment in the monotheistic revolution that came to full fruition only several hundred years later. But from the later perspective of the biblical redactors at least, from Sinai forward the Israelites saw themselves as God's chosen people among the nations and their history as the history of the mighty acts of the one God.

The monotheistic revolution might thus be said to have begun with Abraham or Moses. Historically, we can trace it primarily from the bipartite division of the Israelite kingdom in 922 B.C.E. After this, men and women known as the *prophets* arose. These inspired messengers of God were sent to call their people back from worship of false gods to faith in the one true God, and from immorality to obedience to God's commandments.

The important point in the colorful history of the great and lesser prophets is that their activity was closely linked to the saga of Israelite national success, exile, and return in the mid–first millennium B.C.E. In the biblical interpretation of these events, we can see the progressive consolidation of Judaic religion. This consolidation, even amidst the political demise of the Israelite kingdom, was largely the work of the prophets. Their concern with purifying the Jewish faith, and with morality, focused in particular on two ideas that proved central to Judaic monotheism.

The first seminal idea for the Jews was the significance of history in the divine plan. Calling on the Jews' awareness of the Sinai covenant, the prophets saw in Israel's past and present troubles God's punishment for failing in their covenant duties. Their prophecies of coming disaster from their enemies were based on the conviction that unless Israel changed its ways, more punishment would follow. But they were not only prophets of doom. When the predicted disasters arrived, their vision extended to seeing Israel as the "suffering servant" among the nations, the people who, by their trials, would purify other nations and bring them ultimately to God. Here the nationalistic, particularistic focus of previous Israelite religion gave way to a more complete, universalist monotheism: Yahweh was now God of all, even the Babylonians or Assyrians.

The second central idea emphasized the nature of Yahweh. The prophets saw in Yahweh the transcendent ideal of justice and goodness. From this view followed naturally

Exile of the Israelites. In 722 B.C.E. the northern part of Jewish Palestine, the kingdom of Israel, was conquered by the Assyrians. Its people were driven from their homeland and exiled all over the vast Assyrian Empire. This wall carving in low relief comes from the palace of the Assyrian king Sennacherib at Nineveh. It shows the Jews with their cattle and baggage going into exile. *Erich Lessing/Art Resource, New York.*

the demand for justice and goodness, individually and collectively, among his worshipers. God was a righteous God who expected righteousness from human beings. (See Document, "God's Purpose with Israel".) No longer could he be only the object of a sacrificial cult: he was a moral God who demanded goodness, not blood offerings or empty prayers. A corollary of God's goodness was his love for his people, as the prophet Hosea (late eighth century B.C.E.) emphasized. However much he might have to punish them for their sins, God would finally lead them back to his favor.

The crux of the breakthrough to ethical monotheism lay in linking the Lord of the Universe to history and morality. The Almighty Creator was seen as actively concerned with the actions and fates of his human creatures as exemplified in Israel. This concern was reflected in God's involvement in history, which thus took on transcendent meaning. God had created humankind for an ultimately good purpose; they were called to be just and good like their Creator, for they were involved in the fulfillment of his divine purpose. This fulfillment would come in the restoration of Israel as a people purified of their sins: "I will put my law within them, and I will write it upon their hearts; and I will be their God, and they shall be my people" (Jeremiah 31:33).

Even after the exile, however, the realization of the prophesied days of peace and blessedness under God's rule clearly still had not come. Jews were scattered from Egypt to Babylonia, and their homeland was controlled by foreign powers. This context brought forth the late prophetic

Document God's Purpose with Israel

According to Jewish tradition, the Ten Commandments that Moses received from God for the Israelites are given in two different places in the Torah, with slightly different wording in each. The Exodus passage is one of these; the other is in Deuteronomy 5, the chapter immediately followed by the second passage cited here, Deuteronomy 6:1–9. This latter passage contains the fundamental statement of Judaic faith (verses 4–5), known as the *Shema* ("Hear," the word that begins this divine command).

■ *How do these passages exemplify the moral consciousness and utter faith in God on which Jewish monotheism is built?*

And God spoke all these words, saying,

"I am the Lord your God, who brought you out of the land of Egypt, out of the house of bondage.

"You shall have no other gods before me.

"You shall not make for yourself a graven image, or any likeness of anything that is in heaven above, or that is in the earth beneath, or that is in the water under the earth; you shall not bow down to them or serve them; for I the Lord your God am a jealous God, visiting the iniquity of the fathers upon the children to the third and the fourth generation of those who hate me, but showing steadfast love to thousands of those who love me and keep my commandments.

"You shall not take the name of the Lord your God in vain; for the Lord will not hold him guiltless who takes his name in vain.

"Remember the sabbath day, to keep it holy. Six days you shall labor, and do all your work; but the seventh day is a sabbath to the Lord your God; in it you shall not do any work, you, or your son, or your daughter, your manservant, or your maidservant, or your cattle, or the sojourner who is within your gates; for in six days the Lord made heaven and earth, the sea, and all that is in them and rested the seventh day; therefore the Lord blessed the sabbath day and hallowed it.

"Honor your father and your mother, that your days may be long in the land which the Lord your God gives you.

"You shall not kill.

"You shall not commit adultery.

"You shall not steal.

"You shall not bear false witness against your neighbor.

"You shall not covet your neighbor's house; you shall not covet your neighbor's wife, or his manservant, or his maidservant, or his ox, or his ass, or anything that is your neighbor's."

Exodus 20:1–17

"Now this is the commandment, the statutes and the ordinances which the Lord your God commanded me to teach you, that you may do them in the land to which you are going over, to possess it; that you may fear the Lord your God, you and your son and your son's son, by keeping all his statutes and his commandments, which I command you, all the days of your life; and that your days may be prolonged. Hear therefore, O Israel, and be careful to do them; that it may go well with you, and that you may multiply greatly, as the Lord, the God of your fathers, has promised you, in a land flowing with milk and honey.

"Hear, O Israel: The Lord our God is one Lord, and you shall love the Lord your God with all your heart, and with all your soul, and with all your might. And these words which I command you this day shall be upon your heart; and you shall teach them diligently to your children, and shall talk of them when you sit in your house, and when you walk by the way, and when you lie down, and when you rise. And you shall bind them as a sign upon your hand, and they shall be as frontlets between your eyes. And you shall write them on the doorposts of your house and on your gates.

Deuteronomy 6:1–9

Source: Scripture quotations are from the Revised Standard Version of the Bible. Copyright 1946, 1951, 1971, by the Division of Christian Education of the National Council of Churches of Christ in the USA. Used by permission. Annotations © 1965 Oxford University Press.

Chronology

The Israelites

ca. 1000–961 B.C.E.	Reign of King David
ca. 961–922 B.C.E.	Reign of King Solomon
722 B.C.E.	Assyrian conquest of Israel (Northern Kingdom)
586 B.C.E.	Destruction of Jerusalem; fall of Judah (Southern Kingdom); Babylonian captivity
539 B.C.E.	Restoration of Temple; return of exiles

The Fall. The German artist Albrecht Dürer (1471–1528) engraved this image of the biblical first humans whose creation and fall are recounted in Genesis. God's covenant with humankind is central to his divine plan. However much he might punish people for their sins, God would finally lead them back to his favor.

concept that history's culmination would come in a future Messianic age. Faith and morality were tied to human destiny, even without the still later Jewish idea that a Day of Judgment would cap the golden age of the **Messiah**, the redeemer whom Jews believed would establish the kingdom of God on earth. The significance of these ideas, some of which might have come from the Jews' encounter with Zoroastrian traditions during the exile, did not stop with Judaic religion. They played a key role in similar Christian and Muslim ideas of a Messianic deliverer, resurrection of the body, and a life after death.

Alongside the prophets, the other key element in the monotheistic revolution of the Jews was the Law itself. The Law is embodied in the five books of the Torah (the Pentateuch, or "five books": Genesis, Exodus, Leviticus, Numbers, and Deuteronomy). The central place of the Law in Jewish life was reestablished, after a period of decline, by King Josiah of Judah (ca. 649–609 B.C.E.) shortly before the fall of Jerusalem and the exile. Its presence and importance in Judaic faith enabled the Jews in exile to survive the loss of the Temple and its priestly cult, thereby fixing the Torah even over Jerusalem as the ultimate earthly focus of faith in God. Its centrality for the Judaic nation was reaffirmed after the reestablishment of the Temple by the prophets Ezra and Nehemiah in the fifth century B.C.E.

In the second century B.C.E., the enduring role of the Torah was ensured by its physical compilation, together with the books of the prophets and other writings, into the Holy Scriptures, or Bible (from the Greek *bibloi*, "books"). The Torah has not only the Law itself, but also the record of the Jews' journey to the recognition of God's law for his people. A holy, authoritative, divinely revealed scripture as an element of Judaic monotheism had revolutionary consequences, not only for Jews, but also for Christians and Muslims. It put the seal on the monotheistic revolution that had made the sovereignty and righteousness of God the focal points of faith.

The evolution of Judaic monotheistic faith was the beginning of one of the major traditions of world religion. For the first time, a nation defined itself not primarily by dynastic, linguistic, or geographic considerations, but by shared religious faith and practice. This was something new in human history. It was later to have still greater effects when not only Judaic but also Christian and Muslim traditions would change the face of much of the world.

Greek Philosophy

Greek thought offered different approaches and answers to many of the same concerns as those of the original monotheists. Calling attention to some of those differences will help to identify the distinctive outlook of the Greeks and of the later cultures of Western civilization that have drawn heavily on it.

"The School of Athens." In this painting, the great Italian Renaissance painter Raphael portrayed the ancient Greek philosopher Plato and his student, Aristotle, engaged in debate. Plato, who points to the heavens, believed in a set of ideal truths that exist in their own realm distinct from the earth. Aristotle urged that all philosophy must be in touch with lived reality and confirms this position by pointing to the earth.

The Greek gods had most of the characteristics of the Mesopotamian deities; magic and incantations played a part in Greek lives; and their law was usually connected with divinity. Some Greeks developed ideas that were strikingly different and, in so doing, set a part of humankind on an entirely new path. As early as the sixth century B.C.E., Greeks living in the Ionian cities of Asia Minor raised questions and suggested answers about nature that produced an intellectual revolution. In speculating about the nature of the world and its origin, they made guesses that were completely naturalistic and included no reference to supernatural powers. One historian of Greek thought, discussing the views of Thales (624–545 B.C.E.), the first Greek philosopher, put the case particularly well:

In one of the Babylonian legends it says: "All the lands were sea. Marduk bound a rush mat upon the face of the waters, he made dirt and piled it beside the rush mat." What Thales did was to leave Marduk out. He, too, said

that everything was once water. But he thought that earth and everything else had been formed out of water by a natural process, like the silting up of the Delta of the Nile. It is an admirable beginning, the whole point of which is that it gathers together into a coherent picture a number of observed facts without letting Marduk in.[3]

The same relentlessly rational approach was applied even to the gods themselves. In the same century as Thales, Xenophanes of Colophon expressed the opinion that humans think of the gods as resembling themselves, that like themselves they were born, that they wear clothes like theirs, and that they have voices and bodies like theirs. In the fifth century B.C.E. Protagoras of Abdera (ca. 490–420 B.C.E.) went so far in the direction of agnosticism as to say, "About the gods I can have no knowledge either that they are or that they are not or what is their nature."[4]

This rationalistic, skeptical way of thinking carried over into practical matters as well. The school of medicine led by Hippocrates of Cos (ca. 400 B.C.E.) attempted to understand, diagnose, and cure disease without recourse to supernatural forces or beings. One of the Hippocratics wrote of the mysterious disease epilepsy:

It seems to me that the disease is no more divine than any other. It has a natural cause, just as other diseases have. Men think it divine merely because they do not understand it. But if they called everything divine which they do not understand, why, there would be no end of divine things.[5]

By the fifth century B.C.E., it was possible for the historian Thucydides (ca. 460–400 B.C.E.) to analyze and explain the behavior of humans in society completely in terms of human nature and chance, leaving no place for the gods or supernatural forces.

The relative unimportance of divine or supernatural forces also characterized Greek views of law and justice. Most Greeks, of course, liked to think that law came ultimately from the gods. In practice, however, and especially in the democratic states, they understood that laws were made by humans and should be obeyed because they represented the expressed consent of the citizens. Law, according to the fourth-century B.C.E. statesman Demosthenes (384–322 B.C.E.), was "a general covenant of the whole State, in accordance with which all men in that State ought to regulate their lives."[6]

[3] Benjamin Farrington, *Greek Science* (London: Penguin Books, 1953), p. 37.

[4] Hermann Diels, *Fragmente der Vorsokratiker*, 5th ed., ed. by Walther Kranz (Berlin: Weidmann, 1934–1938), Frg. 4.

[5] Ibid., Frgs. 14–16.

[6] *Against Aristogeiton*, p. 16.

Overview — Four Great Systems of Thought and Religion

In the accompanying flowchart, note the river valleys in which the original civilizations arose. Each was characterized by cities, writing systems, agriculture, and so on. (The Mississippi, Amazon, and Congo lacked such developments.) During the axial age from 500 to 200 B.C.E., the same areas saw the birth of the world religions of Hinduism, Buddhism, and Judaism, and the world philosophies of China and Greece. Each continued to develop, and in the Middle East, by a combination of Judaic and Greek elements, there occurred the rise of Christianity and Islam.

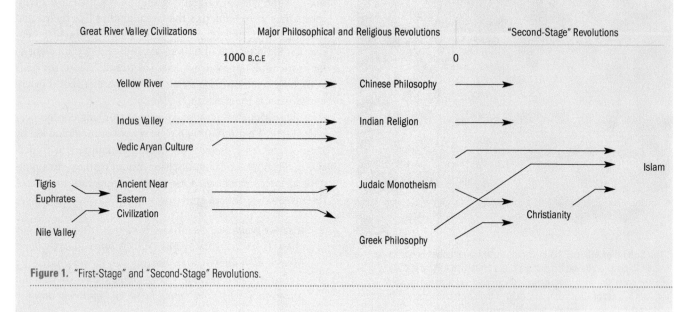

Figure 1. "First-Stage" and "Second-Stage" Revolutions.

These ideas, so different from any that came before the Greeks, open the discussion of most of the issues that appear in the long history of civilization and that remain major concerns in the modern world: What is the nature of the universe, and how can it be controlled? Are there divine powers, and if so, what is humanity's relationship to them? Are law and justice human, divine, or both? What is the place in human society of freedom, obedience, and reverence? The Greeks confronted and intensified these and many other problems.

Reason and the Scientific Spirit

The rational spirit characteristic of Greek culture blossomed in the sixth century B.C.E. into the intellectual examination of the physical world and the place of humankind in it that we call philosophy. The first steps along this path were taken in Ionia on the coast of Asia Minor, which was on the fringe of the Greek world and therefore in touch with foreign ideas and the learning of the East (see Map 2).

Thales of Miletus believed that the earth floated on water and that water was the primary substance. This idea was not new; what was new was the absence of any magical or mythical elements in the explanation. Thales observed, as any person can, that water has many forms: liquid, solid, and gaseous. He saw that it could "create" land by alluvial deposit and that it was necessary for all life. These observations he organized by reason into a single explanation that accounted for many phenomena without any need for the supernatural. The first philosopher thus set the tone for future investigations. Greek philosophers assumed that the world was knowable, rational, and simple.

The search for fundamental rational explanations of phenomena was carried forward by another Milesian, Anaximander (ca. 611–546 B.C.E.). He imagined that the basic element was something undefined, "unlimited." The world emerged from this basic element as the result of an interaction of opposite forces—wet and dry, hot and cold. Anaximander pictured the universe in eternal motion, with all sensible things emerging from the "unlimited," then decaying and returning to it.

Anaximenes, another Milesian who flourished about 546 B.C.E., believed that air was primary. It took different forms as a result of the purely physical processes of rarefaction and condensation.

Map Exploration

To explore this map further, go to **http://www.myhistorylab.com**

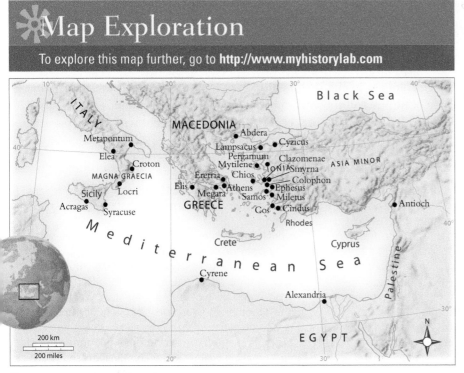

Map 2. Centers of Greek Philosophy.

Heraclitus of Ephesus, who lived near the end of the sixth century B.C.E., carried the dialogue further. His famous saying, "All is motion," raised important problems. If all is constantly in motion, nothing ever really exists. Yet Heraclitus believed that the world order was governed by a guiding principle, the *Logos*, and that though phenomena changed, the *Logos* did not. *Logos* has several meanings, among them "word," "language," "speech," and "reason." So when Heraclitus said that the physical world was governed by *Logos*, he implied that it could be explained by reason. Thus, speculations about the physical world, what we would call natural science, soon led the way toward even more difficult philosophical speculations about language, about the manner of human thought, and about knowledge itself.

In opposition to Heraclitus, the fifth-century B.C.E. philosopher Parmenides of Elea and his pupil Zeno argued that change was only an illusion of the senses. Reason and reflection showed that reality was fixed and unchanging because it seemed evident that nothing could be created out of nothingness. Such fundamental speculations were carried forward by Empedocles of Acragas (fl. ca. 450 B.C.E.), who spoke of four basic elements: fire, water, earth, and air. Like Parmenides, he thought that reality was permanent but not immobile, for the four elements were moved by two primary forces, Love and Strife, or, as we might be inclined to say, attraction and repulsion.

This theory was clearly a step on the road to the atomic theory of Leucippus of Miletus (fl. fifth century B.C.E.) and

Democritus of Abdera (ca. 460–370 B.C.E.). They believed that the world consisted of innumerable tiny, solid particles (atoms) that could not be divided or modified and that moved about in the void. The size of the atoms and the arrangement in which they were joined with others produced the secondary qualities that the senses could perceive, such as color and shape. These qualities—unlike the atoms themselves, which were natural—were merely conventional. Anaxagoras of Clazomenae (ca. 500–428 B.C.E.) had previously spoken of tiny fundamental particles called *seeds* that were put together on a rational basis by a force called *nous*, or "mind." Thus, Anaxagoras suggested a distinction between matter and mind. But the **atomists** regarded "soul," or "mind," as material and believed that everything was guided by purely physical laws. In the arguments of Anaxagoras and the atomists, we have the beginning of the philosophical debate between materialism and idealism that has continued through the ages.

These discussions interested few; indeed, most Greeks were suspicious of such speculations. A far more influential debate was begun by a group of professional teachers who emerged in the mid–fifth century B.C.E. Called **Sophists**, they traveled about and received pay for teaching practical techniques of persuasion, such as rhetoric, which were highly valued in democracies such as Athens. Some claimed to teach wisdom and even virtue. They did not speculate about the physical universe but applied reasoned analysis to human beliefs and institutions. This human focus was characteristic of fifth-century B.C.E. thought, as was the central problem that the Sophists considered: They discovered the tension and even the contradiction between nature and custom, or law. The more traditional among them argued that law itself was in accord with nature, and this view fortified the traditional beliefs about the **polis**, the Greek city-state.

Others argued that laws were merely conventional and not in accord with nature. The law was not of divine origin but just the result of an agreement among people. It could not pretend to be a positive moral force but only had the negative function of preventing people from harming each other. The most extreme Sophists argued that law was contrary to nature, a trick whereby the weak controlled the strong. Critias

Document | The Atomists' Account of the Origin of the World Order

Leucippus and Democritus were Greek thinkers of the fifth century B.C.E. who originated the theory that the world is entirely material, made up of atoms and the void, moving through space without external guidance. As these selections show, they provided a fundamental explanation of things that was purely natural, without divine or mythical intervention. Their view was passed on and later influenced such Renaissance scientists as Galileo.

1. The world-orders arise in this way. Many bodies of all sorts of shapes "split off" from the infinite into a great void where, being gathered together, they give rise to a single vortex, in which, colliding and circling in all sorts of ways, they begin to separate apart, like to like. Being unable to circle in equilibrium any longer because of their congestion, the light bodies go off into the outer void like chaff, while the rest "remain together" and, becoming entangled, unite their motions and produce first a spherical structure. This stands apart like a "membrane," containing in itself all sorts of bodies; and, because of the resistance of the middle, as these revolve the surrounding membrane becomes thin as contiguous bodies continually flow together because of contact with the vortex. And in this way the earth arose, the bodies which were carried to the middle remaining together. Again, the surrounding membrane increases because of the acquisition of bodies from without; and as it moves with the vortex, whatever it touches it adds to itself. Certain of these, becoming entangled, form a structure at first very watery and muddy; but afterward they dry out, being carried about with the rotation of the whole, and ignite to form the substance of the heavenly bodies.

2. Certainly the atoms did not arrange themselves in order by design or intelligence, nor did they propound what movements each should make. But rather myriad atoms, swept along through infinite time or myriad paths by blows and their own weight, have come together in every possible way and tried out every combination that they could possibly create. So it happens that, after roaming the world for aeons of time in making trial of every combination and movement, at length they come together—those atoms whose sudden coincidence often becomes the origin of mighty things: of earth and sea and sky and the species of living things.

Source: The first selection is from Diogenes Laertius 9.31; the second is from Lucretius, *De Rerum Naturae* 5.419–431. Both selections from John Mansley Robinson, *An Introduction to Early Greek Philosophy*. Copyright © 1968 by John Mansley Robinson. Used with permission of the author.

(ca. 460–403 B.C.E.) went so far as to say that the gods themselves had been invented by some clever man to deter people from doing what they wished. Such ideas attacked the theoretical foundations of the *polis* and helped provoke the philosophical responses of Plato and Aristotle in the next century.

Political and Moral Philosophy

Like thinkers in other parts of the world around the middle of the first millennium B.C.E., some Greeks were vitally concerned with the formulation of moral principles for the governance of the state and the regulation of individual life, as well as with more abstract problems of the nature of existence and transcendence. Nowhere is the Greek concern with ethical, political, and religious issues clearer than in the philosophical tradition that began with Socrates in the latter half of the fifth century B.C.E. That tradition continued with Socrates' pupil Plato and with Plato's pupil Aristotle. Aristotle also had great interest in and made great contributions to the scientific understanding of the physical world, but he is perhaps more important for his impact on later Western and Islamic metaphysics.

The three philosophical giants of Hellenic political and moral philosophy were Socrates, Plato, and Aristotle. The starting point for all three was the social and political reality

•••┌Read the Document
Aristotle, excerpts from *Physics and Posterior Analytics* at **MyHistoryLab.com**

of the Greek city-state, or *polis*. The greatest crisis for the *polis* was the Great Peloponnesian War (435–404 B.C.E.). Probably the most complicated response to this crisis may be found in the life and teachings of Socrates (469–399 B.C.E.). Because he wrote nothing, our knowledge of him comes chiefly from his disciples Plato and Xenophon (ca. 435–354 B.C.E.) and from later tradition. Although as a young man Socrates was interested in speculations about the physical world, he later turned to the investigation of ethics and morality. As the Roman writer and statesman Cicero (106–43 B.C.E.) put it, he brought philosophy down from the heavens.

Socrates was committed to the search for truth and for the knowledge about human affairs that he believed reason could reveal. His method was to go among men, particularly those reputed to know something, such as craftsmen, poets, and politicians, to question and cross-examine them. The result was always the same: Those he questioned might have technical information and skills but seldom had any knowledge of the fundamental principles of human behavior. It is understandable that Athenians so exposed should become angry with their examiner, and it is not surprising that they thought Socrates was undermining the beliefs and values of the *polis*. Socrates' unconcealed contempt for democracy, which seemingly relied on ignorant amateurs to make important political decisions without any certain knowledge, created further hostility. Moreover, his insistence on the primacy of his own individualism and his determination to pursue philosophy even against the wishes of his fellow citizens reinforced this hostility and the prejudice that went with it.

Unlike the Sophists, Socrates did not accept pay for his teaching; he professed ignorance and denied that he taught at all. His individualism, moreover, was unlike the worldly hedonism of some of the Sophists. It was not wealth or pleasure or power that he urged people to seek, but "the greatest improvement of the soul." He differed also from the more radical Sophists in denying that the *polis* and its laws were merely conventional. He thought, on the contrary, that they had a legitimate claim on the citizen, and he proved it in the most convincing fashion. In 399 B.C.E., he was condemned to death by an Athenian jury on the charges of bringing new gods into the city and of corrupting its youth. His dialectical inquiries had angered many important people, and his criticism of democracy must have been viewed with suspicion. He was given a chance to escape, but in Plato's *Crito* we are told of his refusal to do so because of his veneration of the laws.

Socrates' career set the stage for later responses to the travail of the *polis*; he recognized its difficulties and criticized its shortcomings. Although he turned away from an active political life, he did not abandon the idea of the *polis*. He fought as a soldier in its defense, obeyed its laws, and sought to use reason to put its values on a sound foundation.

The Cynics One branch of Socratic thought—the concern with personal morality and one's own soul, the disdain for worldly pleasure and wealth, and the withdrawal from political life—was developed and then distorted almost beyond recognition by the Cynic school. Its most famous exemplar was Diogenes of Sinope (ca. 400–325 B.C.E.). Diogenes wore rags and lived in a tub. He performed shameful acts in public and made his living by begging to show his rejection of convention. He believed that happiness lay in satisfying natural needs in the simplest and most direct way. Because actions to this end, being natural, could not be indecent, they could and should be done publicly.

Socrates questioned the theoretical basis for popular religious beliefs; the Cynics ridiculed all religious observances. As Plato said, Diogenes was Socrates gone mad. Beyond that, the way of the Cynics contradicted important Socratic beliefs. Socrates believed that virtue was not a matter of birth but of knowledge, and that people did wrong only through ignorance of what is virtuous. The Cynics, on the contrary, believed that virtue was an affair of deeds and did not need a store of words and learning. Wisdom and happiness came from pursuing the proper style of life, not from philosophy. The Cynics moved even further from Socrates by abandoning the concept of the *polis* entirely. When Diogenes was asked about his citizenship, he answered that he was *kosmopolites*, a citizen of the world. The Cynics plainly had turned away from the past, and their views anticipated those of the Hellenistic Age.

Plato Plato (429–347 B.C.E.) was the most important of Socrates' associates and is a perfect example of the pupil who becomes greater than his master. He was the first systematic philosopher and therefore the first to place political ideas in their full philosophical context. He was also a writer of genius, leaving us twenty-six philosophical discussions. Almost all are in the form of dialogues, which dramatize the examination of difficult and complicated philosophical problems and make them somewhat entertaining.

Born of a noble Athenian family, Plato looked forward to an active political career until he was discouraged by the excesses of Athenian politics and the execution of Socrates. Twice he went to Sicily in the hope of producing

•••┌Read the Document
Plato, The Republic, "On Shadows and Realities in Education" at **MyHistoryLab.com**

a model state at Syracuse under that city's rulers, but without success. In 386 B.C.E., Plato founded the Academy, a center of philosophical investigation and a school for training statesmen and citizens that had a powerful impact on Greek thought and endured until it was closed in the sixth century C.E.

Like Socrates, Plato firmly believed in the *polis* and its values. Its virtues were order, harmony, and justice, and one of its

Document

The Sophists: From Rational Inquiry to Skepticism

The rational spirit inherent in Greek thought was carried to remarkable and dangerous extremes by the Sophists in the fifth century B.C.E. As these three selections suggest, they questioned even the nature, the existence, and the origin of the gods, subjecting these matters to rational analysis.

■ *What was new in the thinking of the Sophists? How was it similar to the thought of the atomists (Democritus and Leucippus)? How was it different? In what ways were Sophist ideas threatening to the Greek way of life?*

1. Concerning the gods, I do not know whether they exist or not. For many are the obstacles to knowledge: the obscurity of the subject and the brevity of human life.

2. Prodicus says that the ancients worshiped as gods the sun, the moon, rivers, springs, and all things useful to human life, simply because of their usefulness—just as the Egyptians deify the Nile. For this reason bread is worshiped as Demeter, wine as Dionysus, water as Poseidon, fire as Hephaestus, and so on for each of the things that are useful to men.

3. There was a time when the life of man was disorderly and bestial and subject to brute force; when there was no reward for the good and no punishment for the bad. At that time, I think, men enacted laws in order that justice might be absolute ruler and have arrogance as its slave; and if anyone did wrong he was punished. Then, when the laws prohibited them from doing deeds of violence, they began to do them secretly. Then, I think, some shrewd and wise man invented fear of the gods for mortals, so that there might be some deterrent to the wicked even if they did or said or thought something in secret. Therefore he introduced the divine, saying that there is a god, flourishing with immortal life, hearing and seeing with his mind, thinking of all things

and watching over them and having a divine nature; who will hear everything that is said among mortals and will be able to see all that is done. And if you plan any evil in secret it will not escape the notice of the gods, for they are of surpassing intelligence. In speaking thus he introduced the prettiest of teachings, concealing the truth under a false account. And in order that he might better strike fear into the hearts of men he told them that the gods dwell in that place which he knew to be a source of fears to mortals—and of benefits too— namely, the upper periphery where they saw lightnings and heard the dreaded rumblings of thunder and saw the starry body of the heaven, the beauteous embroidery of that wise craftsman Time, where the bright glowing mass of the sun moves and whence dark rains descend to earth. With such fears did he surround men, and by means of them he established the deity securely in a place befitting his dignity, and quenched lawlessness. Thus, I think, did some man first persuade mortals to believe in a race of gods.

Source: The first selection is from Diogenes Laertius 9.51; the next two are from Sextus Empiricus, *Against the Schoolmasters* 9.18, 9.54. From John Mansley Robinson, *An Introduction to Early Greek Philosophy.* Copyright © 1968 by John Mansley Robinson. Used with permission of the author.

main objects was to produce good people. Like his master, and unlike the radical Sophists, Plato thought that the *polis* was in accord with nature. He accepted Socrates' doctrine of the identity of virtue and knowledge and made it plain what that knowledge was: *episteme*, science, a body of true and unchanging wisdom open to only a few philosophers whose training, character, and intellect allowed them to see reality. Only such people were qualified to rule; they themselves would prefer the life of pure contemplation but would accept their responsibility and take their turn as philosopher-kings. The training of such men required a specialization of function and a subordination of the individual to the

•••┤Read the Document
Plato, The Republic, "The Philosopher-King" at **MyHistoryLab.com**

community. This specialization would lead to Plato's definition of justice: that each man should do only that one thing to which his nature was best suited.

Plato understood that the *polis* of his day suffered from terrible internal stress, class struggle, and factional divisions. His solution, however, was not that of some Greeks— that is, conquest and resulting economic prosperity. For Plato the answer was in moral and political reform. The way to harmony was to destroy the causes of strife: private property, the family—anything, in short, that stood between the individual citizen and devotion to the *polis*.

Concern for the redemption of the *polis* was at the heart of Plato's system of philosophy. He began by asking the traditional questions: What is a good man, and how is he made? The goodness of a human being was a theme that belonged to moral philosophy, and when it became a function of the state, the question became part of political philosophy. Because goodness depended on knowledge of the good, it required a theory of knowledge and an investigation of what the knowledge was that was required for goodness. The answer must be metaphysical and so required a full examination of metaphysics. Even when the philosopher knew the good, however, the question remained of how the state could bring its citizens to the necessary comprehension of that knowledge. The answer required a theory of education. Even purely logical and metaphysical questions, therefore, were subordinate to the overriding political questions. Plato's need to find a satisfactory foundation for the beleaguered *polis* thus contributed to the birth of systematic philosophy.

Aristotle Aristotle (384–322 B.C.E.) was a pupil of Plato and owed much to the thought of his master, but his different experience and cast of mind led him in new directions. He was born in northern Greece, the son of the court doctor of neighboring Macedon. As a young man, he came to study at the Academy, where he stayed until Plato's death. Then he joined a Platonic colony at Assos in Asia Minor, and from there, he moved to Mytilene. In both places, he carried on research in marine biology, and biological interests played a large part in all his thoughts. In 342 B.C.E., Philip, the king of Macedon, appointed him tutor to his son, the young Alexander. In 336 he returned to Athens, where he founded his own school, the Lyceum (or the Peripatos, as it was also called, based on the covered walk within it). In later years, its members were called Peripatetics. On the death of Alexander in 323 B.C.E., the Athenians rebelled against Macedonian rule, and Aristotle found it wise to leave Athens. He died the following year.

The Lyceum was different from the Academy. Its members took little interest in mathematics and were concerned with gathering, ordering, and analyzing all human knowledge. Aristotle wrote dialogues on the Platonic model, but none has survived. He and his students also prepared many collections of information to serve as the basis for scientific works, but of them only one remains, the *Constitution of the Athenians*, one of 158 constitutional treatises. Almost all we possess of his work is in the form of philosophical and scientific studies, whose loose organization and style suggest that they were lecture notes. The range of treated subjects is astonishing, including logic, physics, astronomy, biology, ethics, rhetoric, literary criticism, and politics.

In each field, the method was the same. Aristotle began with observation of the empirical evidence, which in some cases was physical and in others was common opinion. To this body of information he applied reason and discovered inconsistencies or difficulties. To deal with these, he introduced metaphysical principles to explain the problems or to reconcile the inconsistencies. His view on all subjects, like Plato's, was teleological; that is, he recognized purposes apart from and greater than the will of the individual human being. Plato's purposes, however, were contained in the Ideas, or Forms—transcendental concepts outside the experience of most people. For Aristotle, the purposes of most things were easily inferred by observing their behavior in the world.

Aristotle's most striking characteristics are his moderation and common sense. His epistemology finds room for both reason and experience; his metaphysics gives meaning and reality to both mind and body; his ethics aims at the good life, which is the contemplative life, but recognizes the necessity for moderate wealth, comfort, and pleasure.

All these qualities are evident in Aristotle's political thought. Like Plato, he opposed the Sophists' assertion that the *polis* was contrary to nature and the result of mere convention. His response was to apply to politics the teleology that he saw in all nature. In his view, matter existed to achieve an end, and it developed until it achieved its form, which was its end. There was constant development from matter to form, from potential to actual. Therefore, human primitive instincts could be seen as the matter out of which the human's potential as a political being could be realized. The *polis* made individuals self-sufficient and allowed the full realization of their potentiality. It was therefore natural. It was also the highest point in the evolution of the social institutions that serve the human need to continue the species: marriage, household, village, and finally, *polis*. For Aristotle, the purpose of the *polis* was neither economic nor military, but moral: "The end of the state is the good life," the life lived "for the sake of noble actions," a life of virtue and morality.[7]

Characteristically, Aristotle was less interested in the best state—the utopia that required philosophers to rule it—than in the best state practically possible, one that would combine justice with stability. The constitution for that state he called *politeia*, not the best constitution, but the next best, the one most suited to and most possible for most states. Its quality was moderation, and it naturally gave power to neither the rich nor the poor but to the middle class, which also had to be the most numerous. The middle class possessed many virtues: Because of its moderate wealth, it was free of the arrogance of the rich and the malice of the poor. For this reason, it was the most stable class. The stability of the constitution also came from being a mixed constitution, blending in some way the laws of democracy and those of oligarchy.

All the political thinkers of the fourth century B.C.E. recognized that the *polis* was in danger and hoped to save it. All recognized the economic and social troubles that threatened it. Isocrates (436–338 B.C.E.), a contemporary of Plato and Aristotle, urged a program of imperial conquest as a cure for poverty and revolution. Plato saw the folly of solving a political

---

[7] Aristotle, *Politics*, 1280b, 1281a.

Document

Plato on the Role of Women in His Utopian Republic

The Greek invention of reasoned intellectual analysis of all things led the philosopher Plato to consider the problem of justice, which is the subject of his most famous dialogue, *The Republic*. This inquiry leads him to sketch out a utopian state in which justice may be found and where the most radical arrangements may be necessary. These include the equality of the sexes and the destruction of the family in favor of the practice of men having wives and children in common. In the following excerpts he argues for the fundamental equality of men and women and states that women are no less appropriate than men as Guardians, leaders of the state.

■ *What are Plato's reasons for treating men and women the same? What objections could be raised to that practice? Would that policy, even if appropriate in Plato's utopia, also be suitable to conditions in the real world of classical Athens? In the world of today?*

"If, then, we use the women for the same things as the men, they must also be taught the same things."

"Yes."

"Now music and gymnastics were given to the men."

"Yes."

"Then these two arts, and what has to do with war, must be assigned to the women also, and they must be used in the same ways."

"On the basis of what you say," he said, "it's likely."

"Perhaps," I said, "compared to what is habitual, many of the things now being said would look ridiculous if they were to be done as is said."

"Indeed they would," he said.

"Well," I said, "since we've started to speak, we mustn't be afraid of all the jokes—of whatever kind—the wits might make if such a change took place in gymnastic, in music and, not the least, in the bearing of arms and the riding of horses."

"Then," I said, "if either the class of men or that of women shows its superiority in some art or other practice then we'll say that that art must be assigned to it. But if they look as though they differ in this alone, that the female bears and the male mounts, we'll assert that it has not thereby yet been proved that a woman differs from a man with respect to what we're talking about; rather, we'll still suppose that our Guardians and their women must practice the same things."

"And rightly," he said.

"Therefore, my friend, there is no practice of a city's governors which belongs to woman because she's woman, or to man because he's man; but the natures are scattered alike among both animals; and woman participates according to nature in all practices, and man in all, but in all of them woman is weaker than man."

"Certainly."

"So, shall we assign all of them to men and none to women?"

"How could we?"

"For I suppose there is, as we shall assert, one woman apt at medicine and another not, one woman apt at music and another unmusical by nature."

"Of course."

"And isn't there then also one apt at gymnastic and at war, and another unwarlike and no lover of gymnastic?"

"I suppose so."

"And what about this? Is there a lover of wisdom and a hater of wisdom? And one who is spirited and another without spirit?"

"Yes, there are these too."

"There is, therefore, one woman fit for guarding and another not, or wasn't it a nature of this sort we also selected for the men fit for guarding?"

"Certainly, that was it."

Source: Excerpts from *The Republic of Plato* by Allan Bloom. Copyright © 1991 by Allan Bloom. Reprinted by permission of Basic Books, a member of the Perseus Book Group.

Chronology

Major Greek Philosophers

469–399 B.C.E.	Socrates
429–347 B.C.E.	Plato
384–322 B.C.E.	Aristotle

and moral problem by purely economic means and resorted to the creation of utopias. Aristotle combined the practical analysis of political and economic realities with the moral and political purposes of the traditional defenders of the *polis*. The result was a passionate confidence in the virtues of moderation and of the middle class, and the proposal of a constitution that would give it power. It is ironic that the ablest defense of the *polis* came soon before its demise.

Concern with an understanding of nature in a purely rational, scientific way remained strong through the fifth century B.C.E., culminating in the work of the formulators of the atomic theory, Democritus and Leucippus, and in that of the medical school founded by Hippocrates of Cos. In the mid–fifth century B.C.E., however, men like the Sophists and Socrates turned their attention to humankind and to ethical, political, and religious questions. This latter tradition of inquiry led, by way of Plato, Aristotle (in his metaphysical thought), and the Stoics, to Christianity; it had, as well, a substantial impact on Judaic and Islamic thought. The former tradition of thought, following a line from the natural philosophers, the Sophists, Aristotle (in his scientific thought), and the Epicureans, had to wait until the Renaissance in western Europe to exert an influence. Since the eighteenth century, this line of Greek thought has been the more influential force in Western civilization. It may not be too much to say that since the Enlightenment of that century, the western world has been engaged in a debate between the two strands of the Greek intellectual tradition. As Western influence has spread over the world in recent times, that debate has attained universal importance, for other societies have not separated the religious and philosophical from the scientific and physical realms as radically as has the modern West.

Summary

The Four Great Philosophical and Religious Revolutions.
Between 800 and 300 B.C.E., four philosophical and religious revolutions arose that were to shape the subsequent history of the world. These were Chinese philosophy, Indian religion, Hebrew monotheism, and Greek philosophy.

Chinese Philosophy.
Traditional Chinese philosophical thought, which took shape with the teachings of Confucius in the sixth century B.C.E., remained dominant in China until the early twentieth century. It was concerned with social and political issues and sought to teach human beings how to live harmoniously and ethically under Heaven by prescribing the correct relationships between ruler and subject, father and son, older and younger brother, husband and wife, and friend and friend. Confucianism became the official philosophy of China in the second century B.C.E. Other Chinese philosophies were Daoism, a mystical way of thought that offered a refuge from social responsibilities, and Legalism, which taught that a good society requires a strong state that enforces the law and punishes wrongdoers.

Indian Religion.
Hinduism, the dominant Indian religious tradition, took shape by 400 B.C.E. In Indian religion, existence was an endless alternation between life and death (*samsara*). The escape from this dilemma lay in the concept of *karma*, the idea that good actions, following (*dharma,*) could lead to rebirth as a higher being, even a god, or to escape the cycle entirely and be released entirely from the *samsaric* round of rebirth and re-death (*moksha*).

Another Indian religious tradition, the Jains, sought to liberate the soul from the bonds of the material world by eliminating evil acts.

A third Indian tradition, Buddhism, traces its origins to the teachings of Siddhartha Gautama (b. ca. 566 B.C.E.). Buddhism holds that escape from *samsara* lies in following a moral path of right understanding and actions and in having compassion for all beings.

Hebrew Monotheism.
Monotheism is the faith in a single, all-powerful God as the sole creator, sustainer, and ruler of the universe. The Hebrews were the first people to emphasize the moral demands that the one God, Yahweh, placed on individual and community and to see history as the unfolding of a divine plan. The Hebrews, or Jews, were the first people in history to be defined by shared religious faith and practice. Through the Christian and Muslim traditions, Judaic monotheism would change the face of much of the world.

Greek Philosophy.
The Greeks were the first to initiate the unreservedly rational investigation of the universe. They thus became the forerunners of Western philosophy and science. In the sixth and fifth centuries B.C.E., Greek thinkers, such as Thales of Miletus and Heraclitus, sought to explain natural phenomena without recourse to divine intervention. In the later fifth century and the fourth century B.C.E., philosophers, such as Socrates, Plato, and Aristotle, applied the same rational, inquisitive approach to the study of moral and political issues in the life of the Greek city-state, or *polis*.

Key Terms

atman-Brahman	covenant
atomists	Daoism (daow-ihzm)
Brahmanas	*dharma*

Hindu	**monotheism**
Jains	**polis (POH-lihs)**
karma	**polytheistic**
Legalism	*samsara*
Messiah	**Sophists**

Review Questions

1. Is your outlook on life closer to Confucianism, Daoism, or Legalism? What specifically makes you favor one over the others?

2. Which fundamental assumptions about the world, the individual, and reality do the Jain, Hindu, and Buddhist traditions share? How do these assumptions compare with those that underlie Chinese philosophy, Jewish religious thought, and Greek philosophy?

3. How did the monotheism of the Hebrews differ from that of Egypt's Akhenaten? To what extent did their faith bind the Jews politically? Why was the concept of monotheism so radical for Near Eastern civilization?

4. In what ways did the ideas of the Greeks differ from those of other ancient peoples? How do Aristotle's political and ethical ideas compare with those of Confucius? What were Socrates' contributions to the development of philosophy?

Note: To learn more about the topics in this chapter, please turn to the Suggested Readings at the end of the book. For additional sources related to this chapter please see MyHistoryLab.com.

myhistorylab Connections

Reinforce what you learned in this chapter by studying the many documents, images, maps, review tools, and videos available at **www.myhistorylab.com**.

Read and Review

✓ Study and Review Chapter 2

Read the Document *Origins of the Chinese Civilization–Confucianism, Daoism or Legalism?*
Confucious, selections from the Analects
Confucianism: Government and the Superior (551-479 B.C.E.)
Confucian Political Philosophy: An Excerpt from Mencius
Laozi, excerpt from Tao Te Ching, "The Unvarying Way"
Daoism: The Classic of the Way and Virtue (500s-400s B.C.E.)"
The Way of the State (475-221 B.C.E.) Legalism
Li Si and the Legalist Policies of Qin Shihuang (280-208 B.C.E.)
Selections from the Rig Veda
Jainism: Selections from The Book of Sermons and The Book of Good Conduct 6th century B.C.E.-5th century C.E.
Vardhamana Maharíva, selections from Akaranga-sutra, "Jain Doctrines and Practices of Nonviolence."
Buddha's Sermon at Benares - The Edicts of Ashoka (530 B.C.E., 268-233 B.C.E.)
Rise of Buddhism–Forces for Social Change?
Aristotle, excerpts from Physics and Posterior Analytics
Plato, The Republic, "On Shadows and Realities in Education"
Plato, The Republic, "The Philosopher-King"

Watch the Video *The Old City of Jerusalem*

Research and Explore

View the Image *Buddhist Religious Site*

See the Map *Israel and Judah, Eighth Century B.C.E.*

((•─ **Hear** the **Audio**

Hear the audio file for Chapter 2 at
www.myhistorylab.com.

Suggested Readings

China

R. Bernstein, Ultimate Journey: Retracing the Path of an Ancient Buddhist Monk Who Crossed Asia in Search of Enlightenment (2001). Discusses the diffusion of Buddhism from India to China.

H.G. Creel, What Is Taoism? And Other Studies in Chinese Cultural History (1970).

W.T. de Bary et al., Sources of Chinese Tradition (1960). A reader in China's philosophical and historical literature. It should be consulted for the later periods as well as for the Zhou.

H. Fingarette, Confucius—The Secular as Sacred (1998).

Y.L. Fung, A Short History of Chinese Philosophy, ed. by D. Bodde (1948). A survey of Chinese philosophy from its origins down to recent times.

A. Graham, Disputers of the Tao (1989).

D. Hawkes, Ch'u Tz'u: The Songs of the South (1985).

D.C. Lau, trans., Lao-tzu, Tao Te Ching (1963).

D.C. Lau, trans., Confucius, The Analects (1979).

C. Li, ed., The Sage and the Second Sex: Confucianism, Ethics, and Gender (2000). A good introduction to gender and ethics in Confucian thought.

B.I. Schwartz, The World of Thought in Ancient China (1985).

A. Waley, Three Ways of Thought in Ancient China (1956). An easy yet sound introduction to Confucianism, Daoism, and Legalism.

A. Waley, The Book of Songs (1960).

B. Watson, trans., Basic Writings of Mo Tzu, Hsun Tzu, and Han Fei Tzu (1963).

B. Watson, trans., The Complete Works of Chuang Tzu (1968).

H. Welch, Taoism, The Parting of the Way (1967).

India

A.L. Basham, The Wonder That Was India, rev. ed. (1963). Still unsurpassed by more recent works. Chapter VII, "Religion," is a superb introduction to the Vedic Aryan, Brahmanic, Hindu, Jain, and Buddhist traditions of thought.

W.N. Brown, Man in the Universe: Some Continuities in Indian Thought (1970). A penetrating yet brief reflective summary of major patterns in Indian thinking.

W.T. de Bary et al., Sources of Indian Tradition (1958). 2 vols. Vol. I, From the Beginning to 1800, ed. and rev. by Ainslie T. Embree (1988). Excellent selections from a variety of Indian texts, with good introductions to chapters and individual selections.

P. Harvey, An Introduction to Buddhism (1990). Chapters 1–3 provide an excellent historical introduction.

T.J. Hopkins, The Hindu Religious Tradition (1971). A first-rate, thoughtful introduction to Hindu religious ideas and practice.

K. Klostermaier, Hinduism: A Short History (2000). A relatively compact survey of the history of Hinduism.

J.M. Koller, The Indian Way (1982). A useful, wide-ranging handbook of Indian thought and religion.

R.H. Robinson and W.L. Johnson, The Buddhist Religion, 3rd ed. (1982). An excellent first text on the Buddhist tradition, its thought and development.

R.C. Zaehner, Hinduism (1966). One of the best general introductions to central Indian religious and philosophical ideas.

Israel

A. Bach, ed., Women in the Hebrew Bible: A Reader (1999). Excellent introduction to the ways in which biblical scholars are exploring the role of women in the Bible.

Bright, A History of Israel (1968), 2nd ed. (1972). One of the standard scholarly introductions to biblical history and literature.

W.D. Davies and L. Finkelstein, eds., The Cambridge History of Judaism. Vol. I, Introduction: The Persian Period (1984). Excellent essays on diverse aspects of the exilic period and later.

J. Neusner, The Way of Torah: An Introduction to Judaism (1979). A sensitive introduction to the Judaic tradition and faith.

The Oxford History of the Biblical World, M. D. Coogan, ed. (1998).

Greece

The Cambridge Companion to Greek and Roman Philosophy, D. Sedley ed. (2003).

G.B. Kerferd, The Sophistic Movement (1981). An excellent description and analysis.

J. Lear, Aristotle: The Desire to Understand (1988). A brilliant yet comprehensible introduction to the work of the philosopher.

T.E. Rihil, Greek Science (1999). Good survey of Greek science incorporating recent reseach on the topic.

J.M. Robinson, An Introduction to Early Greek Philosophy (1968). A valuable collection of the main fragments and ancient testimony to the works of the early philosophers, with excellent commentary.

G. Vlastos, The Philosophy of Socrates (1971). A splendid collection of essays illuminating the problems presented by this remarkable man.

G. Vlastos, Platonic Studies, 2nd ed. (1981). A similar collection on the philosophy of Plato.

G. Vlastos, Socrates, Ironist and Moral Philosopher (1991). The results of a lifetime of study by the leading interpreter of Socrates in our time.

Comparative Studies

(Increasingly, world historians are looking at ancient civilizations in relationship to each other rather than as isolated entities to try to understand commonalities and differences in social and cultural development.)

W. Doniger, Splitting the Difference: Gender and Myth in Ancient Greece and India (1999).

G.E.R. Lloyd, The Ambitions of Curiosity: Understanding the World in Ancient Greece and China (2002).

G.E.R. Lloyd, The Way and the Word: Science and Medicine in Early China and Greece (2002).

T. McEvilley, The Shape of Ancient Thought: Comparative Studies of Greek and Indian Philosophies (2002).

Astronomy

CHARTING THE HEAVENS

CHARTING THE HEAVENS

THE FOUNDATIONS OF ASTRONOMY

LEARNING GOALS

Studying this chapter will enable you to

1. Describe how scientists combine observation, theory, and testing in their study of the universe.

2. Explain the concept of the celestial sphere and how we use angular measurement to locate objects in the sky.

3. Describe how and why the Sun and the stars appear to change their positions from night to night and from month to month.

4. Explain why Earth's rotation axis shifts slowly with time, and say how this affects Earth's seasons.

5. Show how the relative motions of Earth, the Sun, and the Moon lead to eclipses.

6. Explain the simple geometric reasoning that allows astronomers to measure the distances and sizes of otherwise inaccessible objects.

Nature offers no greater splendor than the starry sky on a clear, dark night. Silent and jeweled with the constellations of ancient myth and legend, the night sky has inspired wonder throughout the ages—a wonder that leads our imaginations far from the confines of Earth and the pace of the present day and out into the distant reaches of space and cosmic time itself.

Astronomy, born in response to that wonder, is built on two of the most basic traits of human nature: the *need to explore* and the *need to understand*. Through the interplay of curiosity, discovery, and analysis—the keys to exploration and understanding—people have sought answers to questions about the universe since the earliest times. Astronomy is the oldest of all the sciences, yet never has it been more exciting than it is today.

THE BIG PICTURE

Stars are the most fundamental visible component of the universe. Roughly as many stars reside in the observable universe as there are grains of sand in all the beaches of the world—around a hundred sextillion, or about 10^{23}.

LEFT: *High overhead on a clear, dark night, we can see a rich band of stars known as the Milky Way—so-called for its resemblance to a milky band of countless stars. All these stars (and more) are part of a much larger system called the Milky Way Galaxy, of which our star, the Sun, is one member. This single exposure, dubbed "Going to the Stars Road," was made at night with only the Moon's light illuminating the terrain on the continental divide at Logan Pass in Glacier National Park, near the Montana/Alberta border. (© Tyler Nordgren)*

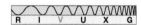

Each photo in this chapter is accompanied by this spectrum icon identifying the wavelength of the electromagnetic radiation used to capture the image, ranging left to right: radio, infrared, visible, ultra-violet, X-ray, and gamma-ray.

1 Our Place in Space

Of all the scientific insights attained to date, one stands out boldly: Earth is neither central nor special. We inhabit no unique place in the universe. Astronomical research, especially within the past few decades, strongly suggests that we live on what seems to be an ordinary rocky *planet* called Earth, one of eight known planets orbiting an average *star* called the Sun, a star near the edge of a huge collection of stars called the Milky Way Galaxy, which is one *galaxy* among billions of others spread throughout the observable universe. To begin to get a feel for the relationships among these very different objects, consult Figures 1 through 4; put them in perspective by studying Figure 5.

We are connected to the most distant realms of space and time not only by our imaginations but also through a common cosmic heritage. Most of the chemical elements that make up our bodies (hydrogen, oxygen, carbon, and many more) were created billions of years ago in the hot centers of long-vanished stars. Their fuel supply spent, these giant stars died in huge explosions, scattering the elements created deep within their cores far and wide. Eventually, this matter collected into clouds of gas that slowly collapsed to give birth to new generations of stars. In this way, the Sun and its family of planets formed nearly five billion years ago. Everything on Earth embodies atoms from other parts of the universe and from a past far more remote than the beginning of human evolution. Elsewhere, other beings—perhaps with intelligence much greater than our own—may at this very moment be gazing in wonder at their own night sky. Our own Sun may be nothing more than an insignificant point of light to them—if it is visible at all. Yet if such beings exist, they must share our cosmic origin.

Simply put, the **universe** is the totality of all space, time, matter, and energy. **Astronomy** is the study of the universe. It is a subject unlike any other, for it requires us to profoundly change our view of the cosmos and to consider matter on scales totally unfamiliar from everyday experience. Look again at the galaxy in Figure 3. It is a swarm of about a hundred billion stars—more stars than the number of people who have ever lived on Earth. The entire assemblage is spread across a vast expanse of space 100,000 **light-years** in diameter. Although it sounds like a unit of time, a light-year is in fact the *distance* traveled by light in a year, at a speed of about 300,000 kilometers per second. Multiplying out, it follows that a light-year is equal to 300,000 kilometers/second $\times$ 86,400 seconds/day $\times$ 365 days or about 10 trillion kilometers, or roughly 6 trillion miles. Typical

15,000 kilometers

▲ **FIGURE 1 Earth** Earth is a planet, a mostly solid object, although it has some liquid in its oceans and core and gas in its atmosphere. In this view, the North and South American continents are clearly visible, though most of the scene shows Pacific waters. *(NASA)*

1,500,000 kilometers

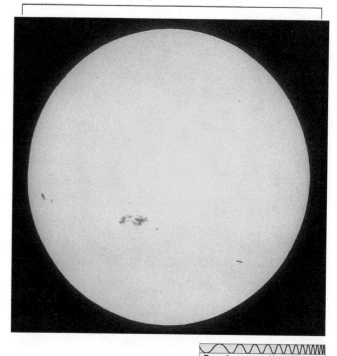

▲ **FIGURE 2 The Sun** The Sun is a star, a very hot ball of gas composed mainly of hydrogen and helium. Much bigger than Earth—more than 100 times larger in diameter—the Sun is held together by its own gravity. The dark blemishes are sunspots. *(AURA)*

galactic systems are truly "astronomical" in size. For comparison, Earth's roughly 13,000-km diameter is less than one-twentieth of a light-*second*.

The light-year is a unit introduced by astronomers to help them describe immense distances. We will encounter many such custom units in our studies. Astronomers frequently augment the standard SI (Système Internationale) metric system with additional units tailored to the particular problem at hand.

A thousand (1000), a million (1,000,000), a billion (1,000,000,000), and even a trillion (1,000,000,000,000)—these words occur regularly in everyday speech. But let's take a moment to understand the magnitude of the numbers and appreciate the differences among them. One thousand is easy enough to understand: At the rate of one number per second, you could count to a thousand in 1000 seconds—about 16 minutes. However, if you wanted to count to a million, you would need more than two weeks of counting at the rate of one number per second, 16 hours per day (allowing 8 hours per day for sleep). To count from one to a billion at the same rate of one number per second and 16 hours per day would take nearly 50 years—the better part of an entire human lifetime.

In this text, we consider *distances* in space spanning not just billions of kilometers, but billions of light-years; *objects* containing not just trillions of atoms, but trillions of stars; and *time intervals* of not just billions of seconds or hours, but billions of years. You will need to become familiar—and comfortable—with such enormous numbers. A good way to begin is learning to recognize just how much larger than a thousand is a million, and how much larger still is a billion. The convenient method used by scientists for writing and manipulating very large and very small numbers is *scientific notation*.

Lacking any understanding of the astronomical objects they observed, early skywatchers made up stories to explain them: The Sun was pulled across the heavens by a chariot drawn by winged horses, and patterns of stars traced heroes and animals placed in the sky by the gods. Today, of course, we have a radically different conception of the universe. The stars we see are distant, glowing orbs hundreds of times larger than our entire planet, and the patterns they form span hundreds of light-years. In this chapter we present some basic methods used by astronomers to chart the space around us. We describe the slow progress of scientific knowledge, from chariots and gods to today's well-tested theories and physical laws, and explain why we now rely on science rather than on myth to help us explain the universe.

About 1000 quadrillion kilometers, or 100,000 light-years

▲ FIGURE 3 **Galaxy** A typical galaxy is a collection of a hundred billion stars, each separated by vast regions of nearly empty space. Our Sun is a rather undistinguished star near the edge of another such galaxy, called the Milky Way. (*NASA*)

About 1,000,000 light-years

▲ FIGURE 4 **Galaxy Cluster** This photograph shows a typical cluster of galaxies, spread across roughly a million light-years of space. Each galaxy contains hundreds of billions of stars, probably planets, and possibly living creatures. (*NASA*)

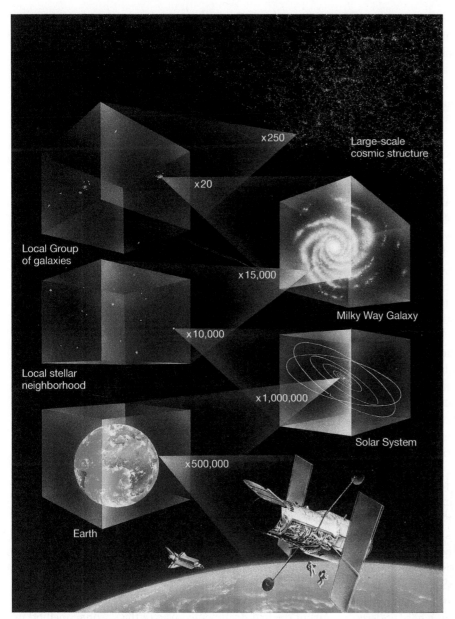

◀ FIGURE 5 **Size and Scale** This artist's conception puts each of the previous four figures in perspective. The bottom of this figure shows spacecraft (and astronauts) in Earth orbit, a view that widens progressively in each of the next five cubes drawn from bottom to top—Earth, our planetary system, the local neighborhood of stars, the Milky Way Galaxy, and the closest cluster of galaxies. The image at the top right depicts the spread of galaxies (white dots) in the universe on extremely large scales—the field of view in this final frame is hundreds of millions of light-years across. The numbers indicate approximately the increase in scale between successive images: Earth is 500,000 times larger than the spacecraft in the foreground, the solar system in turn is some 1,000,000 times larger than Earth, and so on. Modern astronomy is the story of how humans have come to understand the immense scale of the universe, and our place in it. *(D. Berry)*

2 Scientific Theory and the Scientific Method

How have we come to know the universe around us? How do we know the proper perspective sketched in Figure 5? The earliest known descriptions of the universe were based largely on imagination and mythology and made little attempt to explain the workings of the heavens in terms of known earthly experience. However, history shows that some early scientists did come to realize the importance of careful observation and testing to the formulation of their ideas. The success of their approach changed, slowly but surely, the way science was done and opened the door to a fuller understanding of nature. As knowledge from all sources was sought and embraced for its own sake, the influence of logic and reasoned argument grew and the

power of myth diminished. People began to inquire more critically about themselves and the universe. They realized that *thinking* about nature was no longer sufficient—*looking* at it was also necessary. Experiments and observations became a central part of the process of inquiry.

To be effective, a **theory**—the framework of ideas and assumptions used to explain some set of observations and make predictions about the real world—must be continually tested. Scientists accomplish this by using a theory to construct a **theoretical model** of a physical object (such as a planet or a star) or phenomenon (such as gravity or light) that accounts for its known properties. The model then makes further predictions about the object's properties, or perhaps how it might behave or change under new circumstances. If experiments and observations favor those predictions, the theory can be further developed and refined. If they do not, the theory must be reformulated or rejected, no matter how appealing it originally seemed. This approach to investigation, combining thinking and doing—that is, theory and experiment—is known as the **scientific method.** The process, combining theoretical reasoning with experimental testing, is illustrated schematically in Figure 6. It lies at the heart of modern science, separating science from pseudoscience, fact from fiction.

The notion that theories must be tested and may be proven wrong sometimes leads people to dismiss their importance. We have all heard the expression, "Of course, it's only a theory," used to deride or dismiss an idea that someone finds unacceptable. Don't be fooled! Gravity is "only" a theory, but calculations based on it have guided human spacecraft throughout the solar system. Electromagnetism and quantum mechanics are theories, too, yet they form the foundation for most of 20th- (and 21st-) century technology. Facts about the universe are a dime a dozen. Theories are the intellectual "glue" that combine seemingly unrelated facts into a coherent and interconnected whole.

Notice that there is no end point to the process depicted in Figure 6. A theory can be invalidated by a single wrong prediction, but no amount of observation or experimentation can ever prove it "correct." Theories simply become more and more widely accepted as their predictions are repeatedly confirmed. As a class, modern scientific theories share several important defining characteristics:

- They must be *testable*—that is, they must admit the possibility that their underlying assumptions and their predictions can, in principle, be exposed to experimental verification. This feature separates science from, for example, religion, since, ultimately, divine revelations or scriptures cannot be challenged within a religious framework—we can't design an experiment to "verify the mind of God." Testability also distinguishes science from a pseudoscience such as astrology, whose underlying assumptions and predictions have been repeatedly tested and never verified, with no apparent impact on the views of those who continue to believe in it!

- They must continually be *tested,* and their consequences tested, too. This is the basic circle of scientific progress depicted in Figure 6.

- They should be *simple.* Simplicity is less a requirement than a practical outcome of centuries of scientific experience—the most successful theories tend to be the simplest ones that fit the facts. This viewpoint is often encapsulated in a principle known as *Occam's razor:* If two competing theories both explain the facts and make the same predictions, then the simpler one is better. Put another way—"Keep it simple!" A good theory should contain no more complexity than is absolutely necessary.

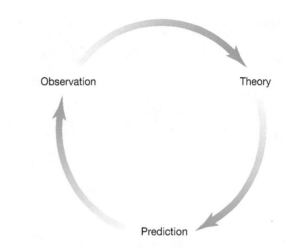

▲ FIGURE 6 **Scientific Method** Scientific theories evolve through a combination of observation, theoretical reasoning, and prediction, which in turn suggests new observations. The process can begin at any point in the cycle (although it usually starts with observations), and it continues forever—or until the theory fails to explain an observation or makes a demonstrably false prediction.

- Finally, most scientists have the additional bias that a theory should in some sense be *elegant.* When a clearly stated simple principle naturally ties together and explains several phenomena previously thought to be completely distinct, this is widely regarded as a strong point in favor of the new theory.

You may find it instructive to apply these criteria to the many physical theories—some old and well established, others much more recent and still developing.

The birth of modern science is usually associated with the Renaissance, the historical period from the late 14th to the mid-17th century that saw a rebirth (*renaissance* in French) of artistic, literary, and scientific inquiry in European culture following the chaos of the Dark Ages. However, one of the first documented uses of the scientific method in an astronomical context was made by Aristotle (384–322 B.C.) some 17 centuries earlier. Aristotle is not normally remembered as a strong proponent of this approach—many of his best known ideas were based on pure thought, with no attempt at experimental test or verification. Nevertheless, his brilliance extended into many areas now thought of as modern science. He noted that, during a lunar eclipse (Section 6), Earth casts a curved shadow onto the surface of the Moon. Figure 7 shows a series of photographs taken during a recent lunar eclipse. Earth's shadow, projected onto the Moon's surface, is indeed slightly curved. This is what Aristotle must have seen and recorded so long ago.

Because the observed shadow seemed always to be an arc of the same circle, Aristotle theorized that Earth, the cause of the shadow, must be round. Don't underestimate the scope of this apparently simple statement. Aristotle also had to reason that the dark region was indeed a shadow and

    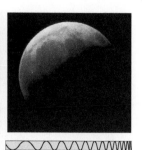

▲ FIGURE 7 **A Lunar Eclipse** This series of photographs shows Earth's shadow sweeping across the Moon during a lunar eclipse. By observing this behavior, Aristotle reasoned that Earth was the cause of the shadow and concluded that Earth must be round. His theory has yet to be disproved. (*G. Schneider*)

that Earth was its cause—facts we regard as obvious today, but far from clear 25 centuries ago. On the basis of this *hypothesis*—one possible explanation of the observed facts—he then predicted that any and all future lunar eclipses would show Earth's shadow to be curved, regardless of our planet's orientation. That prediction has been tested every time a lunar eclipse has occurred. It has yet to be proved wrong. Aristotle was not the first person to argue that Earth is round, but he was apparently the first to offer observational proof using the lunar eclipse method.

This basic reasoning forms the basis of all modern scientific inquiry. Armed only with naked-eye observations of the sky (the telescope would not be invented for almost another 2000 years), Aristotle first made an observation. Next, he formulated a hypothesis to explain that observation. Then he tested the validity of his hypothesis by making predictions that could be confirmed or refuted by further observations. *Observation, theory, and testing*—these are the cornerstones of the scientific method, a technique whose power will be demonstrated again and again throughout our text.

Today, scientists throughout the world use an approach that relies heavily on testing ideas. They gather data, form a working hypothesis that explains the data, and then proceed to test the implications of the hypothesis using experiment and observation. Eventually, one or more "well-tested" hypotheses may be elevated to the stature of a physical law and come to form the basis of a theory of even broader applicability. The new predictions of the theory will in turn be tested, as scientific knowledge continues to grow. Experiment and observation are integral parts of the process of scientific inquiry. Untestable theories, or theories unsupported by experimental evidence, rarely gain any measure of acceptance in scientific circles. Used properly over a period of time, this rational, methodical approach enables us to arrive at conclusions that are mostly free of the personal bias and human values of any one scientist. The scientific method is designed to yield an objective view of the universe we inhabit.

PROCESS OF SCIENCE CHECK
✔ Can a theory ever become a "fact," scientifically speaking?

3 The "Obvious" View

To see how astronomers have applied the scientific method to understand the universe around us, let's start with some very basic observations. Our study of the cosmos, the modern science of astronomy, begins simply, with looking at the night sky. The overall appearance of the night sky is not so different now from what our ancestors would have seen hundreds or even thousands of years ago, but our *interpretation* of what we see has changed immeasurably as the science of astronomy has evolved and grown.

Constellations in the Sky

Between sunset and sunrise on a clear night, we can see about 3000 points of light. If we include the view from the opposite side of Earth, nearly 6000 stars are visible to the unaided eye. A natural human tendency is to see patterns and relationships among objects even when no true connection exists, and people long ago connected the brightest stars into configurations called **constellations,** which ancient astronomers named after mythological beings, heroes, and animals—whatever was important to them. Figure 8 shows a constellation especially prominent in the nighttime sky from October through March: the hunter named Orion. Orion was a mythical Greek hero famed, among other things, for his amorous pursuit of the Pleiades, the seven daughters of the giant Atlas. According to Greek mythology, to protect the Pleiades from Orion, the gods placed them among the stars, where Orion nightly stalks them across the sky. Many constellations have similarly fabulous connections with ancient lore.

Perhaps not surprisingly, the patterns have a strong cultural bias—the astronomers of ancient China saw mythical figures different from those seen by the ancient Greeks, the Babylonians, and the people of other cultures, even though they were all looking at the same stars in the night sky. Interestingly, different cultures often made the same basic *groupings* of stars, despite widely varying interpretations of what they saw. For example, the group of seven stars usually known in North America as "the Dipper" is known as "the Wagon" or "the Plough" in western Europe. The ancient

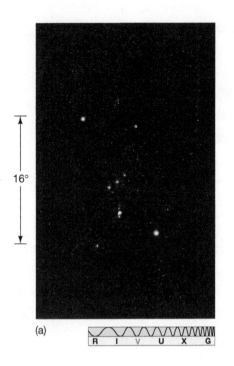

(a)

R I V U X G

(b)

16°

Interactive FIGURE 8
Constellation Orion (a) A photograph of the group of bright stars that make up the constellation Orion. (b) The stars are connected to show the pattern visualized by the Greeks: the outline of a hunter. The Greek letters serve to identify some of the brighter stars in the constellation (see also Figure 9). You can easily find Orion in the northern winter sky by identifying the line of three bright stars in the hunter's "belt." *(S. Westphal)*
From Chapter 1 of *Astronomy Today*, Seventh Edition, Eric Chaisson, Steve McMillan.

Greeks regarded these same stars as the tail of "the Great Bear," the Egyptians saw them as the leg of an ox, the Siberians as a stag, and some Native Americans as a funeral procession.

Early astronomers had very practical reasons for studying the sky. Some constellations served as navigational guides. The star Polaris (part of the Little Dipper) indicates north, and the near constancy of its location in the sky, from hour to hour and night to night, has aided travelers for centuries. Other constellations served as primitive calendars to predict planting and harvesting seasons. For example, many cultures knew that the appearance of certain stars on the horizon just before daybreak signaled the beginning of spring and the end of winter.

In many societies, people came to believe that there were other benefits in being able to trace the regularly changing positions of heavenly bodies. The relative positions of stars and planets at a person's birth were carefully studied by *astrologers*, who used the data to make predictions about that person's destiny. Thus, in a sense, astronomy and astrology arose from the same basic impulse—the desire to "see" into the future—and, indeed, for a long time they were indistinguishable from one another. Today, most people recognize that astrology is nothing more than an amusing diversion (although millions still study their horoscope in the newspaper every morning!). Nevertheless, the ancient astrological terminology—the names of the constellations and many terms used to describe the locations and motions of the planets—is still used throughout the astronomical world.

Generally speaking, as illustrated in Figure 9 for the case of Orion, the stars that make up any particular constellation are not actually close to one another in space, even by astronomical standards. They merely are bright enough to observe with the naked eye and happen to lie in roughly the same direction in the sky as seen from Earth.

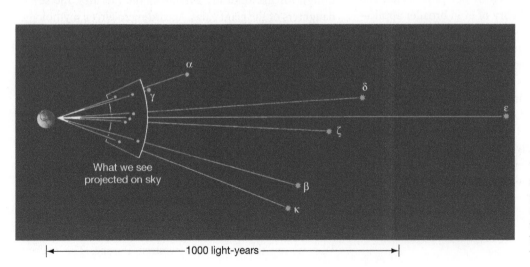

What we see projected on sky

◄ FIGURE 9 Orion in 3-D
The true three-dimensional relationships among the most prominent stars in Orion. The distances were determined by the *Hipparcos* satellite in the 1990s.

1000 light-years

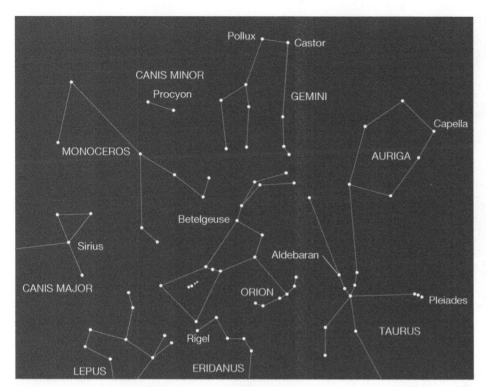

but of Earth. Polaris indicates the direction—due north—in which Earth's rotation axis points. Even though we now know that the celestial sphere is an incorrect description of the heavens, we still use the idea as a convenient fiction that helps us visualize the positions of stars in the sky. The points where Earth's axis intersects the celestial sphere are called the **celestial poles.** In the Northern Hemisphere, the north celestial pole lies directly above Earth's North Pole. The extension of Earth's axis in the opposite direction defines the south celestial pole, directly above Earth's South Pole. Midway between the north

Still, the constellations provide a convenient means for astronomers to specify large areas of the sky, much as geologists use continents or politicians use voting precincts to identify certain localities on planet Earth. In all, there are 88 constellations, most of them visible from North America at some time during the year. Figure 10 shows how the conventionally defined constellations cover a portion of the sky in the vicinity of Orion.

The Celestial Sphere

Over the course of a night, the constellations seem to move smoothly across the sky from east to west, but ancient skywatchers were well aware that the *relative* locations of stars remained unchanged as this nightly march took place.* It was natural for those observers to conclude that the stars must be firmly attached to a **celestial sphere** surrounding Earth—a canopy of stars resembling an astronomical painting on a heavenly ceiling. Figure 11 shows how early astronomers pictured the stars as moving with this celestial sphere as it turned around a fixed, unmoving Earth. Figure 12 shows how all stars appear to move in circles around a point very close to the star Polaris (better known as the Pole Star or North Star). To the ancients, this point represented the axis around which the entire celestial sphere turned.

Today we recognize that the apparent motion of the stars is the result of the spin, or **rotation,** not of the celestial sphere,

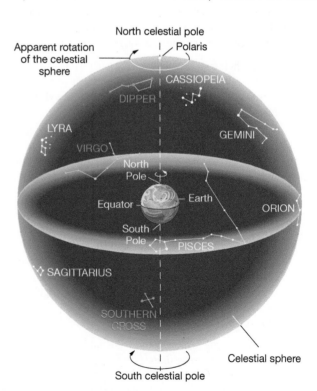

▲ FIGURE 11 **Celestial Sphere** Planet Earth sits fixed at the hub of the celestial sphere, which contains all the stars. This is one of the simplest possible models of the universe, but it doesn't agree with all the facts that astronomers now know about the universe.

*We now know that stars do in fact move relative to one another, but this proper motion *across the sky* is too slow to be discerned with the naked eye.

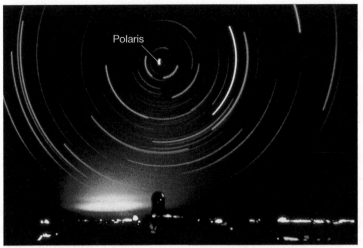

Polaris

Interactive FIGURE 12 **Northern Sky** A time-lapse photograph of the northern sky. Each curved trail is the path of a single star across the night sky. The duration of the exposure is about 5 hours, and each star traces out approximately 20 percent of a circle. The concentric circles are centered near the North Star, Polaris, whose short, bright arc is labeled. *(AURA)*

From Chapter 1 of *Astronomy Today*, Seventh Edition, Eric Chaisson, Steve McMillan.

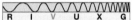

R I V U X G

and south celestial poles lies the **celestial equator,** representing the intersection of Earth's equatorial plane with the celestial sphere. These parts of the celestial sphere are marked on Figure 11.

When discussing the locations of stars "on the sky," astronomers naturally talk in terms of *angular* positions and separations. *More Precisely 1* presents some basic information on angular measure.

MORE PRECISELY 1

Angular Measure

Size and scale are often specified by measuring lengths and angles. The concept of length measurement is fairly intuitive to most of us. The concept of *angular measurement* may be less familiar, but it, too, can become second nature if you remember a few simple facts:

- A full circle contains 360 *degrees* (360°). Thus, the half-circle that stretches from horizon to horizon, passing directly overhead and spanning the portion of the sky visible to one person at any one time, contains 180°.

- Each 1° increment can be further subdivided into fractions of a degree, called *arc minutes*. There are 60 arc minutes (written 60′) in 1°. (The term "arc" is used to distinguish this angular unit from the unit of time.) Both the Sun and the Moon project an angular size of 30 arc minutes (half a degree) on the sky. Your little finger, held at arm's length, has a similar angular size, covering about a 40′ slice of the 180° horizon-to-horizon arc.

- An arc minute can be divided into 60 *arc seconds* (60″). Put another way, an arc minute is $\frac{1}{60}$ of a degree, and an arc second is $\frac{1}{60} \times \frac{1}{60} = \frac{1}{3600}$ of a degree. An arc second is an extremely small unit of angular measure—the angular size of a centimeter-sized object (a dime, say) at a distance of about 2 kilometers (a little over a mile).

The accompanying figure illustrates this subdivision of the circle into progressively smaller units.

Don't be confused by the units used to measure angles. Arc minutes and arc seconds have nothing to do with the measurement of time, and degrees have nothing to do with temperature. Degrees, arc minutes, and arc seconds are simply ways to measure the size and position of objects in the universe.

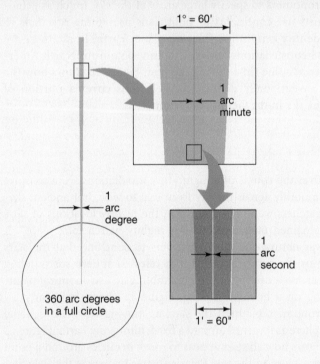

1° = 60′

1 arc minute

1 arc degree

360 arc degrees in a full circle

1 arc second

1′ = 60″

The angular size of an object depends both on its actual size and on its distance from us. For example, the Moon at its present distance from Earth has an angular diameter of 0.5°, or 30′. If the Moon were twice as far away, it would appear half as big—15′ across—even though its actual size would be the same. Thus, *angular size by itself is not enough to determine the actual diameter of an object—the distance to the object must also be known.* We return to this topic in more detail in *More Precisely 2.*

CONCEPT CHECK

✔ Why do astronomers find it useful to retain the fiction of the celestial sphere to describe the sky? What vital piece of information about stars is lost when we talk about their locations "on" the sky?

4 Earth's Orbital Motion

Day-to-Day Changes

We measure time by the Sun. Because the rhythm of day and night is central to our lives, it is not surprising that the period from one noon to the next, the 24-hour **solar day,** is our basic social time unit. The daily progress of the Sun and the other stars across the sky is known as *diurnal motion.* As we have just seen, it is a consequence of Earth's rotation. But the stars' positions in the sky do *not* repeat themselves exactly from one night to the next. Each night, the whole celestial sphere appears to be shifted a little relative to the horizon compared with the night before. The easiest way to confirm this difference is by noticing the stars that are visible just after sunset or just before dawn. You will find that they are in slightly different locations from those of the previous night. Because of this shift, a day measured by the stars—called a **sidereal day** after the Latin word *sidus,* meaning "star"—differs in length from a solar day. Evidently, there is more to the apparent motion of the heavens than simple rotation.

The reason for the difference between a solar day and a sidereal day is sketched in Figure 13. It is a result of the fact that Earth moves in two ways simultaneously: It rotates on its central axis while at the same time **revolving** around the Sun. Each time Earth rotates once on its axis, it also moves a small distance along its orbit about the Sun. Earth therefore has to rotate through slightly more than 360° (360 degrees—see *More Precisely 1*) for the Sun to return to the same apparent location in the sky. Thus, the interval of time between noon one day and noon the next (a solar day) is slightly greater than one true rotation period (one sidereal day). Our planet takes 365 days to orbit the Sun, so the additional angle is 360°/365 = 0.986°. Because Earth, rotating at a rate of 15° per hour, takes about 3.9 minutes to rotate through this angle, the solar day is 3.9 minutes longer than the sidereal day (i.e., 1 sidereal day is roughly $23^\text{h}56^\text{m}$ long).

Seasonal Changes

Figure 14(a) illustrates the major stars visible from most locations in the United States on clear summer evenings. The brightest stars—Vega, Deneb, and Altair—form a conspicuous triangle high above the constellations Sagittarius and Capricornus, which are low

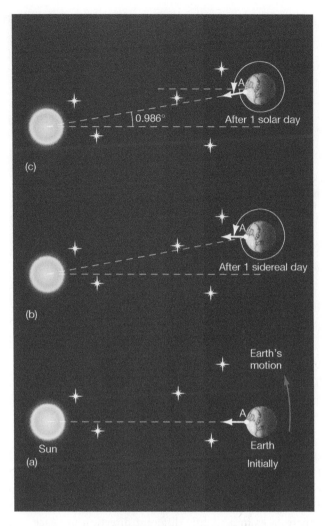

▲ **FIGURE 13 Solar and Sidereal Days** A sidereal day is Earth's true rotation period—the time taken for our planet to return to the same orientation in space relative to the distant stars. A solar day is the time from one noon to the next. The difference in length between the two is easily explained once we understand that Earth revolves around the Sun at the same time as it rotates on its axis. Frames (a) and (b) are one sidereal day apart. During that time, Earth rotates exactly once on its axis and also moves a little in its solar orbit—approximately 1°. Consequently, between noon at point A on one day and noon at the same point the next day, Earth actually rotates through about 361° (frame c), and the solar day exceeds the sidereal day by about 4 minutes. Note that the diagrams are not drawn to scale; the true 1° angle is in reality much smaller than shown here.

on the southern horizon. In the winter sky, however, these stars are replaced as shown in Figure 14(b) by several other, well-known constellations, including Orion, Leo, and Gemini. In the constellation Canis Major lies Sirius (the Dog Star), the brightest star in the sky. Year after year, the same stars and constellations return, each in its proper season. Every winter evening, Orion is high overhead; every summer, it is gone. (For more

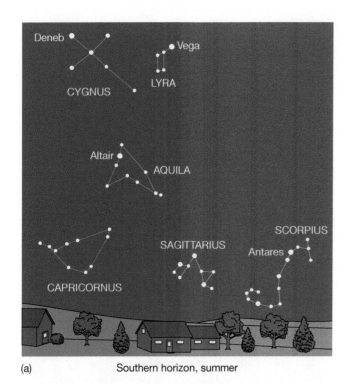

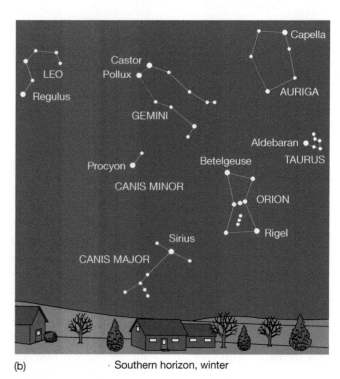

(a) Southern horizon, summer

(b) Southern horizon, winter

▲ **FIGURE 14 Typical Night Sky** (a) A typical summer sky above the United States. Some prominent stars (labeled in lowercase letters) and constellations (labeled in all capital letters) are shown. (b) A typical winter sky above the United States.

detailed maps of the sky at different seasons, consult the star charts.)

These regular seasonal changes occur because of Earth's **revolution** around the Sun: Earth's darkened hemisphere faces in a slightly different direction in space each evening. The change in direction is only about 1° per night (Figure 13)—too small to be easily noticed with the naked eye from one evening to the next, but clearly noticeable over the course of weeks and months, as illustrated in Figure 15. After 6 months, Earth has reached the opposite side of

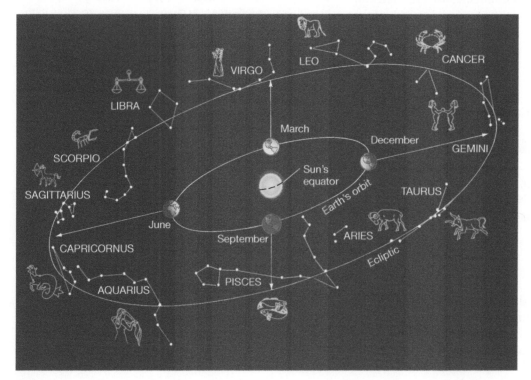

◄ **Interactive** FIGURE 15
The Zodiac The view of the night sky changes as Earth moves in its orbit about the Sun. As drawn here, the night side of Earth faces a different set of constellations at different times of the year. The 12 constellations named here make up the astrological zodiac. The arrows indicate the most prominent zodiacal constellations in the night sky at various times of the year. For example, in June, when the Sun is "in" Gemini, Sagittarius and Capricornus are visible at night. From Chapter 1 of *Astronomy Today*, Seventh Edition, Eric Chaisson, Steve McMillan.

its orbit, and we face an entirely different group of stars and constellations at night. Because of this motion, the Sun appears (to an observer on Earth) to move relative to the background stars over the course of a year. This apparent motion of the Sun on the sky traces out a path on the celestial sphere known as the **ecliptic.**

The 12 constellations through which the Sun passes as it moves along the ecliptic—that is, the constellations we would see looking in the direction of the Sun if they weren't overwhelmed by the Sun's light—had special significance for astrologers of old. These constellations are collectively known as the **zodiac.**

As illustrated in Figure 16, the ecliptic forms a great circle on the celestial sphere, inclined at an angle of 23.5° to the celestial equator. In reality, as illustrated in Figure 17, the plane of the ecliptic is *the plane of Earth's orbit around the Sun.* Its tilt is a consequence of the *inclination* of our planet's rotation axis to the plane of its orbit.

The point on the ecliptic where the Sun is at its northernmost point above the celestial equator is known as the **summer solstice** (from the Latin words *sol,* meaning "sun," and *stare,* "to stand"). As indicated in Figure 17, it represents the location in Earth's orbit where our planet's North Pole comes closest to pointing in the direction of the Sun. This occurs on or near June 21—the exact date varies slightly from year to year because the actual length of a year is not a whole number of days. As Earth rotates, points north of the equator spend the greatest fraction of their time in sunlight on that date, so the summer solstice corresponds to the longest day of the year in

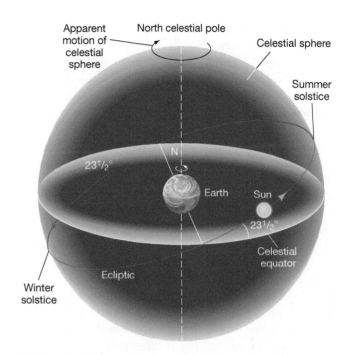

▲ **FIGURE 16 Ecliptic** The apparent path of the Sun on the celestial sphere over the course of a year is called the ecliptic. As indicated on the diagram, the ecliptic is inclined to the celestial equator at an angle of 23.5°. In this picture of the heavens, the seasons result from the changing height of the Sun above the celestial equator. At the summer solstice, the Sun is at its northernmost point on its path around the ecliptic; it is therefore highest in the sky, as seen from Earth's Northern Hemisphere, and the days are longest. The reverse is true at the winter solstice. At the vernal and autumnal equinoxes, when the Sun crosses the celestial equator, day and night are of equal length.

▶ **Interactive** FIGURE 17 **Seasons**
   In reality, the Sun's apparent motion along the ecliptic is a consequence of Earth's orbital motion around the Sun. The seasons result from the inclination of our planet's rotation axis with respect to its orbit plane. The summer solstice corresponds to the point on Earth's orbit where our planet's North Pole points most nearly toward the Sun. The opposite is true of the winter solstice. The vernal and autumnal equinoxes correspond to the points in Earth's orbit where our planet's axis is perpendicular to the line joining Earth and the Sun. The insets show how rays of sunlight striking the ground at an angle (e.g., during northern winter) are spread over a larger area than rays coming nearly straight down (e.g., during northern summer). As a result, the amount of solar heat delivered to a given area of Earth's surface is greatest when the Sun is high in the sky.
From Chapter 1 of *Astronomy Today,*
Seventh Edition, Eric Chaisson,
Steve McMillan.

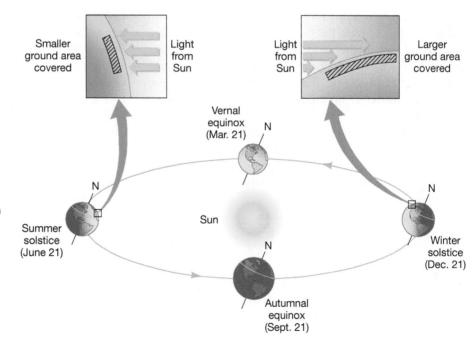

the Northern Hemisphere and the shortest day in the Southern Hemisphere.

Six months later, the Sun is at its southernmost point below the celestial equator (Figure 16)—or, equivalently, the North Pole points farthest from the Sun (Figure 17). We have reached the **winter solstice** (December 21), the shortest day in Earth's Northern Hemisphere and the longest in the Southern Hemisphere.

The tilt of Earth's rotation axis relative to the ecliptic is responsible for the **seasons** we experience—the marked difference in temperature between the hot summer and cold winter months. As illustrated in Figure 17, two factors combine to cause this variation. First, there are more hours of daylight during the summer than in winter. To see why this is, look at the yellow lines on the surfaces of the drawings of Earth in the figure. (For definiteness, they correspond to a latitude of 45°—roughly that of the Great Lakes or the south of France.) A much larger fraction of the line is sunlit in the summertime, and more daylight means more solar heating. Second, as illustrated in the insets in Figure 17, when the Sun is high in the sky in summer, rays of sunlight striking Earth's surface are more concentrated—spread out over a smaller area—than in winter. As a result, the Sun feels hotter. Therefore summer, when the Sun is highest above the horizon and the days are longest, is generally much warmer than winter, when the Sun is low and the days are short.

A popular misconception is that the seasons have something to do with Earth's distance from the Sun. Figure 18 illustrates why this is *not* the case. It shows Earth's orbit "face on," instead of almost edge-on, as in Figure 17. Notice that the orbit is almost perfectly circular, so the distance from Earth to the Sun varies very little (in fact, by only about 3 percent) over the course of a year—not nearly enough to explain the seasonal changes in temperature. What's more, Earth is actually *closest* to the Sun in early January, the dead of winter in the Northern Hemisphere, so distance from the Sun cannot be the main factor controlling our climate.

The two points where the ecliptic intersects the celestial equator (Figure 16)—that is, where Earth's rotation axis is perpendicular to the line joining Earth to the Sun (Figure 17)—are known as **equinoxes.** On those dates, day and night are of equal duration. (The word *equinox* derives from the Latin for "equal night.") In the fall (in the Northern Hemisphere), as the Sun crosses from the Northern into the Southern Hemisphere, we have the **autumnal equinox** (on September 21). The **vernal equinox** occurs in northern spring, on or near March 21, as the Sun crosses the celestial equator moving north. Because of its association with the end of winter and the start of a new growing season, the vernal equinox was particularly important to early astronomers and astrologers. It also plays an important role

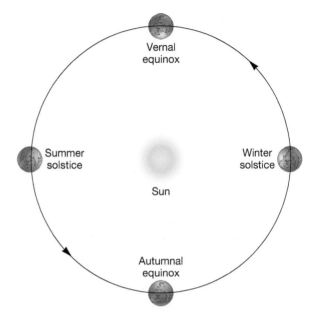

▲ **FIGURE 18 Earth's Orbit** Seen face on, Earth's orbit around the Sun is almost indistinguishable from a perfect circle. The distance from Earth to the Sun varies only slightly over the course of a year and is *not* the cause of the seasonal temperature variations we experience.

in human timekeeping: The interval of time from one vernal equinox to the next—365.2422 mean solar days—is known as one **tropical year.**

Long-Term Changes

Earth has many motions—it spins on its axis, it travels around the Sun, and it moves with the Sun through our Galaxy. We have just seen how some of these motions can account for the changing nighttime sky and the changing seasons. In fact, the situation is even more complicated. Like a spinning top that rotates rapidly on its own axis while that axis slowly revolves about the vertical, Earth's axis changes its *direction* over the course of time (although the angle between the axis and a line perpendicular to the plane of the ecliptic always remains close to 23.5°). Illustrated in Figure 19, this change is called **precession.** It is caused by torques (twisting forces) on Earth due to the gravitational pulls of the Moon and the Sun, which affect our planet in much the same way as the torque due to Earth's own gravity affects a top. During a complete cycle of precession—about 26,000 years—Earth's axis traces out a cone.

The time required for Earth to complete exactly one orbit around the Sun, relative to the stars, is called a **sidereal year.** One sidereal year is 365.256 mean solar days long—about 20 minutes longer than a tropical year. The

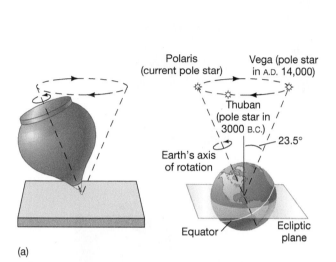

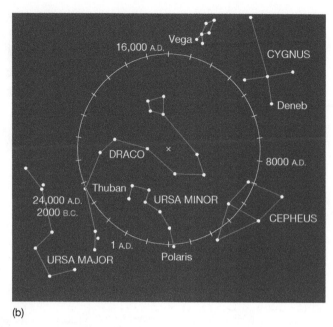

(a)

(b)

Interactive FIGURE 19 **Precession** (a) Earth's axis currently points nearly toward the star Polaris. About 12,000 years from now—almost halfway through one cycle of precession—Earth's axis will point toward a star called Vega, which will then be the "North Star." Five thousand years ago, the North Star was a star named Thuban in the constellation Draco. (b) The circle shows the precessional path of the north celestial pole among some prominent northern stars. Tick marks indicate intervals of a thousand years.
From Chapter 1 of *Astronomy Today*, Seventh Edition, Eric Chaisson, Steve McMillan.

reason for this slight difference is Earth's precession. Recall that the vernal equinox occurs when Earth's rotation axis is perpendicular to the line joining Earth and the Sun, and the Sun is crossing the celestial equator moving from south to north. In the absence of precession, this combination of events would occur exactly once per sidereal orbit, and the tropical and sidereal years would be identical. However, because of the slow precessional shift in the orientation of Earth's rotation axis, the instant when the axis is next perpendicular to the line from Earth to the Sun occurs slightly *sooner* than we would otherwise expect. Consequently, the vernal equinox drifts slowly around the zodiac over the course of the precession cycle.

The tropical year is the year that our calendars measure. If our timekeeping were tied to the sidereal year, the seasons would slowly march around the calendar as Earth precessed—13,000 years from now, summer in the Northern Hemisphere would be at its height in late February! By using the tropical year, we ensure that July and August will always be (northern) summer months. However, in 13,000 years' time, Orion will be a summer constellation.

CONCEPT CHECK

✔ In astronomical terms, what are *summer* and *winter,* and why do we see different constellations during those seasons?

5 The Motion of the Moon

The Moon is our nearest neighbor in space. Apart from the Sun, it is the brightest object in the sky. Like the Sun, the Moon appears to move relative to the background stars. Unlike the Sun, however, the Moon really does revolve around Earth. It crosses the sky at a rate of about 12° per day, which means that it moves an angular distance equal to its own diameter—30 arc minutes—in about an hour.

Lunar Phases

The Moon's appearance undergoes a regular cycle of changes, or **phases,** taking roughly 29.5 days to complete. Figure 20 illustrates the appearance of the Moon at different times in this monthly cycle. Starting from the *new Moon,* which is all but invisible in the sky, the Moon appears to *wax* (or grow) a little each night and is visible as a growing *crescent* (photo 1 of Figure 20). One week after new Moon, half of the lunar disk can be seen (photo 2). This phase is known as a *quarter Moon.* During the next week, the Moon continues to wax, passing through the *gibbous* phase (photo 3) until, 2 weeks after new Moon, the *full Moon* (photo 4) is visible. During the next 2 weeks, the Moon *wanes* (or shrinks), passing in turn through the gibbous, quarter, crescent phases (photos 5–7) and eventually becoming new again.

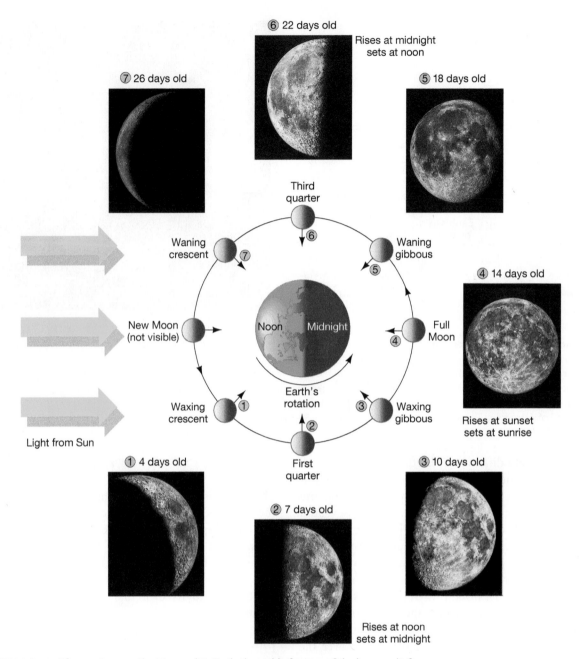

⑥ 22 days old
Rises at midnight
sets at noon

⑦ 26 days old

⑤ 18 days old

Third quarter

Waning crescent

⑦

⑥

Waning gibbous

⑤

④ 14 days old

New Moon (not visible)

Noon   Midnight

④

Full Moon

Earth's rotation

Rises at sunset
sets at sunrise

Waxing crescent

①

②

③

Waxing gibbous

Light from Sun

① 4 days old

First quarter

③ 10 days old

② 7 days old

Rises at noon
sets at midnight

▲ FIGURE 20 **Lunar Phases** Because the Moon orbits Earth, the visible fraction of the lunar sunlit face varies from night to night, although the Moon always keeps the same face toward our planet. (Note the location of the small, straight arrows, which mark the same point on the lunar surface at each phase shown.) The complete cycle of lunar phases, shown here starting at the waxing crescent phase and following the Moon's orbit counterclockwise, takes 29.5 days to complete. Rising and setting times for some phases are also indicated. *(UC/Lick Observatory)*

The position of the Moon in the sky relative to the Sun, as seen from Earth, varies with lunar phase. For example, the full Moon rises in the east as the Sun sets in the west, while the first quarter Moon actually rises at noon, but sometimes becomes visible only late in the day as the Sun's light fades. By this time the Moon is already high in the sky. Some connections between the lunar phase and the rising and setting times of the Moon are indicated in Figure 20.

The Moon doesn't actually change its size and shape from night to night, of course. Its full circular disk is present at all times. Why, then, don't we always see a full Moon? The answer to this question lies in the fact that, unlike the Sun and the other stars, the Moon emits no light of its own. Instead, it shines by reflected sunlight. As illustrated in Figure 20, half of the Moon's surface is illuminated by the Sun at any instant. However, not all of the Moon's sunlit face can be seen because of the Moon's position with respect to Earth and the Sun. When the Moon is full, we see the entire "daylit" face because the Sun and the Moon are in opposite directions from Earth in the sky. In the case of a new Moon, the Moon and the Sun are in almost the same part of the sky, and the sunlit side of the Moon is oriented away from us. At new Moon, the Sun must be almost behind the Moon, from our perspective.

As the Moon revolves around Earth, our satellite's position in the sky changes with respect to the stars. In 1 **sidereal month** (27.3 days), the Moon completes one revolution and returns to its starting point on the celestial sphere, having traced out a great circle in the sky. The time required for the Moon to complete a full cycle of phases, one **synodic month,** is a little longer—about 29.5 days. The synodic month is a little longer than the sidereal month for the same reason that a solar day is slightly longer than a sidereal day: Because of Earth's motion around the Sun, the Moon must complete slightly more than one full revolution to return to the same phase in its orbit (Figure 21).

Eclipses

From time to time—but only at new or full Moon—the Sun and the Moon line up precisely as seen from Earth, and we observe the spectacular phenomenon known as an **eclipse.** When the Sun and the Moon are in exactly *opposite* directions, as seen from Earth, Earth's shadow sweeps across the Moon, temporarily blocking the Sun's light and darkening the Moon in a **lunar eclipse,** as illustrated in Figure 22. From Earth, we see the curved edge of Earth's shadow begin to cut across the face of the full Moon and slowly eat its way into the lunar disk. Usually, the alignment of the Sun, Earth, and Moon is imperfect, so the shadow

▲ **Interactive FIGURE 21 Sidereal Month** The difference between a *synodic* and a *sidereal* month stems from the motion of Earth relative to the Sun. Because Earth orbits the Sun in 365 days, in the 29.5 days from one new Moon to the next (1 synodic month), Earth moves through an angle of approximately 29°. Thus, the Moon must revolve more than 360° between new Moons. The sidereal month, which is the time taken for the Moon to revolve through exactly 360°, relative to the stars, is about 2 days shorter.

never completely covers the Moon. Such an occurrence is known as a **partial lunar eclipse.** Occasionally, however, the entire lunar surface is obscured in a **total lunar eclipse,** such as that shown in the inset of Figure 22. Total lunar

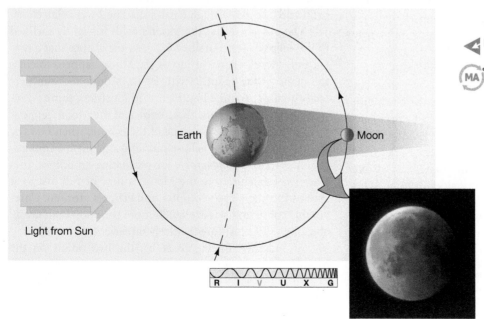

◄ **Interactive FIGURE 22 Lunar Eclipse** A lunar eclipse occurs when the Moon passes through Earth's shadow. At these times, we see a darkened, copper-colored Moon, as shown by the partial eclipse in the inset photograph. The red coloration is caused by sunlight deflected by Earth's atmosphere onto the Moon's surface. An observer on the Moon would see Earth surrounded by a bright, but narrow, ring of orange sunlight. Note that this figure is not drawn to scale, and only Earth's umbra (see text and Figure 24) is shown. *(Inset: G. Schneider)*
From Chapter 1 of *Astronomy Today,* Seventh Edition, Eric Chaisson, Steve McMillan.

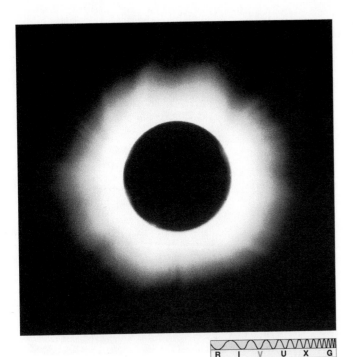

R I V U X G

◀ FIGURE 23 **Total Solar Eclipse** During a total solar eclipse, the Sun's corona becomes visible as an irregularly shaped halo surrounding the blotted-out disk of the Sun. This was the August 1999 eclipse, as seen from the banks of the Danube River near Sofia, Bulgaria. (*M. Tsavkova/B. Angelov*)

eclipses last only as long as is needed for the Moon to pass through Earth's shadow—no more than about 100 minutes. During that time, the Moon often acquires an eerie, deep red coloration—the result of a small amount of sunlight reddened by Earth's atmosphere (for the same reason that sunsets appearred and refracted (bent) onto the lunar surface, preventing the shadow from being completely black.

When the Moon and the Sun are in exactly the *same* direction, as seen from Earth, an even more awe-inspiring event occurs. The Moon passes directly in front of the Sun, briefly turning day into night in a **solar eclipse.** In a *total solar eclipse,* when the alignment is perfect, planets and some stars become visible in the daytime as the Sun's light is reduced to nearly nothing. We can also see the Sun's ghostly outer atmosphere, or *corona* (Figure 23).* In a *partial solar eclipse,* the Moon's path is slightly "off center," and only a portion of the Sun's face is covered. In either case, the sight of the Sun apparently being swallowed up by the black disk of the Moon is disconcerting even today. It must surely have inspired fear in early observers. Small wonder that the ability to predict such events was a highly prized skill.

Unlike a lunar eclipse, which is simultaneously visible from all locations on Earth's night side, a total solar eclipse can be seen from only a small portion of Earth's daytime side. The Moon's shadow on Earth's surface is about 7000 kilometers wide—roughly twice the diameter

of the Moon. Outside of that shadow, no eclipse is seen. However, within the central region of the shadow, called the **umbra,** the eclipse is total. Within the shadow, but outside the umbra, in the **penumbra,** the eclipse is partial, with less and less of the Sun obscured the farther one travels from the shadow's center.

The connections among the umbra, the penumbra, and the relative locations of Earth, Sun, and Moon are illustrated in Figure 24. The umbra is always very small. Even under the most favorable circumstances, its diameter never exceeds 270 kilometers. Because the shadow sweeps across Earth's surface at over 1700 kilometers per hour, the duration of a total eclipse at any given point on our planet can never exceed 7.5 minutes.

The Moon's orbit around Earth is not exactly circular. Thus, the Moon may be far enough from Earth at the moment of an eclipse that its disk fails to cover the disk of the Sun completely, even though their centers coincide. In that case, there is no region of totality—the umbra never reaches Earth at all, and a thin ring of sunlight can still be seen surrounding the Moon. Such an occurrence, called an **annular eclipse,** is illustrated in Figure 24(c) and shown more clearly in Figure 25. Roughly half of all solar eclipses are annular.

Eclipse Seasons

Why isn't there a solar eclipse at every new Moon and a lunar eclipse at every full Moon? That is, why doesn't the Moon pass directly between Earth and the Sun once per orbit and directly through Earth's shadow 2 weeks later?

The answer is that the Moon's orbit is slightly inclined to the ecliptic (at an angle of 5.2°), so the chance that a new (or full) Moon will occur just as the Moon happens to cross the plane of the ecliptic (with Earth, Moon, and Sun perfectly aligned) is quite low. Figure 26 illustrates some possible configurations of the three bodies. If the Moon happens to lie above or below the plane of the ecliptic when new (or full), a solar (or lunar) eclipse cannot occur. Such a configuration is termed *unfavorable* for producing an eclipse. In a *favorable* configuration, the Moon is new or full just as it crosses the plane of the ecliptic, and eclipses are seen. Unfavorable configurations are much more common than favorable ones, so eclipses are relatively rare events.

As indicated on Figure 26(b), the two points on the Moon's orbit where it crosses the plane of the ecliptic are known as the *nodes* of the orbit. The line joining the nodes, which is also the line of intersection of Earth's and the Moon's orbital planes, is known as the *line of nodes.* When the line of

Actually, although a total solar eclipse is undeniably a spectacular occurrence, the visibility of the corona is probably the most important astronomical aspect of such an event today. It enables us to study this otherwise hard-to-see part of our Sun.

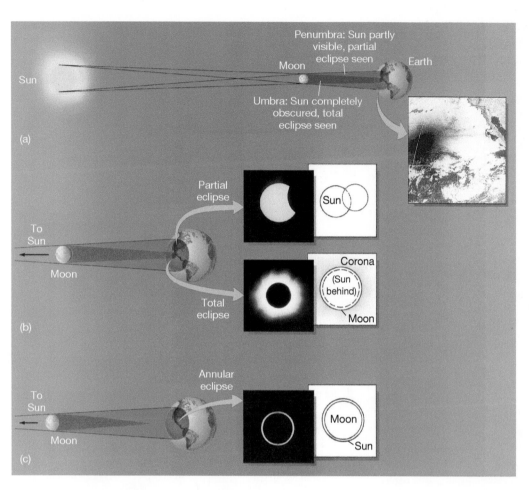

Interactive FIGURE 24 **Types of Solar Eclipse** (a) The Moon's shadow consists of two parts: the umbra, where no sunlight is seen, and the penumbra, where a portion of the Sun is visible. (b) If we are in the umbra, we see a total eclipse; in the penumbra, we see a partial eclipse. (c) If the Moon is too far from Earth at the moment of the eclipse, the umbra does not reach Earth and there is no region of totality; instead, an annular eclipse is seen. (Note that these figures are not drawn to scale.) *(Insets: NOAA; G. Schneider)*

From Chapter 1 of *Astronomy Today*, Seventh Edition, Eric Chaisson, Steve McMillan.

nodes is not directed toward the Sun, conditions are unfavorable for eclipses. However, when the line of nodes briefly lies along the Earth–Sun line, eclipses are possible. These two periods, known as **eclipse seasons,** are the only times at which an eclipse can occur. Notice that there is no guarantee that an eclipse *will* occur. For a solar eclipse, we must have a new Moon during an eclipse season. Similarly, a lunar eclipse can occur only at full Moon during an eclipse season.

Because we know the orbits of Earth and the Moon to great accuracy, we can predict eclipses far into the future. Figure 27 shows the location and duration of all total eclipses of the Sun between 2010 and 2030. It is interesting to note that the eclipse tracks run from west to east—just the opposite of more familiar phenomena such as sunrise and sunset, which are seen earlier by observers located farther east. The reason is that the Moon's shadow sweeps

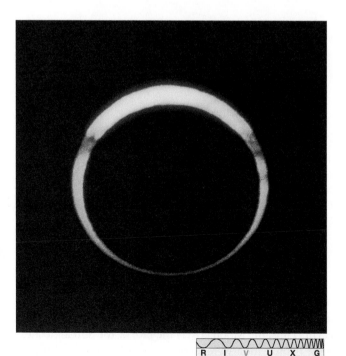

◀ FIGURE 25 **Annular Solar Eclipse** During an annular solar eclipse, the Moon fails to completely hide the Sun, so a thin ring of light remains. No corona is seen in this case because even the small amount of the Sun still visible completely overwhelms the corona's faint glow. This was the December 1973 eclipse, as seen from Algiers. (The gray fuzzy areas at the top left and right are clouds in Earth's atmosphere.) *(G. Schneider)*

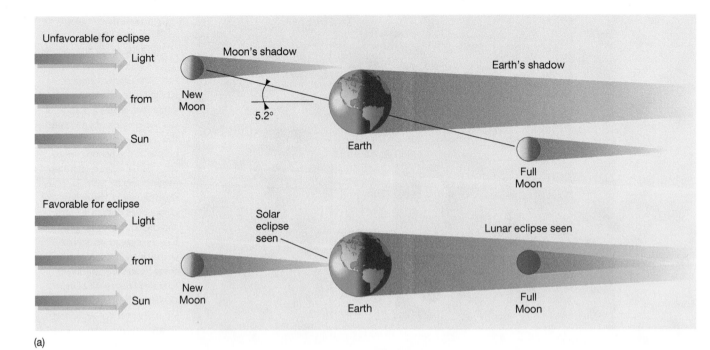

▲ FIGURE 26 **Eclipse Geometry** (a) An eclipse occurs when Earth, Moon, and Sun are precisely aligned. If the Moon's orbital plane lay in exactly the plane of the ecliptic, this alignment would occur once a month. However, the Moon's orbit is inclined at about 5° to the ecliptic, so not all configurations are favorable for producing an eclipse. (b) For an eclipse to occur, the line of intersection of the two planes must lie along the Earth–Sun line. Thus, eclipses can occur just at specific times of the year. Only the umbra of each shadow is shown, for clarity (see Figure 24).

across Earth's surface faster than our planet rotates, so the eclipse actually *overtakes* observers on the ground.

The solar eclipses that we do see highlight a remarkable cosmic coincidence. Although the Sun is many times farther away from Earth than is the Moon, it is also much larger. In fact, the ratio of distances is almost exactly the same as the ratio of sizes, so the Sun and the Moon both have roughly the *same* angular diameter—about half a degree, seen from Earth. Thus, the Moon covers the face of the Sun almost exactly. If the Moon were larger, we would never see annular

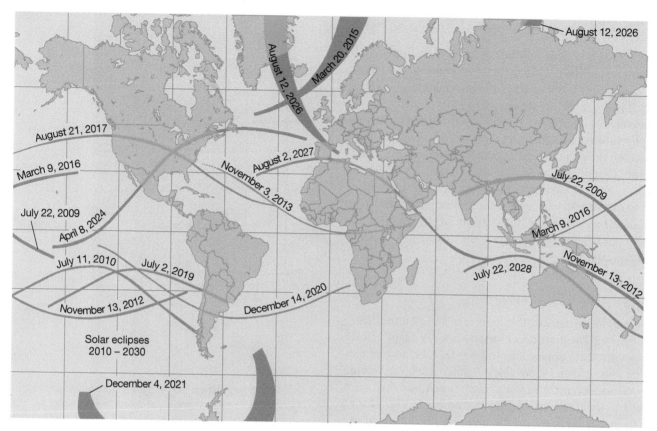

▲ FIGURE 27 **Eclipse Tracks** Regions of Earth that saw or will see total solar eclipses between the years 2010 and 2030. Each track represents the path of the Moon's umbra across Earth's surface during an eclipse. The width of the track depends upon the latitude on Earth and the distance from Earth to the Moon during the eclipse. High-latitude tracks are broader because sunlight strikes Earth's surface at an oblique angle near the poles (and also because of the projection of the map). The closer the Moon is to Earth during a total eclipse, the wider is the umbra (see Figure 24).

eclipses, and total eclipses would be much more common. If the Moon were a little smaller, we would see only annular eclipses.

The gravitational tug of the Sun causes the Moon's orbital orientation, and hence the direction of the line of nodes, to change slowly with time. As a result, the time between one orbital configuration with the line of nodes pointing at the Sun and the next (with the Moon crossing the ecliptic in the same sense in each case) is not exactly 1 year, but instead is 346.6 days—sometimes called one *eclipse year*. Thus, the eclipse seasons gradually progress backward through the calendar, occurring about 19 days earlier each year. For example, in 1999 the eclipse seasons were in February and August, and on August 11 much of Europe and southern Asia was treated to the last total eclipse of the millennium (Figure 23). By 2002, those seasons had drifted into December and June, and eclipses actually occurred on June 10 and December 4 of that year. By studying Figure 27, you can follow the progression of the eclipse seasons through the calendar. (Note that two partial eclipses in 2004 and two in 2007 are not shown in the figure.)

The combination of the eclipse year and the Moon's synodic period leads to an interesting long-term cycle in solar (and lunar) eclipses. A simple calculation shows that 19 eclipse years is almost exactly 223 lunar months. Thus, every 6585 solar days (actually 18 years, 11.3 days) the "same" eclipse recurs, with Earth, the Moon, and the Sun in the same relative configuration. Several such repetitions are evident in Figure 27—see, for example, the similarly shaped December 4, 2002, and December 14, 2020, tracks. (Note that we must take leap years properly into account to get the dates right!) The roughly 120° offset in longitude corresponds to Earth's rotation in 0.3 day. This recurrence is called the *Saros cycle*. Well known to ancient astronomers, it undoubtedly was the key to their "mystical" ability to predict eclipses!

CONCEPT CHECK

✔ What types of solar eclipses would you expect to see if Earth's distance from the Sun were to double? What if the distance became half its present value?

6 The Measurement of Distance

We have seen a little of how astronomers track and record the positions of the stars in the sky. But knowing the direction to an object is only part of the information needed to locate it in space. Before we can make a systematic study of the heavens, we must find a way of measuring *distances,* too. One distance-measurement method, called **triangulation,** is based on the principles of Euclidean geometry and finds widespread application today in both terrestrial and astronomical settings. Surveyors use these age-old geometric ideas to measure the distance to faraway objects indirectly. Triangulation forms the foundation of the family of distance-measurement techniques making up the **cosmic distance scale.**

Triangulation and Parallax

Imagine trying to measure the distance to a tree on the other side of a river. The most direct method is to lay a tape across the river, but that's not the simplest way (nor, because of the current, may it even be possible). A smart surveyor would make the measurement by visualizing an *imaginary* triangle (hence *triangulation*), sighting the tree on the far side of the river from two positions on the near side, as illustrated in Figure 28. The simplest possible triangle is a right triangle, in which one of the angles is exactly 90°, so it is usually convenient to set up one observation position directly opposite the object, as at point A. The surveyor then moves to another observation position at point B, noting the distance covered between points A and B. This distance is called the **baseline** of the imaginary triangle. Finally, the surveyor, standing at point B, sights toward the tree and notes the angle at point B between this line of sight and the baseline. Knowing the value of one side (AB) and two angles (the right angle at point A and the angle at point B) of the right triangle, the surveyor geometrically constructs the remaining sides and angles and establishes the distance from A to the tree.

To use triangulation to measure distances, a surveyor must be familiar with *trigonometry,* the mathematics of geometrical angles and distances. However, even if we knew no trigonometry at all, we could still solve the problem by graphical means, as shown in Figure 29. Suppose that we pace off the baseline AB, measuring it to be 450 meters, and measure the angle between the baseline and the line from B to the tree to be 52°, as illustrated in the figure. We can transfer the problem to paper by letting one box on our graph represent 25 meters on the ground. Drawing the line AB on paper and completing the other two sides of the triangle, at angles of 90° (at A) and 52° (at B), we measure the distance on paper from A to the tree to be 23 boxes—that is, 575 meters. We have solved the real problem by *modeling* it on paper. The point to remember here is this: Nothing more complex than basic geometry is needed to infer the distance,

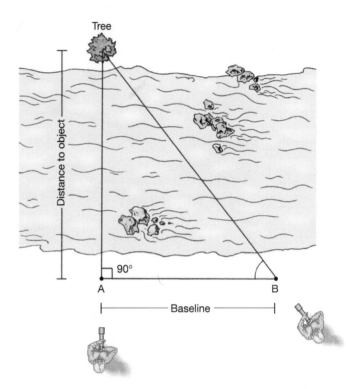

▲ FIGURE 28 **Triangulation** Surveyors often use simple geometry and trigonometry to estimate the distance to a faraway object by triangulation. By measuring the angles at A and B and the length of the baseline, the distance can be calculated without the need for direct measurement.

the size, and even the shape of an object that is too far away or inaccessible for direct measurement.

Obviously, for a fixed baseline the triangle becomes longer and narrower as the tree's distance from A increases. Narrow triangles cause problems, because it becomes hard to measure the angles at A and B with sufficient accuracy. The measurements can be made easier by "fattening" the triangle—that is, by lengthening the baseline—but there are limits on how long a baseline we can choose in astronomy. For example, consider an imaginary triangle extending from Earth to a nearby object in space, perhaps a neighboring planet. The triangle is now extremely long and narrow, even for a relatively nearby object (by cosmic standards). Figure 30(a) illustrates a case in which the longest baseline possible on Earth—Earth's diameter, measured from point A to point B—is used.

In principle, two observers could sight the planet from opposite sides of Earth, measuring the triangle's angles at A and B. However, in practice it is easier to measure the third angle of the imaginary triangle. Here's how. The observers sight toward the planet, taking note of its position *relative to some distant stars* seen on the plane of the sky. The observer at point A sees the planet at apparent location A′ relative to those stars, as indicated in Figure 30(a). The observer at B sees the planet at point B′. If each observer takes a photograph of the

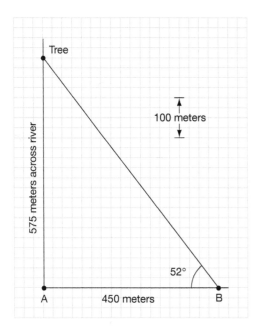

▲ FIGURE 29 **Geometric Scaling** Not even trigonometry is needed to estimate distances indirectly. Scaled estimates, like this one on a piece of graph paper, often suffice.

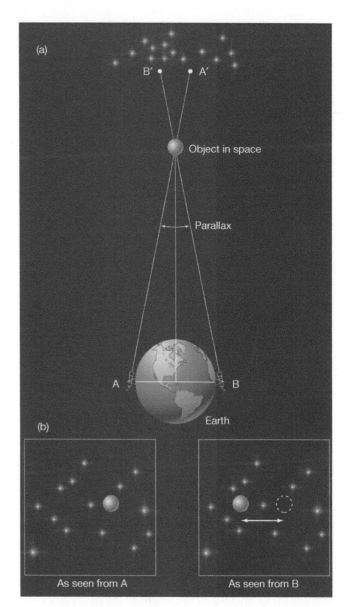

▲ FIGURE 30 **Parallax** (a) This imaginary triangle extends from Earth to a nearby object in space (such as a planet). The group of stars at the top represents a background field of very distant stars. (b) Hypothetical photographs of the same star field showing the nearby object's apparent displacement, or shift, relative to the distant undisplaced stars. Elementary geometry is one of the basic distance-measurement techniques that enable astronomers to study the immense universe in which we live.

appropriate region of the sky, the planet will appear at slightly different places in the two images. The planet's photographic image is slightly displaced, or shifted, relative to the field of distant background stars, as shown in Figure 30(b). The background stars themselves appear undisplaced because of their much greater distance from the observer.

This apparent displacement of a foreground object relative to the background as the observer's location changes is known as **parallax**. The size of the shift in Figure 30(b), measured as an angle on the celestial sphere, is the third, small angle in Figure 30(a). In astronomical contexts, the parallax is usually very small. For example, the parallax of a point on the Moon, viewed using a baseline equal to Earth's diameter, is about 2°; the parallax of the planet Venus at closest approach (45 million km), is just 1′ (see *More Precisely 2*).

The closer an object is to the observer, the larger is the parallax. Figure 31 illustrates how you can see this for yourself. Hold a pencil vertically in front of your nose and concentrate on some far-off object—a distant wall, perhaps. Close one eye, and then open it while closing the other. You should see a large shift in the apparent position of the pencil projected onto the distant wall—a large parallax. In this example, one eye corresponds to point A, the other eye to point B, the distance between your eyeballs to the baseline, the pencil to the planet, and the distant wall to a remote field of stars. Now hold the pencil at arm's length, corresponding to a more distant object (but still not as far away as the even more distant stars). The apparent shift of the pencil will be less. You might even be able to verify that the apparent shift is in-

versely proportional to the distance to the pencil. By moving the pencil farther away, we are narrowing the triangle and decreasing the parallax (and also making accurate measurement more difficult). If you were to paste the pencil to the wall, corresponding to the case where the object of interest is as far away as the background star field, blinking would produce no apparent shift of the pencil at all.

The amount of parallax is thus inversely proportional to an object's distance. Small parallax implies large distance, and

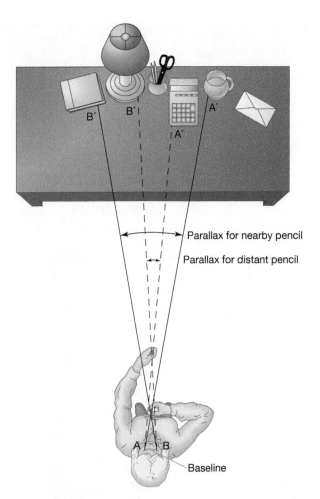

▲ FIGURE 31 **Parallax Geometry** Parallax is inversely proportional to an object's distance. An object near your nose has a much larger parallax than an object held at arm's length.

large parallax implies small distance. Knowing the amount of parallax (as an angle) and the length of the baseline, we can easily derive the distance through triangulation. *More Precisely 2* explores the connection between angular measure and distance in more detail, showing how we can use elementary geometry to determine both the distances and the dimensions of far away objects.

Surveyors of the land routinely use such simple geometric techniques to map out planet Earth. As surveyors of the sky, astronomers use the same basic principles to chart the universe.

Sizing Up Planet Earth

Now that we have studied some of the tools available to astronomers, let's end the chapter with a classic example of how the scientific method, combined with the basic geometric techniques just described, enabled an early scientist to perform a calculation of truly "global" proportions.

In about 200 B.C., a Greek philosopher named Eratosthenes (276–194 B.C.) used simple geometric reasoning to calculate the size of our planet. He knew that at noon on the first day of summer observers in the city of Syene (now called Aswan) in Egypt saw the Sun pass directly overhead. This was evident from the fact that vertical objects cast no shadows and sunlight reached to the very bottoms of deep wells, as shown in the insets in Figure 32. However, at noon of the same day in Alexandria, a city 5000 *stadia* to the north, the Sun was seen to be displaced slightly from the vertical. (The *stadium* was a Greek unit of length, roughly equal to 0.16 km—the modern town of Aswan lies about 780 km, or 490 miles, south of Alexandria.) By measuring the length of the shadow of a vertical stick and applying elementary trigonometry, Eratosthenes determined the angular displacement of the Sun from the vertical at Alexandria to be 7.2°.

What could have caused this discrepancy between the two measurements? It was not the result of measurement error—the same results were obtained every time the observations were repeated. Instead, as illustrated in Figure 32, the explanation is simply that Earth's surface is not flat, but *curved.* Our planet is a sphere. Eratosthenes was not the first person to

▶ FIGURE 32 **Measuring Earth's Radius** The Sun's rays strike different parts of Earth's surface at different angles. The Greek philosopher Eratosthenes realized that the difference was due to Earth's curvature, enabling him to determine Earth's radius by using simple geometry.

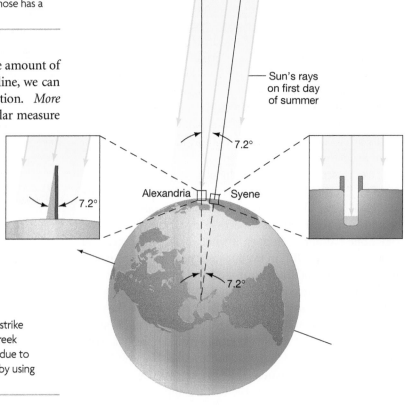

MORE PRECISELY 2

Measuring Distances with Geometry

Simple geometrical reasoning forms the basis for almost every statement made in this text about size and scale in the universe. In a very real sense, our modern knowledge of the cosmos depends on the elementary mathematics of ancient Greece. Let's take a moment to look in a little more detail at how astronomers use geometry to measure the distances to, and sizes of, objects near and far.

We can convert baselines and parallaxes into distances, and vice versa, by using arguments made by the Greek geometer Euclid. The first figure represents Figure 30(a), but we have changed the scale and added the circle centered on the target planet and passing through our baseline on Earth:

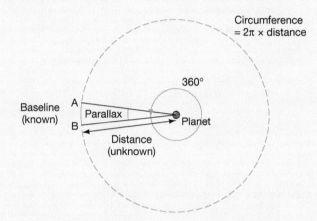

To see how the planet's parallax relates to its distance, we note that the ratio of the baseline AB to the circumference of the large circle shown in the figure must be equal to the ratio of the parallax to one full revolution, 360°. Recall that the circumference of a circle is always 2π times its radius (where π—the Greek letter "pi"—is approximately equal to 3.142). Applying this relation to the large circle in the figure, we find that

$$\frac{\text{baseline}}{2\pi \times \text{distance}} = \frac{\text{parallax}}{360°},$$

from which it follows that

$$\text{parallax} = (360°/2\pi) \times \frac{\text{baseline}}{\text{distance}}.$$

The angle $360°/2\pi \approx 57.3°$ in the preceding equation is usually called 1 *radian*.

EXAMPLE 1 The planet Venus lies roughly 45,000,000 km from Earth at closest approach. Two observers 13,000 km apart (i.e., at opposite ends of Earth's diameter) looking at the planet would measure a parallax of $57.3° \times (13,000 \text{ km}/45,000,000 \text{ km}) = 0.017° = 1.0$ arc minutes, as stated in the text.

Alternatively, if we know the parallax (from direct measurement, such as the photographic technique described in Section 6), we can rearrange the above equation to tell us the distance to the planet:

$$\text{distance} = \text{baseline} \times \frac{57.3°}{\text{parallax}}.$$

EXAMPLE 2 Two observers 1000 km apart looking at the Moon might measure a parallax of 9.0 arc minutes—that is, 0.15°. It then follows that the distance to the Moon is 1000 km × $(57.3/0.15) \approx 380,000$ km. (More accurate measurements, based on laser ranging using equipment left on the lunar surface by *Apollo* astronauts, yield a mean distance of 384,000 km.)

Knowing the distance to an object, we can determine many other properties. For example, by measuring the object's *angular diameter*—the angle from one side of the object to the other as we view it in the sky—we can compute its size. The second figure illustrates the geometry involved:

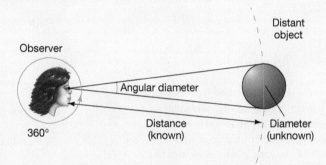

Notice that this is basically the same diagram as the previous one, except that now the angle (the angular diameter) and distance are known, instead of the angle (the parallax) and baseline. Exactly the same reasoning as before then allows us to calculate the diameter. We have

$$\frac{\text{diameter}}{2\pi \times \text{distance}} = \frac{\text{angular diameter}}{360},$$

so

$$\text{diameter} = \text{distance} \times \frac{\text{angular diameter}}{57.3°}.$$

EXAMPLE 3 The Moon's angular diameter is measured to be about 31 arc minutes—a little over half a degree. From the preceding discussion, it follows that the Moon's actual diameter is 380,000 km × $(0.52°/57.3°) \approx 3450$ km. A more precise measurement gives 3476 km.

Study the foregoing reasoning carefully. We will use these simple arguments, in various forms, many times throughout this text.

realize that Earth is spherical—the philosopher Aristotle had done that over 100 years earlier (see Section 2), but he was apparently the first to build on this knowledge, combining geometry with direct measurement to infer the size of our planet. Here's how he did it.

Rays of light reaching Earth from a very distant object, such as the Sun, travel almost parallel to one another. Consequently, as shown in the figure, the angle measured at Alexandria between the Sun's rays and the vertical (i.e., the line joining Alexandria to the center of Earth) is equal to the angle between Syene and Alexandria, as seen from Earth's center. (For the sake of clarity, the angle has been exaggerated in the figure.) As discussed in *More Precisely 2,* the size of this angle in turn is proportional to the fraction of Earth's circumference that lies between Syene and Alexandria:

$$\frac{7.2° \text{ (angle between Syene and Alexandria)}}{360° \text{ (circumference of a circle)}}$$
$$= \frac{5000 \text{ stadia}}{\text{Earth's circumference}}.$$

Earth's circumference is therefore 50×5000, or 250,000 stadia, or about 40,000 km, so Earth's radius is $250{,}000/2\pi$ stadia, or 6366 km. The correct values for Earth's circumference and radius, now measured accurately by orbiting spacecraft, are 40,070 km and 6378 km, respectively.

Eratosthenes' reasoning was a remarkable accomplishment. More than 20 centuries ago, he estimated the circumference of Earth to within 1 percent accuracy, using only simple geometry and basic scientific reasoning. A person making measurements on only a small portion of Earth's surface was able to compute the size of the entire planet on the basis of observation and pure logic—an early triumph of the scientific method.

CONCEPT CHECK

✔ Why is elementary geometry essential for measuring distances in astronomy?

CHAPTER REVIEW

SUMMARY

1 The **scientific method** is a methodical approach employed by scientists to explore the universe around us in an objective manner. A **theory** is a framework of ideas and assumptions used to explain some set of observations and construct **theoretical models** that make predictions about the real world. These predictions in turn are amenable to further observational testing. In this way, the theory expands and science advances.

2 Early observers grouped the thousands of stars visible to the naked eye into patterns called **constellations,** which they imagined were attached to a vast **celestial sphere** centered on Earth. Constellations have no physical significance, but are still used to label regions of the sky. The points where Earth's axis of rotation intersects the celestial sphere are called the north and south **celestial poles.** The line where Earth's equatorial plane cuts the celestial sphere is the **celestial equator.**

3 The nightly motion of the stars across the sky is the result of Earth's **rotation** on its axis. The time from one noon to the next is called a **solar day.** The time between successive risings of any given star is one **sidereal day.** Because of Earth's **revolution** around the Sun, we see different stars at night at different times of the year, and the Sun appears to move relative to the stars. The Sun's apparent yearly path around the celestial sphere (or the plane of Earth's orbit around the Sun) is called the **ecliptic.** We experience **seasons** because Earth's rotation axis is inclined to the ecliptic plane. At the **summer solstice,** the Sun is highest in the sky and the length of the day is greatest. At the **winter solstice,** the Sun is lowest and the day is shortest. At the **vernal** and **autumnal equinoxes,** Earth's axis of rotation is perpendicular to the line joining Earth to the Sun, so day and night are of equal length. The interval of time from one vernal equinox to the next is one **tropical year.**

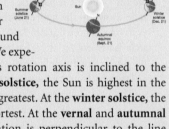

4 In addition to its rotation about its axis and its revolution around the Sun, Earth has many other motions. One of the most important of these is **precession,** the slow "wobble" of Earth's axis due to the influence of the Moon. As a result, the **sidereal year** is slightly longer than the tropical year, and the particular constellations that happen to be visible during any given season change over the course of thousands of years.

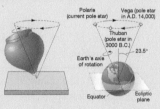

5 The Moon emits no light of its own, but instead shines by reflected sunlight. As the Moon orbits Earth, we see **lunar phases** as the amount of the Moon's sunlit face visible to us varies. A **lunar eclipse** occurs when the Moon enters Earth's shadow. A **solar eclipse** occurs when the Moon passes between Earth and the Sun. An eclipse may be **total** if the body in question (Moon or Sun) is completely obscured, or **partial** if only a portion of the surface is affected. If the Moon happens to be too far from Earth for its disk to completely hide the Sun, an **annular eclipse** occurs. Because the Moon's orbit around Earth is slightly inclined with respect to the ecliptic, solar and lunar eclipses do not occur every month, but only during **eclipse seasons** (twice per year).

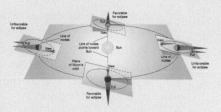

6 Surveyors on Earth use **triangulation** to determine the distances to faraway objects. Astronomers use the same technique to measure the distances to planets and stars. The **cosmic distance scale** is the family of distance-measurement techniques by which astronomers chart the universe. **Parallax** is the apparent motion of a foreground object relative to a distant background as the observer's position changes. The larger the **baseline**—the distance between the two observation points—the greater is the parallax. The same basic geometric reasoning is used to determine the sizes of objects whose distances are known. The Greek philosopher Eratosthenes used elementary geometry to determine Earth's radius.

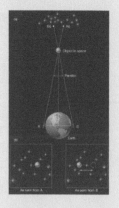

Mastering ASTRONOMY *For instructor-assigned homework go to www.masteringastronomy.com*

Problems labeled **POS** explore the process of science | **VIS** problems focus on reading and interpreting visual information

REVIEW AND DISCUSSION

1. Compare the size of Earth with that of the Sun, the Milky Way Galaxy, and the entire universe.

2. What does an astronomer mean by "the universe"?

3. How big is a light-year?

4. **POS** What is the scientific method, and how does science differ from religion?

5. What is a constellation? Why are constellations useful for mapping the sky?

6. Why does the Sun rise in the east and set in the west each day? Does the Moon also rise in the east and set in the west? Why? Do stars do the same? Why?

7. How and why does a day measured with respect to the Sun differ from a day measured with respect to the stars?

8. How many times in your life have you orbited the Sun?

9. Why do we see different stars at different times of the year?

10. Why are there seasons on Earth?

11. What is precession, and what causes it?

12. Why don't the seasons move around the calendar as Earth precesses?

13. If one complete hemisphere of the Moon is always lit by the sun, why do we see different phases of the Moon?

14. What causes a lunar eclipse? A solar eclipse?

15. Why aren't there lunar and solar eclipses every month?

16. **POS** Do you think an observer on another planet might see eclipses? Why or why not?

17. What is parallax? Give an everyday example.

18. Why is it necessary to have a long baseline when using triangulation to measure the distances to objects in space?

19. What two pieces of information are needed to determine the diameter of a faraway object?

20. **POS** If you traveled to the outermost planet in our solar system, do you think the constellations would appear to change their shapes? What would happen if you traveled to the next-nearest star? If you traveled to the center of our Galaxy, could you still see the familiar constellations found in Earth's night sky?

CONCEPTUAL SELF-TEST: MULTIPLE CHOICE

1. If Earth rotated twice as fast as it currently does, but its motion around the Sun stayed the same, then **(a)** the night would be twice as long; **(b)** the night would be half as long; **(c)** the year would be half as long; **(d)** the length of the day would be unchanged.

2. A long, thin cloud that stretched from directly overhead to the western horizon would have an angular size of **(a)** 45°; **(b)** 90°; **(c)** 180°; **(d)** 360°.

3. **VIS** According to Figure 15 ("The Zodiac"), in January the Sun is in the constellation **(a)** Cancer; **(b)** Gemini; **(c)** Leo; **(d)** Aquarius.

4. If Earth orbited the Sun in 9 months instead of 12, then, compared with a sidereal day, a solar day would be **(a)** longer; **(b)** shorter; **(c)** unchanged.

5. When a thin crescent of the Moon is visible just before sunrise, the Moon is in its (a) waxing phase; (b) new phase; (c) waning phase; (d) quarter phase.

6. If the Moon's orbit were a little larger, solar eclipses would be (a) more likely to be annular; (b) more likely to be total; (c) more frequent; (d) unchanged in appearance.

7. If the Moon orbited Earth twice as fast but in the same orbit the frequency of solar eclipses would (a) double; (b) be cut in half; (c) stay the same.

8. **VIS** In Figure 28 ("Triangulation"), using a longer baseline would result in (a) a less accurate distance to the tree; (b) a more accurate distance to the tree; (c) a smaller angle at point B; (d) a greater distance across the river.

9. **VIS** In Figure 30 ("Parallax"), a smaller Earth would result in (a) a smaller parallax angle; (b) a shorter distance measured to the object; (c) a larger apparent displacement; (d) stars appearing closer together.

10. Today, distances to stars are measured by (a) bouncing radar signals; (b) reflected laser beams; (c) travel time by spacecraft; (d) geometry.

Communications

Managing Conflict

From Chapter 8 of *Communicating in Small Groups,* Tenth Edition. Steven A. Beebe, John T. Masterson. Copyright © 2012 by Pearson Education, Inc. Published by Pearson Allyn & Bacon. All rights reserved.

Managing Conflict

"When we all think alike, then no one is thinking."
—Walter Lippman

CHAPTER OUTLINE

What Is Conflict?

Types of Conflict

Conflict and Diversity in Small Groups

Conflict-Management Styles

Collaborative Conflict Management:
Principles and Skills

When People Are Not Cooperative: Dealing
with Difficult Group Members

Case Study: Practice in Applying Principles

Groupthink: Conflict Avoidance

Consensus: Reaching Agreement Through
Communication

Study Guide: Putting Group Principles into
Practice

OBJECTIVES

After studying this chapter, you will be able to:

■ Explain why conflict occurs in small groups.
■ Describe the negative impact of conflict on group communication.
■ List three misconceptions about conflict.
■ Describe five conflict-management styles.
■ Identify strategies for managing different types of conflict.
■ Describe four conflict-management principles.
■ Define groupthink.
■ Identify six symptoms of groupthink.
■ Apply techniques for reducing groupthink.
■ Define consensus.
■ Apply techniques for managing conflict and reaching consensus in
small groups.

A dolph and his brother Rudolph lived in a small German town and had heard about the American sprinter Jesse Owens, who was coming to Germany to compete in the 1936 Berlin Olympics. The two brothers had a small cobbler shop and thought they would try making sports shoes for the famed runner. They approached Owens and asked if he would wear their shoes during the Olympic competition. Owens quickly accepted the offer of free shoes and then won four gold medals. The two brothers parlayed that good fortune into making their small shoe shop into a major producer of running shoes. Just one problem: The two brothers didn't get along. In fact, they fought a lot. Eventually, because of the constant conflict, they decided to go their separate ways. Adolph, whose nickname was "Adi," took half of the shoe-making machines and started his own company on one side of the river in their town. You know it today as Adidas. Rudolph stayed on the other side of the river and called his new shoe company Puma. Their family conflict had thus created two giant running shoe corporations.[1]

Conflict is a fact of life. Throughout history, people have been involved in conflicts ranging from family feuds that spawned rival shoe companies to nations that waged war against each other. Communication researchers and social psychologists conclude that when people interact with one another they inevitably disagree.[2]

This chapter gives you some ideas about the causes of conflict in groups and teams and presents some strategies for managing it. We're not going to tell you how to eliminate group conflict but rather how to understand it and its importance in your group deliberations.

Despite the prevalence of conflict in group and team deliberations, communication researchers Steven Farmer and Jonelle Rothe note that much of what we know about group conflict has been generalized from research that has investigated interpersonal conflict.[3] The prime objective of this chapter is to help you understand how conflict in groups and teams can be both useful and detrimental to collaborative decision making.

What Is Conflict?

Conflict is about disagreement. Communication experts William Wilmot and Joyce Hocker define conflict as including four elements: (1) an expressed struggle (2) between at least two interdependent people (3) who perceive incompatible goals, scarce resources, and interference from others, (4) to achieve specific goals.[4]

- *Expressed struggle:* A conflict becomes a concern to a group when the disagreement is expressed verbally or, more often, nonverbally. Early signs of conflict include furrowed brows, grimacing facial expressions, and flashes of frustration evident in the voice. If the conflict persists, words are usually exchanged and unmanaged tempers may flare.
- *Between at least two interdependent people:* From a systems theory perspective, people in a group are *interdependent*; what happens to one person has an impact on others in the group. A conflict between even just two people in a group of five will undoubtedly have an impact on the dynamics of the entire group.
- *Incompatible goals, scarce resources, and interference:* Conflict often occurs because two or more people want the same thing, yet both can't have it. If resources are scarce or if something or someone is blocking what others want, conflict is likely.
- *Achieving a goal:* People in conflict want something. Understanding what the people in conflict want is an important step toward finding a way to manage the conflict.

If a group experienced no conflict, it would have little to discuss. One value of conflict is that it makes a group test and challenge ideas. Conflict can, however, be detrimental to group interaction and group decision making. Conflict has a negative impact on a group when it (1) keeps the group from completing its task, (2) interferes with the quality of the group's decision or productivity, or (3) threatens the existence of the group.[5]

Causes of Conflict

What causes conflict in groups and teams? Conflict results from differences between group members—differences in perception, personality, information, culture, and power or influence. Differences in group members' tolerance for taking risks also contributes to group conflict; some people are comfortable with risk, others aren't.[6] Because people are unique, their different attitudes, beliefs, and values will inevitably surface and cause conflict. No matter how much they try to empathize with others, people still have individual perspectives on the world. People also differ in the amount of knowledge they have on various topics. In groups, they soon realize that some members are more experienced or more widely read than others. This difference in information contributes to different attitudes. People also have different levels of power, status, and influence over others—differences that can increase conflict. People with power often try to use that power to influence others, and most do not like to be told what to do or think. Conflict can also occur because of disagreement about processes and procedures. Research suggests that entrenched disagreements about process issues (such as how decisions will be made and what the rules and norms are for expressing disagreement) can be more disruptive over the long haul than a simple disagreement about a specific task issue.[7]

Conflict does not just happen. You can often discern phases or stages of conflict development. Communication scholar B. Aubrey Fisher found that group deliberations can be organized around four phases: orientation, conflict, emergence, and reinforcement.[8] Several researchers have discovered that the conflict phase in groups often emerges in predictable stages.[9]

Conflict in groups can be directed toward people (interpersonal conflict), ideas (task conflict), or both people and ideas.[10] One research team found that conflict often occurs because of perceived inequity; if we think someone has more resources or is getting more than his or her fair share, conflict often results.[11] When the conflict is directed toward people, we may first try to manage the conflict by avoiding the individual or the topic of conflict. If the conflict is more task-centered, we usually first try more integrative approaches by seeking solutions that are agreeable to all parties. One of the prime effects of conflict and discord that occurs in groups is that the seeming lack of progress toward the group's goals results in a lack of motivation to keep working at a solution to resolve the conflict.[12] Two of the biggest triggers of conflict occur when people believe they haven't been treated fairly or that they are entitled to something that they didn't receive.

Misconceptions about Conflict

People often have misconceptions about the role of conflict in groups because they think that conflict is bad and should be avoided. With higher rates of divorce, crime, and international political tensions, it is understandable that people view conflict negatively. The following discussion of myths will examine some of the feelings you may have about conflict and point out how a different attitude might improve the quality of your group discussions.[13]

Misconception 1: Conflict Should Be Avoided at All Costs   Conflict is a natural byproduct of communication; unless participants in your group share the same attitudes, beliefs, and values (an unlikely situation), there will be some conflict. Several researchers have discovered that conflict is an important, indeed useful, part of group communication.[14] Members who believe that conflict is unhealthy become frustrated when conflict erupts in a group. They should realize that conflict probably will occur and that it is a natural and healthy part of group communication.

Research suggests that when conflict occurs, group members are often challenged to research issues in greater detail and learn more about the issues under discussion.[15] In the end, conflict can enhance learning and encourage more in-depth analysis.

Group conflict can also spur group members to share more information with one another than they would if everyone simply agreed on the issues discussed. Research has found that dissent in a group can uncover hidden agendas. So the quality of group discussion increases when people express different ideas, opinions, and perspectives.[16]

Misconception 2: All Conflict Occurs Because People Do Not Understand One Another   Have you ever been in a heated disagreement with someone and found yourself blurting out "You just don't understand me!"? You easily assume that conflict occurs because another person does not understand your position. Not all conflict occurs because of misunderstandings, however. You may believe that if others really understood you, they would agree with you. Sometimes, however, conflict occurs because you *have* communicated your position clearly; it's just that others disagree with that position.[17] Yes, of course conflict can result from not understanding what someone says, but some conflicts intensify when a person clarifies his or her point.

Misconception 3: All Conflict Can Be Resolved   Perhaps you consider yourself an optimist. You like to think that problems can be solved. You may also feel that if a conflict arises, a compromise will resolve it. However, you should realize that not all conflicts can be resolved. Many disagreements are not simple. For example, fundamental differences between those who oppose abortion and those who support it can obviously not be resolved easily, if at all. Some ideologies are so far apart that resolving conflicts between them is unlikely. This does not mean that whenever a conflict arises in your group, you should despair and say, "Oh, well, no use trying to solve this disagreement." That position also oversimplifies the conflict-management process. Because some conflicts cannot be resolved, group members may have to focus on differences on which they *can* most likely reach agreement.

Types of Conflict

Communication scholars Gerald Miller and Mark Steinberg identify three classic types of interpersonal conflict: (1) pseudo-conflict, (2) simple conflict, and (3) ego conflict.[18] They suggest that by identifying the type of conflict in a group, you will be better able to manage it. The following sections look at these three types of conflict in the context of a small group.

Pseudo-Conflict: When People Misunderstand One Another

Some conflict occurs because of misunderstandings. **Pseudo-conflict** occurs when individuals agree, but, because of poor communication, they believe that they disagree. *Pseudo* means fake or false. Thus, pseudo-conflict is conflict between people who really agree on issues but who do not understand that their differences are caused by misunderstandings or misinterpretations. "Oh, I see," said Mark after several minutes of heatedly defending a position he had suggested to the group. "I just misunderstood you. I guess we really agree."

To manage pseudo-conflict, consider these strategies:

- Ask others what they mean by terms or phrases they use.
- Establish a supportive rather than a defensive climate if misunderstandings occur.
- Become an active listener:
  Stop: Tune in to what your partner says rather than to your own thoughts.
  Look: Pay attention to unspoken messages and monitor the emotional climate.
  Listen: Focus on key details and link them to major ideas.

Groups must find ways of managing conflict and channeling energy constructively. How might conflict be healthy?

© 06 Dist. By Universal Press Synd. 2-23.

Question: Ask appropriate questions about information or ideas that are unclear to you.

Paraphrase content: To test your understanding, summarize your conception of what your partner says.

Paraphrase feelings: When appropriate, check your perception of your partner's feelings.

Research clearly supports the importance of good listening skills in small groups and teams.[19]

Simple Conflict: When People Disagree about Issues

Simple conflict occurs when two people's goals or ideas are mutually exclusive or incompatible. "Simple conflict involves one person saying, 'I want to do X,' and another saying, 'I want to do Y,' when X and Y are incompatible forms of behavior."[20] Although the conflict may seem far from simple, it's called "simple conflict" because the issues are clear and each party understands the problem. For example, in a corporation with only a limited amount of money to invest, one board member may want to invest in real estate and another may want to make capital improvements. The issue is clear; the individuals simply believe the company should take different courses of action.

When you understand what someone says but simply disagree with his or her point, consider using these skills:

- Clarify your perception and your partner's perception of the message.
- Keep the discussion focused on issues, not personalities.
- Use facts that support your point rather than opinions or emotional arguments.
- Use a structured problem-solving approach to organize the discussion: Define, analyze, identify several solutions, evaluate the solutions, select the best one.
- When appropriate, look for ways to compromise.
- Make the conflict a group concern rather than a conflict between just two people; ask others for information and data.
- If there are several issues, decide which issues are the most important, and then tackle them one at a time.
- Find areas of agreement.
- If possible, postpone decisions until additional research can be conducted. Such a delay may also lessen tensions.

Ego Conflict: When Personalities Clash

Ego conflict occurs when individuals become defensive about their positions because they think they are being personally attacked. Of the types of conflict under discussion, this one is the most difficult to manage. Ego conflicts are charged with emotion, and defensiveness in one individual often causes defensiveness in others. Underlying many ego conflicts are power struggles.[21] "Just because you're the chair of the group doesn't give *you* the right to railroad decision making," snaps Frank. "Well, you're just jealous. You think you should have been elected chairperson," retorts Ed. Based on his study of small group communication, Dennis Devine suggests that a disagreement about issues (simple conflict) can quickly evolve into a more emotionally charged discussion that becomes personal (ego conflict) unless group members consciously monitor how they interact with one another.[22]

If you are trying to mediate an ego conflict, find issues the disagreeing parties can agree on. Identify and emphasize the common ground between them, and encourage them to describe the sequence of events that created the conflict. A key immediate concern when ego conflict flares up in a group is to permit the disagreement to be verbalized without heightening the emotional tension. Just venting anger and irritation won't lessen tensions, nor will simply ignoring the conflict make the tension go away. Research clearly documents that the emotional climate in a group shapes how effectively the conflict will be managed.

Here are additional strategies that may help manage the clash of egos:[23]

- Encourage active listening.
- Return the discussion to the key issues under discussion.
- Try to turn the discussion into a problem to be solved rather than a conflict someone has to win.

REVIEW

▶ SUMMARY OF THREE CONFLICT TYPES

SOURCE OF CONFLICT

Pseudo-Conflict

Individuals misunderstanding each other's perceptions of a problem.

Simple Conflict

Disagreement over a course of action, idea, policy, or procedure.

Ego Conflict

Defense of ego: Individual believes he or she is being attacked personally.

SUGGESTIONS FOR MANAGING CONFLICT

Pseudo-Conflict

1. Ask for clarification of perceptions.
2. Establish a supportive rather than a defensive climate.
3. Employ active listening:
   - Stop
   - Look
   - Listen
   - Question
   - Paraphrase content
   - Paraphrase feelings

Simple Conflict

1. Listen and clarify perceptions.
2. Make sure issues are clear to all group members.
3. Use a problem-solving approach to manage differences of opinion.
4. Keep discussion focused on the issues.
5. Use facts rather than opinions as evidence.
6. Look for alternatives or compromise positions.
7. Make the conflict a group concern rather than an individual concern.
8. Determine which conflicts are the most important to resolve.
9. If appropriate, postpone the decision while additional research is conducted. This delay also helps relieve tensions.

Ego Conflict

1. Let members express their concerns, but do not permit personal attacks.
2. Employ active listening.
3. Call for a cooling-off period.
4. Try to keep discussion focused on issues (simple conflict).
5. Encourage parties to be descriptive rather than evaluative and judgmental.
6. Use a problem-solving approach to manage differences of opinion.
7. Speak slowly and calmly.
8. Agree to disagree.

- Seek to cool the emotional climate by lowering your voice and speaking more calmly, not in a patronizing way but in a way that signals your interest in dialogue rather than emotional argument.
- Be descriptive rather than evaluative or judgmental when discussing the issues of contention.
- Develop rules or procedures that permit differences of opinion.
- Unless the disagreement is central to the nature of the group, agree to disagree and return to areas of agreement.

Conflict and Diversity in Small Groups

As we noted, the root of most conflicts are differences—differences in understanding, perception, attitudes, or preferred action. Yet one of the key advantages of working in groups and teams is the opportunity to capitalize on the different perspectives that group and team members have. As the saying goes, if both of us agree, then one of us is irrelevant. The challenge is to use group diversity without becoming locked in intractable conflict. Although we've emphasized that not all conflict is bad and not all of it should be avoided, entrenched conflict decreases a group's effectiveness. The key to understanding how differences lead to conflict is understanding how group members communicate with one another when conflict occurs. Effective communication helps manage the conflict.[24] Two frameworks for describing cultural differences shed light on how some conflicts develop and fester.

Approaches to Conflict in Individualistic and Collectivistic Cultures

Some cultures expect and nurture a team or collective approach to working with others; more individualistic cultures, such as that of the United States, place greater value on individual achievement.[25] This culturally learned difference can explain why individuals who place different values on the role of the individual or the team manage conflict as they do. Stella Ting-Toomey suggests that people in individualistic cultures are more likely to use direct, confrontational methods of managing disagreements than people who value a collective or team approach to group work.[26] She also suggests that people from collectivistic cultures, especially cultures that place considerable stock in nonverbal messages, prefer nonconfrontational and indirect methods of resolving differences. She suspects this difference may be because people from individualistic cultures tend to approach problem solving from a linear, step-by-step perspective, whereas people from collectivistic cultures often use a more intuitive problem-solving process. Ting-Toomey finds that people from individualistic cultures are more likely to use facts or principles as a basis for approaching conflict, negotiation, or persuasion situations.[27] People from collectivistic cultures adopt more relationship-based messages to manage differences. It is important for people from collectivistic cultures to save face by not being perceived as having lost a confrontation.

Approaches to Conflict in High-Context and Low-Context Cultures

A high-context culture is one in which considerable weight is given to the context of unspoken messages. In a low-context culture, such as that of the United States, more emphasis is placed on words and their explicit meaning than on implicit, nonverbal cues.[28] Researchers have found that people in low-context cultures give

THEORY INTO PRACTICE

Managing Conflict in Diverse Groups: Surface and Deep Diversity

One of the most interesting questions that group communication researchers have explored is how diversity in group membership affects group performance. Although one of the benefits of working in groups is learning from diverse perspectives, do differences in race, ethnicity, culture, age, or gender enhance group quality? Is it only diversity that a person can physically see that influences the communication in groups and teams? And how does the diversity of group members, whether surface-level or deep-level, affect the conflict-management process?

Researchers have made distinctions between surface-level diversity and deep-level diversity. **Surface-level diversity** is defined as the social differences that are easily visible to us—such as differences in ethnicity, race, age,

sex, and other social and observable categories. **Deep-level diversity** includes differences in attitudes, opinions, values, information, and other factors that take time to become evident in groups. They are differences that emerge only after conversation occurs and are not apparent just by looking at someone. As one research team noted, "People who look the same on the surface are expected to share the same task perspective, and people who look different are expected to have a different task perspective to share, even when the surface-level characteristic is not related to the task.[29] Researchers found that we expect people who look like us and hold similar surface-level features to agree with us, and that we are surprised when someone with our own surface-level characteristics disagrees with us.[30] Another communication researcher, Ralph Rodriguez, also found that it's not differences in such demographic characteristics as race, gender, and other observable factors that affect group performance, but rather,

greater importance to task or instrumental issues than do people in high-context cultures.[31] In high-context cultures, the expressive or emotional aspects of managing conflict take on special importance. In expressive conflict, the goal is often to express feelings and release tension.[32] Keeping the relationship in balance, maintaining the friendship, and managing the emotional climate often take a higher priority in a high-context culture than achieving a particular outcome. Here again, saving face and avoiding embarrassment for all parties are more important in high-context cultures than in low-context cultures.

In your group deliberations, knowing that culture and gender differences exist can help you decide which strategies will be more effective than others. We caution you, however, to avoid stereotyping others by cultural, national, ethnic, or gender differences alone. For example, it would be most inappropriate to draw a stereotyped conclusion that all Asians will emphasize expressive rather than instrumental objectives in conflict. Similarly, taking an egocentric view (that is, assuming your perspective is correct) or an ethnocentric view (assuming your cultural methods of managing conflict are superior to those used by others) can be detrimental to effective communication.

Approaches to Conflict When There Are Gender Differences

Gender is another factor that sometimes makes a difference in how people express and manage conflict in groups and teams. Research suggests that people with a feminine style of differences in underlying values or approaches to problems.[33]

Real-Life Applications

What are the best strategies for managing conflict that may stem from differing cultural, racial, ethnic, or gender- or age-based points of view? Consider the following suggestions.

If you are in the minority in a group:

- Make sure that you tactfully, yet assertively, express your ideas, opinions, facts, and information to the group.
- Ask the group to consider an alternative point of view. Your world view is your fundamental outlook on reality. Help the group understand that those with a different life experience or racial, ethnic, or cultural world view may see the issue differently.

If you are in the majority in the group:

- Don't monopolize the conversation; be a gatekeeper by inviting those who have not spoken up to participate in the conversation.
- Encourage people to share ideas and information via e-mail. Some quieter group members may be more likely to participate in this way than by voicing their opinion in person.
- Be cautious of making sweeping generalizations about those who are from a culture different from your own. Each person's opinions and ideas are unique and may not necessarily be shared by others in the same racial or ethnic group.
- Don't expect a person from a minority group to be a spokesperson for others in that group. Don't, for example, turn to an African American student and say, "So, what do blacks think about this topic?" You can ask what an individual may think or believe, but don't ask someone to speak for a particular group.

managing conflict (either men or women could have a feminine style) are more likely to be interested in issues of equity, empathy, caring, and closeness; to encourage mutual involvement; and generally to focus on relationship issues. A masculine style of conflict management emphasizes achieving specific goals and protecting self-interests, and it is concerned with equality of rights, fairness, and generally focusing on the task.[34] Research further finds sex differences (here the research notes differences between men and women—not just gender differences) in conflict-management styles: women tend to emphasize more expressive goals in conflict, whereas men emphasize instrumental or task objectives.[35]

Although we've noted these generalizations about sex and gender differences, we emphasize that not all men use a masculine conflict-management style and not all women use a feminine style. Such generalizations need to be tempered by considering each individual as unique.

Conflict-Management Styles

Regardless of our cultural backgrounds or the types of conflict we experience, research suggests that each of us behaves in predictable ways to manage disagreements with others. What is your conflict-management style? Do you tackle conflict head-on or seek ways to remove yourself from the fray? Although these are not the only options available for managing conflict, reduced to its essence, conflict-management style often boils down to fight or flight.

"And should there be a sudden loss of consciousness during this meeting, oxygen masks will drop from the ceiling."

© 1999 Ted Goff

3M Meeting Network.

Ralph Kilmann and Kenneth Thomas suggest that your conflict-management style is based on two factors: (1) how concerned you are for other people and (2) how concerned you are for yourself.[36] These two factors, or dimensions, result in five conflict-management styles, shown in Figure 1. The five styles are (1) avoidance, (2) accommodation, (3) competition, (4) compromise, and (5) collaboration. The following sections examine each style in some detail.

Avoidance

Some people just don't like to deal with conflict, so they avoid it. The **avoidance** conflict-management style is one in which a person attempts to ignore disagreements. Why do people sometimes avoid conflict? People who sidestep conflict may not like the hassle of dealing with a difficult, uncomfortable situation; or they may be unassertive and afraid of standing up for their rights. At other times people avoid conflict because they don't want to hurt someone's feelings.

There are disadvantages to ignoring conflict. If people avoid directly addressing the conflict, the cause of the conflict may remain and emotions may escalate, making the conflict worse. Avoiding conflict may also signal to others that you simply don't care about the needs and interests of others in your group.

When may it be advantageous to avoid conflict? Taking a break from addressing a difficult, conflict-producing issue may be just what a group needs in some circumstances. Avoiding conflict could give the group time to cool off or to think about the issues that are the source of the conflict. If the conflict is about something trivial or unimportant, it may not be worth the time and effort to manage the conflict.

Accommodation

Some people simply give in to avoid a major blow-up or controversy. The **accommodation** style is another approach used to try to make conflict go away by giving in to the wishes of

FIGURE 1
Conflict-Management Styles. The five conflict management styles in relation to concern for others and concern for self.

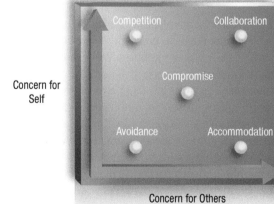

Concern for Self

Competition

Collaboration

Compromise

Avoidance

Accommodation

Concern for Others

others. This style is sometimes called a "lose-win" approach. People may accommodate for several reasons. Perhaps they have a high need for approval, and they want others to like them. Or they may want to reduce threats to their sense of self-worth, so they decide to give in rather than defend their own views on the issue. Some people who accommodate appear to maintain their cool, doing what others want them to do; but in reality they are using accommodation to serve their own needs—to get other people to like them.

There may be times when it's disadvantageous to accommodate others during conflict. Giving in too quickly to what others want may cause the group to make a bad decision because the issues underlying the conflict have not been thoroughly examined. Remember, conflict is not inherently bad; it is normal and to be expected. If several people quickly accommodate, then the group has lost a key advantage of using different points of view to hash out the best solution or decision.

But there are also advantages in being accommodating to the views of others. To agree with others can indicate that you are reasonable and that you want to help. If the issue is a trivial matter, it may be best to let it slide. If you realize that your position is wrong, then by all means go ahead and agree with others. If you admit your errors, then others may be more likely to admit their mistakes as well, which can help create a climate of trust. Stubbornly clinging to your position, even when you realize it's wrong, creates a defensive climate. Research suggests that one way to break an upward spiral of conflict is to find something about which members can agree.[37] So, accommodating can help the group develop a supportive climate; just don't make a habit of *always* accommodating quickly to squelch *all* disagreement.

Competition

People who have power or want more power often seek to compete with others so that others will accept their point of view as the best position. The **competition** conflict-management style occurs when people stress winning a conflict at the expense of one or more other people. Think of the competition style of conflict management as an arm-wrestling match: One person tries to win so that the other person will lose. Winning is often about power, and power is about exerting control over others. Group members who seek power and position are often the ones who talk the most.[38] Research has found that if you're in a group with a competitive, even contentious and cutthroat atmosphere, it's hard to break that cycle and evolve into a more collaborative environment.[39] It takes both an awareness of the contentious climate and then talking about how to break out of the competitive environment to develop a more collaborative approach to managing conflict.

There are several disadvantages to creating a group climate built on competition. The competitive style may result in greater defensiveness, messages that blame others, and efforts to control other group members. We've stressed that it's important for group and team members to have a common goal and to work toward the common good. If some group members seek to promote their own interests over the group interests, then the undue competition diminishes the overall power of the group.

We don't want to leave the impression that it's always wrong to compete: If you are certain that you have accurate information and that your insights and experiences can help the group achieve its goal, then stick to your position and seek to persuade others. Likewise, if some group members advocate a course of action that is immoral or illegal or that violates your personal instincts of what is right and wrong, it's appropriate to advocate a different course of action.

But competing with others can be a problem if you try to control without being sensitive to their needs or rights. To compete can also be detrimental if your method of competition is simply to outlast or out-shout others, threaten them, or use unethical means of persuasion, such as knowingly using false information to win. When assertiveness crosses the line into aggression (trying to force others to support your point), most group members find that the competition style becomes tiresome over the course of several group meetings.

Compromise

The **compromise** style of conflict management attempts to find a middle ground—a solution that somewhat meets the needs of all concerned. The word *somewhat* is important. Although on the surface a compromise can look like a "win-win" approach, it can also create a lose-lose result if nobody gets what he or she actually wants or needs. Often when people give up some of what they hope to achieve, no one gets precisely what they want. When trying to reach a compromise, you're really expected to lose something and win something simultaneously; you also expect others to lose and win. As shown in Figure 1, when you compromise, you have some concern for others, as well as some concern for yourself.

Although compromise sounds good in principle, it may not be best in practice. If, for example, no one feels that the compromise solution is a good one, then it probably isn't the best solution. If group members quickly try to reach a compromise without hashing out why they disagree, the group may not make the best solution or decision. Compromise can be tempting because it seemingly gives in to each position. An old joke says that a camel is a horse designed by a committee. When groups compromise, the final product may not quite be what anyone had in mind, and it may not really solve the problem.

Although we've cautioned against too quickly reaching a compromise to manage conflict, there are obvious advantages to crafting a compromise solution. If a decision is needed quickly and a compromise can be achieved to meet the time demands of the situation, then compromise may be best. Compromise may help everyone save face, especially after a long, contentious conflict. Compromise may also maintain the balance of power in a group. A compromise on one issue can create a climate of cooperation and support that will serve the group well as it faces other challenges and disagreements.

Collaboration

To **collaborate** is to have a high concern for both yourself and others. Group members who use a collaboration style of conflict management view conflict as a problem to be solved rather than as a game in which some people win and others lose. In the long run, groups that take the time to collaborate have better results.[40] When group members work side-by-side, rather then jostling for power and supremacy, the result may be a win-win outcome.[41] Several research studies have found that when there are cultural differences among group members, a collaborative approach to conflict management works best.[42] Essential elements of a collaborative style include leaving personal grievances out of the discussion and describing problems without being judgmental or evaluative of other people. To compromise is to realize that each person loses something as well as wins something; to collaborate is to take the time to find a solution in which all parties are comfortable with the outcome rather than harboring a sense of loss and sacrifice.

The main disadvantage of a collaboration style is the time, effort, and skill it takes to collaborate. Collaboration requires patience. If your group needs a quick decision, group members may find that taking time to reach a truly "win-win" outcome is more trouble than the issue at hand is worth. Additionally, some people may use the appearance of collaboration as a pretense to compete: A person who is skilled in negotiation and who uses words well can manipulate a collaborative effort and ultimately "win."

The obvious advantage to investing time and energy in collaboration is the prospect of both a better solution to issues facing the group and more satisfied group members. Collaboration is also advantageous when the group needs fresh, new ideas because the old approaches of trying to hammer out a solution simply haven't worked. Working to develop a true consensus on a solution that all individuals support is a good goal for most groups to consider.

It may sound like the collaborative approach is always the best conflict-management style to use. And we do think it's worth pursuing in many, if not most, cases. But the best conflict-management style depends on a variety of factors. Research suggests that most people find three things about conflict uncomfortable: (1) the participants fail to reach a clear solution, (2) the conflict is managed poorly, and (3) the participants avoid discussing the key issues and true sources of the conflict.[43] There is no specific conflict-management style that "works" in all situations. However, we will discuss research conclusions that identify specific strategies and practices for collaboration that increase the likelihood that all individuals involved in a conflict will be satisfied.

Collaborative Conflict Management: Principles and Skills

What principles and strategies can help a group manage conflict collaboratively? No simple checklist of techniques will miraculously resolve or manage group differences. Research supports the principle that focusing on shared interests and developing a collaborative conflict-management style are usually preferred over more combative conflict-management styles.[44] However, based on several studies of what works and what does not work when managing conflict, Roger Fisher and William Ury identified the four conflict-management principles discussed in the following sections.[45]

Separate the People from the Problem

When conflict becomes personal and egos become involved, it is very difficult to develop a positive climate in which differences can be managed. If people feel they are being evaluated and strategically manipulated, they will respond with defensiveness. Separating the person from the problem means valuing the other individual as a person, treating her or him as an equal, and empathizing with her or his feelings. A key to valuing others is to use good listening skills. It is also useful to acknowledge the other person's feelings. Emotion is the fuel of conflict. Several scholars agree that efforts to manage our feelings facilitate the conflict-management process.[46]

One strategy for constructively expressing how you feel toward others in conflict is to use the approach John Gottman and his colleagues call the **X-Y-Z formula.**[47] According to this method, you say "When you do X, in situation Y, I feel Z." Here's an example: "When you are 15 minutes late to our staff meetings, I feel like you don't care about us or our meetings."

When you are the recipient of someone's wrath, you could use the X-Y-Z formula to explain how being yelled at makes it difficult for you to listen effectively. Trying to understand and manage your own and others' feelings helps separate personal issues from issues of substance. Joyce Hocker and William Wilmot suggest that when you are the receiver of someone's emotional outburst, you could consider the following actions.[48]

1. *Acknowledge the person's feelings.*
2. *Determine what specific behavior is causing the intense feelings.*
3. *Assess the intensity and importance of the issue.*
4. *Invite the other person to join you in working toward solutions.*
5. *Make a positive relational statement.*

Research also supports the value of using well-crafted arguments rather than emotion-laden opinions to help those in conflict sort through periods of contention.[49] No technique or simple formula exists to help you manage the challenging task of separating personal from substantive issues. Using good listening skills, acknowledging how others feel, and expressing your own feelings (without ranting and raving) make a good start toward mediating challenging conflict situations.

Another strategy to help separate personal issues from the differences team members have about the task is to use computer-mediated messages to help the team focus on just the task issues. Posting anonymous messages on a message board or brainstorming anonymously may help deflect team members' fleeting irritation with other team members and keep everyone focused on the issues rather than on personality differences.[50]

Focus on Shared Interests

The words to one old song begin with the advice "Accentuate the positive. Eliminate the negative." A collaborative style focuses on areas of agreement and what all parties have in common.[51] If, for example, you are in a group debating whether public schools should distribute condoms, group members are more likely to have a productive discussion if they verbalize the goals and values they hold in common. A comment such as "We all agree that we want to reduce the spread of AIDS" might be a good place to start such a discussion.

Conflict is goal-driven. The individuals embroiled in the conflict want something. Unless goals are clear to everyone, it will be difficult to manage the conflict well. If you are involved in conflict, determine what your goals are. Then identify your partner's goals. Finally, identify where goals overlap and where there are differences.

Do not confuse a goal with the strategy for achieving what you and a feuding group member want. For example, you may ask the group to make fewer copies on the copy machine. Your goal is to save money because you are in charge of managing the office. Asking that your colleagues make fewer copies is a strategy that you have suggested for achieving your goal. Clarifying the underlying goal rather than only debating the merits of one strategy for achieving it should help unravel clashes over issues or personalities.

Generate Many Options to Solve Problems

During negotiation, group members who adamantly hold to only one solution create a competitive climate. Collaborative conflict managers are more likely to use brainstorming or the nominal-group technique or other strategies for identifying a variety of options to manage the disagreement; they seek several solutions to overcome obstacles. Research by Shaila Miranda suggests that using e-mail or other electronic support systems to generate and evaluate ideas can also be a productive way of increasing the number of options a group or team might consider.[52] Sometimes feuding group members become fixated on only one approach to their goal. When conflict management degenerates into a verbal arm-wrestling match, where combatants perceive only one way to win, the conflict is less likely to be managed successfully.

Base Decisions on Objective Criteria

Criteria are the standards for an acceptable solution to a problem. Typical criteria are such things as a limit to how much the solution can cost or a deadline by which a solution must be implemented. If, for example, group members agree that a solution must decrease the spread of AIDS but also not cost more than $1 million to implement, the group is using criteria to help identify an acceptable solution.

When People Are Not Cooperative: Dealing with Difficult Group Members

Evidence suggests that managers spend up to 25 percent of their time dealing with conflict.[53] One author boldly claims that 98 percent of the problems we face are "people problems."[54] Scholars call them "group deviants"; you may call them a pain in the neck. Even though we hope that you will not have to deal with difficult or cantankerous group members, we are not naive. Not all group members will separate people from the problem, focus on shared interests, be eager to search for more alternatives, or base decisions on objective criteria. Our individualistic cultural traditions often make it challenging to develop collaborative groups and teams. Research suggests that if you think you are a typical group member who abides by the norms and rules of the group, you are more likely to be upset by someone who obstructs the group process.[55] You're more likely to label someone a deviant if you think you are not deviant in your own team behavior. It sometimes takes special "people skills" to deal with some group members. Drawing on the principles and skills of the collaborative conflict-management style, we offer the following tips for dealing with the more difficult group members.

Manage Your Emotions

When we are emotionally charged, we may find it difficult to practice rational, logical methods of managing conflict. One researcher offers this description of what happens to our bodies when we become upset:

> Our adrenaline flows faster and our strength increases by about 20 percent. . . . The veins become enlarged and the cortical centers where thinking takes place do not perform nearly as well. . . . the blood supply to the problem-solving part of the brain is severely decreased because, under stress, a greater portion of blood is diverted to the body's extremities.[56]

It's normal to feel angry when someone seems constantly to say or do things that make you feel judged or evaluated. In that situation, you may say or do something you later regret. Although some people advocate expressing anger to "clear the air," expressing uncensored emotions can make matters worse. On the other hand, communication researchers Barbara Gayle and Raymond Preiss confirmed what most of us know intuitively: Unresolved conflict is a breeding ground for emotional upheaval in groups and organizations.[57] Although it's been said that time heals all wounds, there are instances

CASE STUDY

→ Practice in Applying Principles

You would think that board members of the Buckner Valley food bank would be, for the most part, pleasant, selfless people who were trying to give something back to the community by volunteering their time to help provide food for those who needed a little help. Yet the board members often found themselves embroiled in conflict, due in part to some of their personalities.

Jeff meant well, but he seemed to have a need to dominate the board. He talked too much; and although he was not the current board chair, he wanted to insist that his ideas were the ones to be implemented. Jeff's dominance made other board members reactively reject his ideas, even when the ideas were good ones, such as purchasing a new van to make food deliveries. Tired of Jeff's overly bombastic style of trying to get his way, they usually disagreed with him regardless of the merit of his suggestions.

Aiden also meant well, but he missed about half of the twice-monthly meetings. He often didn't follow through on assignments. Yet he liked being on the board because it looked good on his resume; he was planning on running for city council next year and wanted to demonstrate his concern for the community by being on the board. Even when Aiden was present he seemed mentally absent; he didn't say much, even though as manager of the local grocery store he had much to offer.

Jessica was a hard worker—maybe too hard. She always followed through on her assignments and had little patience for people who didn't do what they were supposed to do. She did more than just raise her voice when expressing her concerns; she yelled and often screamed obscenities at members who made the smallest errors or mistakes. Because of her hard work, the board needed her; but members were frankly a bit afraid of her wrath and just kept quiet when she hollered at them. They didn't want to upset her further because they knew she would holler even louder.

Hudson always thought the food bank was running out of money (even when it wasn't). He longed for the good old days when just he and C. J. ran the food bank. So Hudson was typically against any new idea,

BIZARRO © 2005 Dan Piraro. King Features Syndicate.

when ignoring hurt feelings can make the conflict escalate. Leaders and team members need to recognize when to be active in addressing emotional volatility.[58] Research has confirmed that teams comprised of people with a well-developed sense of emotional intelligence (that is, they have empathy for others and are better able to manage their emotions) have less contentious and more productive meetings.[59]

Consider the following five strategies for managing your emotions during conflict.

1. *Be aware of your anger level.* Candidates for anger management programs don't monitor their emotions well; before they know it, their emotions boil over. Uncensored emotional outbursts rarely enhance the quality of communication. An emotional purge may make you feel empowered momentarily, but it usually only escalates conflict and tension.[60]

2. *Breathe.* It may sound too simple, but it works. As you become aware of your increased emotional arousal, take a

especially anything that cost money. When strategies were suggested to raise more funds, Hudson was against it; he didn't agree with the philosophy "It takes money to raise money," so he blocked most new ideas.

C. J., current board chair, was the glue that held the board together. She was mild-mannered yet hard-working and talented at keeping the other board members moving forward (most of the time). Yet she was getting weary of the constant bickering, power struggles, and inactivity on the part of some.

It was time for the board to organize the annual holiday gift basket program for Buckner Valley, yet the board just wasn't making progress. The need was greater this year than ever because of the downturn in the economy. Many people had lost their jobs and would have no holiday if it weren't for the food bank. Jeff had a good idea for streamlining the operation so that more families could be fed, but other members rejected his idea because they didn't want Jeff to get credit for the idea. Since Aiden ran the grocery store he could make a major difference in the community, but he didn't have time to attend many meetings. He just didn't seem to have time or interest. Hudson didn't want to spend a dime more than what was spent last year and was against any new plan that

might cost more money. Jessica was at her prickly best, and, although she could do the work, she had nothing but critical comments for her fellow board members. C. J. knew the Buckner Valley community was depending on the board, so she was intent on doing whatever she could to feed even more people this year—families were depending on it.

Questions for Analysis

1. Based on the descriptions of pseudo, simple and ego conflict, what type or types of conflict do you see evident on the board?
2. What different styles of conflict management do you see among the board members? How do those different styles affect the level of conflict among board members?
3. Which collaborative conflict-management principles and skills presented on pages 185-87 would be helpful for board members to implement to address the recurring conflicts they were experiencing?
4. Based on the strategies presented in Table 1 what suggestions would you make to help manage the array of personalities present on the board?

slow, deep breath. A deep breath can help calm you and manage the physiological changes that adrenaline creates. A slow, deep breath can help soothe your spirit and give you another focus besides lashing out at others.

3. *Use self-talk.* Your thoughts are linked to your feelings. You can affect your emotional state by first being aware that you are becoming upset and then telling yourself to calm down and stay focused on the issues at hand. Eleanor Roosevelt's observation that "no one can make you feel inferior without your consent" is an acknowledgment of the power of self-talk to affect your emotional response to what others say and do.

4. *Monitor your nonverbal messages.* Emotions are usually communicated nonverbally rather than verbally. Monitoring your emotional signals (such as noting whether your voice gets louder, your facial expression less friendly, and your gestures more dramatic or emphatic) can help de-escalate an emotionally charged situation before it erupts. Speaking more slowly and calmly, maintaining direct eye contact, and adopting a neutral facial expression can help ensure a climate of civility and decorum. We're not suggesting that you manipulate your nonverbal behavior so that you feel inauthentic or that you speak in a patronizing tone. However, being aware of how your nonverbal messages contribute to the emotional climate can help bring the emotional temperature down a degree or two.

5. *Avoid personal attacks.* When conflict gets personal (ego conflict) it becomes more difficult to manage. Calling people names and hurling negative personal messages at others usually adds to a deteriorating emotional group climate.

Don't **gunny-sack.** Gunny-sacking is dredging up old problems and issues from the past, like pulling them out of an old bag, or gunny sack, to use against your partner. Bringing up old problems that can't be changed now only serves to make matters worse, especially when emotions are raw. Focus on the present and what can be discussed now and changed in the future, rather than reliving past problems.

Describe What Is Upsetting You

Try to avoid lashing back at the offending person. Use a descriptive "I" message to explain to the other person how you are feeling; for example, "I find it difficult to listen to you when you raise your voice at me," or "I notice that is the fourth time you have interrupted me when I was trying to explain my point." Keep in mind that the goal is not to increase the conflict. "You shouldn't yell at me" or "You shouldn't interrupt me" are examples of "you" statements. Such statements are evaluative and are likely to increase resentment and anger. Although we recommend that you manage your emotions during the heat of conflict, we're not suggesting that you can't express your feelings. In fact, one study found that team members who constructively express how they feel can enhance the decision-making process.[61] Individuals who are aware of their own feelings and positively manage what one team of researchers called *affective influence* tend to develop better solutions and make better decisions.

Disclose Your Feelings

After describing the behavior that offends or irritates you, tell how you feel when the behavior occurs: "When I'm interrupted, I feel that my opinion isn't valued," or "I become increasingly

---

COLLABORATING ETHICALLY

What Would You Do?

Imagine that you are a member of a work team whose job is to recommend new software purchases for your company. Your team is led by the talented Tim, who runs a good team meeting. There are, however, two members of the team, Rita and Rob, who seem to be jealous of Tim's consistent ability to accomplish his objectives. In reality both Rita and Rob would like to lead the team. But as long as Tim enjoys the support of the other three team members, they figure they'll just have to wait until Tim's leadership skill and knowledge is challenged.

Having lunch at the company cafeteria, you overhear Rita and Rob, the two want-to-be-leaders, plotting to challenge Tim at the next meeting. They are planning to lodge a critical attack on Tim's new software initiative. They think the conflict they stir up will cause other team members to question Tim's leadership abilities and provide an opening for their own ascendency to co-leading the group. If Tim knew about the planned attack he could be prepared to respond to Rita and Rob's criticism. Although you're not particularly a friend of Tim's, should you tell him about the planned leadership challenge, or just keep quiet and see how Tim deals with the conflict at the next team meeting?

What would you do?

frustrated when I try to contribute to our meeting but I don't feel you are listening." When disclosing your feelings, try to avoid such emotional overstatement as "I've never been so upset in all my life." Such hyperbole raises the emotional stakes and can trigger a new volley of retorts.

Two researchers have found that simply prefacing a statement with the word "I," as we suggested you do when using "I" language, may sometimes be too subtle to help defuse a conflict.[62] You may need to add a longer justification when you provide negative emotional information to another group member. We call this using *extended "I" language,* which is a brief preface to a feedback statement. You might begin by saying something like "I don't want you to take this the wrong way. I really do care about you and I need to share something with you," or "I don't think this is completely your fault. Yet I find myself becoming more frustrated when I hear that you've talked to others about me." These extended comments may have a better chance of taking the sting out of a negative message than simply beginning a sentence with the word *I* instead of the word *you.* There are no magic words that will de-escalate conflict. Being sensitive and thoughtful about how others may respond to your messages can help you express your ideas in ways that are more likely to be heard rather than immediately rejected.

Return to the Issue of Contention

The only way to return to a collaborative style is to get back to the issue that is fueling the disagreement. Avoiding the issue will not resolve the issue.[63] Sometimes one of those in conflict has a hidden agenda that makes it difficult to confront the key issues. A wise person once said, "Often what we fight about is not what we fight about." Although an argument may seem on the surface to be about a substantive issue—such as which solution to adopt or whose research to use—the underlying issue may be about power and control. Only if the underlying issue is exposed and addressed will the conflict be managed.

These general suggestions provide basic principles for dealing with difficult group members, but you may need more specific strategies for managing such people. Table 1 offers several specific ways to deal with group members who perform such self-focused roles as dominator and blocker or who are irresponsible or unethically aggressive. Remember: *No one can change the behavior of another person.* But competent communicators have the knowledge, skill, and motivation to respond appropriately and effectively to others' behavior, even when that behavior is difficult, self-serving, or unethical.

Groupthink: Conflict Avoidance

Groupthink is the illusion of agreement[64]—a type of thinking that occurs when a group strives to minimize conflict, maximize cohesiveness, and reach a consensus without critically testing, analyzing, and evaluating ideas. Columnist William Safire notes that the term *groupthink* first appeared in a 1952 *Fortune* magazine article by William H. Whyte, Jr.[65] When a group reaches decisions too quickly, it does not properly consider the implications of its decisions. Groupthink results in an ineffective consensus; too little conflict often lowers the quality of group decisions. When a group does not take time to examine the positive and negative consequences of alternative decisions, the quality of its decision is likely to suffer.[66]

Sociologist Irving Janis believes that many poor decisions and policies are the result of groupthink.[67] In 1999, eleven students at Texas A&M University were tragically killed when the traditional pre-football-game bonfire they were building collapsed; many other students

TABLE 1

How to Deal with Difficult Group Members

What the Group Member Does	Options for Managing the Problem
Dominates: Tries to tell people what to do without seeking permission from the group; tells rather than asks; monopolizes the conversation	1. Use gatekeeping skills to invite other group members to participate; explicitly state that you'd like to hear what others have to say. 2. In private, ask the dominating group member to be less domineering and to give others an opportunity to participate. 3. Channel the dominator's energy by giving him or her a specific task to accomplish, such as recording the minutes of the meeting or periodically summarizing the group's progress. 4. The group or team may collectively decide to confront the domineering member; clearly describe the behavior that the group perceives as inappropriate.
Blocks Progress: Has a negative attitude. Is often stubborn and disagreeable without a clear reason. When the group is making progress, the blocker seems to keep the group from achieving its goal.	1. Ask for specific evidence as to why the blocker does not support the group's position. 2. Calmly confront the blocker and explain how consistently being negative creates a negative group climate. 3. Use humor to help defuse the tension that the blocker creates. 4. Assign the blocker the role of devil's advocate before the group makes a decision; giving the blocker permission to be negative at certain times can help the group avoid groupthink.
Is Irresponsible: Does not carry through with assignments; is often absent from or late to meetings	1. Speak to the offending group member privately and convince him or her to pull his or her own weight. Explain how his or her irresponsibility is hurting other group members and the overall success of the group. 2. Assign a mentor. Call the person or send an e-mail to remind him or her to attend the meeting. Ask for a progress report on the status of assigned work. Work one-on-one trying to help the irresponsible member see how his or her behavior hurts the group. Provide more structure. 3. If confronting the offending group member first privately and then collectively does not get results, ask for help from a supervisor or instructor. 4. Clarify who will get the credit. To minimize social loafing, tell the offending member that when the final product is complete, the group will clearly indicate her or his lack of participation.
Is Unethically Aggressive: Is verbally abusive toward other group members or purposefully disconfirms others. Tries to take credit for the work of others	1. Do not accept unethical behavior in silence. Immediately describe the offensive behavior to the aggressor, and indicate its negative effect on individuals or the entire group. 2. Several group members may confront the offending group member collectively. The group as a whole should not tolerate mean-spirited actions toward others. 3. Become an advocate for other group members; support those who are attacked or singled out. 4. Seek help from an instructor or supervisor or from someone in authority outside the group to stop the unethical, offending behavior. Sometimes a bully only responds to a person of greater power.

were injured. Investigators found that a structural engineering professor had for years tried to warn university officials that the bonfire's design was unsafe; other engineering faculty members who also thought the bonfire was a disaster waiting to happen finally stopped trying to influence the university because no one would listen.[68] The decision to launch the flawed space shuttle *Challenger* on that unforgettable January morning in 1986 was also tinged by groupthink.[69] Corporate executives and others did not challenge assumptions in the construction and launch procedures; disaster resulted. The pressure for consensus resulted in groupthink. In hindsight, one contributing cause of the 2002 *Columbia* shuttle disaster was believed to have been groupthink as well.

Yet another example: The Congressional 9/11 commission, investigating why U.S. intelligence organizations were not as vigilant as they should have been in anticipating the terrorists attacks on September 11, 2001, concluded that groupthink was a contributing factor. The commission also found that leaders and analysts in intelligence organizations reached conclusions about the presence of weapons of mass destruction in Iraq that were based on unchallenged assumptions and unverified information.[70]

The Texas A&M bonfire tragedy, the *Challenger* and *Columbia* shuttle disasters, and the terrorist attacks of September 11 are dramatic examples of how groupthink has contributed to faulty decision making. The groups and teams in which you participate are equally susceptible to this illusion of agreement.

Groups with highly esteemed leaders are most prone to groupthink. Because these leaders' ideas are often viewed as sacrosanct, few members disagree with them. A group may also suffer from groupthink if its members consider themselves highly cohesive and take pride in getting along well with one another and providing support and encouragement for members' ideas.

One research study found that groupthink is most likely to occur when (1) the group is apathetic about the task, (2) group members have low expectations about their ability to be successful, (3) there is at least one highly qualified, credible group member, (4) one group member is exceptionally persuasive, and (5) there is a norm that group members should conform rather than express negative opinions.[71] Research further suggests that you are more likely to think groupthink is a problem in your group after your group has struggled and gotten off the track.[72] Teams are better able to diagnose groupthink as the culprit in making groups wobble *after* the wobbling is over rather than during a group's struggle. So it's important that you recognize the symptoms of groupthink while your group is demonstrating those symptoms rather than after the damage has been done.

Although some small group communication scholars question the theoretical soundness of the theory of groupthink, it continues to serve as a useful and practical way of helping groups understand why they make poor decisions.[73]

Symptoms of Groupthink

Can you identify groupthink when it occurs in groups to which you belong? Here are some of the common symptoms of groupthink.[74]

Critical Thinking Is Not Encouraged or Rewarded   If you are working in a group that considers disagreement or controversy counterproductive, chances are that groupthink is alive and well in that group. One advantage of working in groups is having an opportunity to evaluate ideas so that you can select the best possible solution. If group members seem proud that peace and harmony prevail at their meetings, they may suffer from groupthink.

Members Believe That Their Group Can Do No Wrong   During the 1972 presidential election, members of the committee to reelect President Nixon did not consider that they might fail to obtain information from Democratic headquarters. They thought their group was invulnerable. But the burglary of the Watergate office and the subsequent coverup ultimately led to the resignation of President Nixon. This sense of invulnerability is a classic symptom of groupthink. Another symptom is that members dismiss potential threats to the group as minor problems. If your group is consistently overconfident in dealing with problems that may interfere with its goals, it may suffer from groupthink.[75]

Members Are Too Concerned about Justifying Their Actions   Members of highly cohesive groups like to feel that they are acting in their group's best interests. Therefore, groups that experience groupthink like to rationalize their positions on issues. A group susceptible to groupthink is too concerned about convincing itself that it has made proper decisions in the past and will make good decisions in the future.

Members Apply Pressure to Those Who Do Not Support the Group   Have you ever voiced an opinion contrary to the majority opinion and quickly realized that other members were trying to pressure you into going along with the rest of the group? Groups prone to groupthink have a low tolerance for members who do not "go along." They see controversy and conflict injected by a dissenting member as a threat to *esprit de corps*. Therefore, a person voicing an idea different from the group's position is often punished.[76]

Sometimes pressure is subtle, taking the form of frowns or grimaces. Group members may not socialize with the dissenting member, or they may not listen attentively to the dissident. Usually their first response is to try to convince this member to reconsider his or her position. But if the member still does not agree with the others, he or she may be expelled from the group. Of course, if a group member is just being stubborn, the others should try to reason with the dissenter. Do not, however, be too quick to label someone as a troublemaker simply because he or she has an opinion different from that of other group members.

Members Often Believe That They Have Reached a True Consensus   A significant problem in groups that suffer from groupthink is that members are not aware of the phenomenon. They think they have reached genuine consensus. For example, suppose you and your friends are trying to decide which movie to rent on Friday night. Someone suggests *The Lord of the Rings*. Even though you've already seen the movie, you don't want to be contentious, so you agree with the suggestion. Other group members also agree.

After your group has seen the movie, you overhear another one of your friends say, "I enjoyed the movie better when I saw it the first time." After a quick poll of the group, you discover that most of your friends had already seen the movie! They agreed to see it only because they did not want to hurt anyone's feelings. They thought everyone else was in agreement. Although the group appeared to reach consensus, only a few people actually agreed with the decision. Therefore, even if you think that the rest of the group agrees and that you are the only dissenter, your group could still be experiencing groupthink. Just because your group seems to have reached a consensus does not necessarily mean that all the members truly agree.

Members Are Too Concerned about Reinforcing the Leader's Beliefs   Leaders of small groups often emerge because they suggest some of the best ideas, motivate group members, or devote themselves to group goals more than others do. If group members place too much emphasis on the credibility or infallibility of their leader, groupthink may occur. Leaders who like to be surrounded by yes people (those who always agree with their ideas) lose the advantage of having their ideas tested. Most people do not like criticism and do not like to be told that their ideas are inept or inappropriate. Therefore, group leaders are understandably attracted to those who agree with them. Leaders sensitive to the problem of groupthink will solicit and tolerate all viewpoints because testing the quality of solutions requires different opinions.

One researcher has found empirical support for the symptoms of groupthink. Rebecca Cline found that groups exhibiting groupthink do express more agreement without clarification and also use simpler and fewer substantiated agreements than groups that avoid groupthink.[77] She also found that groups that experience groupthink spend about 10 percent more of their discussion time making statements of agreement or disagreement than other groups. Groups that experience groupthink perpetuate the illusion of agreement by sprinkling in frequent comments such as "Yeah, I see what you're saying," "That's right," or "Sure."

REVIEW

▶ SYMPTOMS OF GROUPTHINK

- Critical thinking is not encouraged or rewarded.
- Members think their group can do no wrong.
- Members are too concerned about justifying their actions.

- Members apply pressure to those who do not support the group.
- Members often believe that they have reached a true consensus.
- Members are too concerned about reinforcing the leader's beliefs.

Suggestions for Reducing Groupthink

How can you reduce the chances of groupthink's occurring in your group? Consider the following specific suggestions, based on Janis's initial observations as well as on the theories and the research of several small group communication researchers.

Encourage Critical, Independent Thinking The leader should make clear that he or she does not want the group to reach agreement until each member has critically evaluated

Technicians examine debris from the space shuttle *Columbia* at Cape Canaveral. Some blame the disaster, in part, on groupthink at NASA.

Reuters/CORBIS

the issues. Most group leaders want to command the respect of their groups, but a leader's insistence that the group always agree with him or her does not encourage respect; instead, it may demonstrate a fear of disagreement. Thus, if you find yourself a leader in a small group, you should encourage disagreement—not just for the sake of argument, but to eliminate groupthink. Even if you are not a leader, you can encourage a healthy discussion by voicing any objections you have to the ideas being discussed. Do not permit instant, uncritical agreement in your group.

Be Sensitive to Status Differences That May Affect Decision Making Group members should not yield to status differences when evaluating ideas, issues, and solutions to problems. Instead, they should consider the merits of suggestions, weigh evidence, and make decisions about the validity of ideas without being too concerned about the status of those making suggestions. Of course, this is easier said than done.

Numerous studies suggest that a person with more status is going to be more persuasive.[78] Cereal companies know this when they hire famous athletes to sell breakfast food. The implied message is "Don't worry about the quality of the product. If this Olympic gold-medal winner eats this stuff, you'll like it too." The athlete's fame and status do not necessarily make the cereal good; however, you still might buy the cereal, making a decision based on emotion rather than fact. Group members sometimes make decisions this way, too. Avoid agreeing with a decision just because of the status or credibility of the person making it. Evaluate the quality of the solution on its own merits.

Invite Someone from Outside the Group to Evaluate the Group's Decision-Making Process Sometimes an objective point of view from outside the group can identify unproductive group norms more readily than group members can and thereby help prevent groupthink.[79] Many large companies hire consultants to evaluate organizational decision making, but you do not have to be part of a multinational corporation to ask someone to analyze your group's decision-making process. Ask someone from outside your group to sit in on one of your meetings. At the end of the meeting, ask the observer to summarize his or her observations and evaluations of the group. An outside observer may make some members uncomfortable, but if you explain why the visitor is there, the group will probably accept the visitor and eagerly await objective observations.

Assign a Group Member the Role of Devil's Advocate If no disagreement develops in a group, members may enjoy getting along and never realize that their group suffers from groupthink. If you find yourself in a group of pacifists, play devil's advocate by trying to raise objections and potential problems. Assign someone to consider the negative aspects of a suggestion before it is implemented. It could save the group from groupthink and enhance the quality of the decision.

Research by Ernest Borman suggests that some groups include a person who assumes the **central negative role**.[80] It's called a central negative role because the person seems to be a central figure in routinely having negative things to say about the leader's ideas or other group members' suggestions. The central negative person may offer negative comments to challenge the leader's power and position in the group. Although having someone play a strong central negative role in the group can be annoying, it can also be useful. Rather than routinely trying to shut down the central negative role person, acknowledge the value than can come from having someone periodically challenge the ideas and opinions of the leader, other members, or the entire group. It's important, however, that the central negative person not make his or her critiques personal. If the criticism is focused on issues and not personalities, the central negative person can fulfill a useful purpose in helping the group avoid groupthink.

VIRTUAL COMMUNICATION

Whether you're interacting in person or using e-mail or other mediated messages, the same factors that contribute to conflict can arise. The limited amount of nonverbal cues in mediated settings appears to have an effect on how mediated teams manage conflict.

One research group found that when groups negotiate differences in computer-mediated settings, as conflict escalates group members tend to decrease the intensity of forcefully insisting how the conflict should be resolved.[81] In addition, the researchers found that as conflict increases, negotiators generally tend to avoid conflict rather than addressing it head on. When communicating face-to-face during conflict, team members are more likely to try to control the behavior of others, and there is a more reciprocal, tit-for-tat escalation of conflict than in mediated settings.

Another study found that when attempting to brainstorm and generate ideas, members of computer-mediated groups experience more negative conflict management behaviors than those in face-to-face groups; the computer-mediated groups are less effective in managing conflict.[82] The results suggest that it may be more difficult to mange conflict in a productive way in computer-mediated groups than in face-to-face groups.

Research has also found that if a group has relational conflict, especially if the conflict is intensely personal, it may be best to sort the conflict out in person rather than using e-mail or other mediated methods. If the issue is a difference of opinion about a technical issue, then e-mail can be a useful way of clarifying and sharing information. But if it's a pesky relational conflict, it's best to meet in person.[83]

Another research study explored the effects on conflict-management styles of participating in virtual teams—whether team members are avoidant, competitive, or collaborative.[84] They found that it's not a good idea to suppress ideas and suggestions that are in conflict with those of other virtual team members. Avoiding conflict had a negative effect on team performance. Confronting conflict directly typically resulted in a more positive team outcome. The researchers also found that without the accompanying nonverbal cues, team members' attempts to negatively evaluate others had less of a sting. Collaboration was perceived as a positive strategy in both virtual teams and face-to-face teams. And attempting to reach a compromise, especially an early compromise before team members have a chance to discuss the issues, is not as productive in virtual groups as it is in face-to-face groups.

Putting Research into Practice

What are the best ways to manage conflict when it occurs in mediated or online groups?

- Select the most appropriate conflict-management style. Cooperation and collaboration appears to be the best first approach to use when conflict occurs in mediated settings.
- Don't sweep disagreements under the rug. Address differences of opinion, but do so thoughtfully and politely. Without contemptuous nonverbal cues, you may be able to express your differences of opinion with less of a bite because the receivers won't also hear your sarcastic nonverbal tone.
- When relational conflict erupts online, it may be time to meet face-to-face rather than try to manage the conflict online.

Ask Group Members to Subdivide into Small Groups to Consider Potential Problems with the Suggested Solutions In large groups, not all members will be able to voice their objections and reservations. The U.S. Congress does most of its work in committees. Members of Congress realize that in order to hear and thoroughly evaluate bills and resolutions, small groups of representatives must work together in committees. If you are working in a group too large for everyone to discuss the issues, suggest breaking into groups of two or three, with each group composing a list of objections to the proposals. The lists could be forwarded to the group secretary, who then could weed out duplicate objections and identify common points of contention. Even in a group of seven or eight, two subcommittees could evaluate the recommendations of the group. Group members should be able to participate frequently and evaluate the issues carefully. Individuals could also write down their objections to the proposed recommendations and then present them to the group.

One technique that may reduce groupthink is to have groups divide into two teams to debate an issue. The principle is simple: Develop a group structure that encourages critical thinking. Vigilant thinking fosters quality decisions.

Consider Using Technology to Help Your Group Gather and Evaluate Ideas One study found that having group members share and test ideas and evidence through the use of a computerized group decision support system (GDSS) rather than always meeting face to face may facilitate more extensive testing of ideas and opinions.[85] Some of the groups you participate in may not have access to such systems. Considerable research, however, suggests that the quality of group decisions can be enhanced if group members contribute ideas by using e-mail or other software programs to help gather and evaluate ideas.[86] Research also suggests, though, that being separated from other group members geographically can increase the likelihood of conflict.[87] One advantage to using GDSS methods in reducing groupthink is that ideas can be presented anonymously. Certain software programs let group members share ideas without revealing whether a member is the boss or the new intern. GDSS technology also helps separate the process of generating ideas from evaluating ideas.

Identifying and correcting groupthink should help improve the quality of your group's decisions by capitalizing on opposing viewpoints. A textbook summary of suggestions for dealing with groupthink may lead you to think that this problem can be corrected easily. It cannot. Because many people think that conflict should be avoided, they need specific guidelines for identifying and avoiding groupthink. In essence, be critical of ideas, not people. Remember that some controversy is useful. A decision-making group uses conflict to seek the best decision everyone can agree on—it seeks consensus. The last section of this chapter discusses managing conflict in the search for consensus.

REVIEW

▶ SUGGESTIONS FOR REDUCING GROUPTHINK

- Encourage critical, independent thinking.
- Be sensitive to status differences that may affect decision making.
- Invite someone from outside the group to evaluate the group's decision-making process.
- Assign a group member the role of devil's advocate.

- Ask group members to subdivide into small groups (or to work individually) to consider potential problems with suggested solutions.
- Use e-mail and other electronic technology to permit people to make anonymous contributions; this will reduce the effects of group member status differences.

Consensus: Reaching Agreement Through Communication

Some conflict is inevitable in groups, but this does not mean that all group discussions are doomed to end in disagreement. Conflict can be managed. **Consensus** occurs when all group members support and are committed to a decision. Even if a group does not reach consensus on key issues, it is not necessarily a failure. Good decisions can certainly emerge from groups whose members do not all completely agree on decisions. The U.S. Congress, for example, rarely achieves consensus; that does not mean, however, that its legislative process is ineffective.

Although conflict and controversy can improve the quality of group decision making, it is worthwhile to aim for consensus.[88] The following sections suggest some specific ways to help your group reach agreement.

The Nature of Consensus

Consensus should not come too quickly. If it does, your group is probably a victim of groupthink. Nor does consensus usually come easily. Sometimes group agreement is built on agreements on minor points raised during the discussion. To achieve consensus, group members should try to emphasize these areas of agreement. This can be a time-consuming process, and some members may lose patience before they reach agreement. Regardless of how long a group takes to reach consensus, consensus generally results from careful and thoughtful communication between members of the group.

Is taking the time to reach consensus worth the effort? Groups that reach consensus (not groupthink) and also effectively use good discussion methods, such as testing and challenging evidence and ideas, achieve a better quality decision.[89] Evidence also suggests that groups that achieve consensus are likely to maintain agreement even after several weeks.[90]

To achieve consensus, some personal preferences must be surrendered for the overall well-being of the group. Group members must decide, both individually and collectively, whether they can achieve consensus. If two or three members refuse to change their minds on their positions, the rest of the group may decide that reaching consensus is not worth the extra time. Some group communication theorists suggest that groups might do better to postpone a decision if consensus cannot be reached, particularly if the group making the decision will also implement it. If several group members oppose the solution, they will be less eager to put it into practice. Ultimately, if consensus cannot be reached, a group should generally abide by the decision of the majority.

Suggestions for Reaching Consensus

Communication researchers agree that group members usually go through considerable effort before reaching consensus. Using specific communication strategies may help members more readily foster consensus in group and team meetings.[91]

We suggest you keep three key pieces of advice in mind when striving for group consensus.

1. Because groups have a tendency to get off track, help keep the group oriented toward its goal. Groups and teams often fail to reach agreement because they engage in discussion that is not relevant to the issue at hand—groups digress.

2. Be other-oriented and sensitive to the ideas and feelings of others. Listen without interrupting. Make an honest effort to set aside your own ideas and seek to understand the ideas of others.

3. (Promote honest interaction and dialogue.) Genuine consensus is more likely to occur if group and team members honestly express their thoughts and feelings; withholding ideas and suggestions may lead to groupthink.

How to Orient the Group Toward Its Goal   The following strategies can help your group reach consensus by staying focused and on task.

- *Use metadiscussional phrases:* **Metadiscussion** is discussion about discussion. In other words, a metadiscussional statement focuses on the discussion process rather than on the topic under consideration.[92] Metadiscussional statements include "Aren't we getting a little off the subject?" or "John, we haven't heard from you yet. What do you think?" or "Let's summarize our areas of agreement." These statements contain information and advice about the problem-solving process rather than about the issue at hand. Several studies show that groups whose members help orient the group toward its goal by (1) relying on facts rather than opinions, (2) making useful, constructive suggestions, and (3) trying to resolve conflict are more likely to reach agreement than groups whose members do not try to keep the group focused on its goal.[93]

   One of the essential task competencies is to maintain a focus on the group's task. Metadiscussional phrases help to keep the group or team focused on the task or meeting agenda. This is an exceptionally powerful and useful skill to learn because you can offer metadiscussional statements even if you are not the designated leader of the group. Research clearly supports the importance of metadiscussion; simply having someone periodically reflect on where the group is on the agenda and review what has been accomplished can pay big dividends in helping the group stay on track and reach consensus.[94]

- *Keep the focus on the group's goal rather than on specific strategies to achieve the goal:* Focusing on shared interests and reminding the group what the goals are can help the group move on from debating only one or two strategies to achieving the goal. Group members sometimes fall in love with an idea or strategy and won't let go of it. In order to move forward, explicitly and frequently remind the group of the overarching goal you are trying to achieve.

- *Display known facts for all group members to see:* Consider using a chalkboard, *PowerPoint,* or flipchart to display what is really known about the issues confronting the group. When group members cannot agree, they often retreat to restating opinions rather than advocating an idea based on hard evidence. If all group members can be reminded of what is known, consensus may be more easily obtained.

   One way to display facts is to use the is/is not technique. Draw a line down the middle of the chalkboard or flip chart. On one side of the line, note what is known about the present issue. On the other side, identify what is unknown or is mere speculation. Separating facts from speculation can help group members focus on data rather than on unproven inferences.[95]

- *Do not wait until the very end of the deliberations to suggest solutions:* Research suggests that groups that delay identifying specific solutions until the very end of the discussion are less likely to reach consensus than those groups that think about solutions earlier in the deliberations.[96] Of course, before jumping to solutions, groups need to analyze and assess the present situation.

How to Be Other-Oriented: Listen to the Ideas of Others   What follows are tips and suggestions to help manage the relational tension that usually occurs when groups can't reach consensus.

- *Give your idea to the group:* People often defend a solution or suggestion just because it is theirs. Here is a suggestion that may help you develop a more objective point of view: If you find yourself becoming defensive over an idea you suggest, assume that your idea has become the property of the group; it no longer belongs to you. Present your position as clearly as possible, then listen to other members' reactions and consider them carefully before you push for your point. Just because people disagree with your idea does not necessarily mean they respect you less.

- *Do not assume that someone must win and someone must lose:* When discussion becomes deadlocked, try not to view the discussion in terms of "us" versus "them" or "me" versus "the group." Try not to view communication as a game that someone wins and others lose. Be willing to compromise and modify your original position. Of course, if compromising means finding a solution that is marginally acceptable to everyone but does not really solve a problem, then seek a better solution.

- *Use group-oriented rather than self-oriented pronouns:* Harry likes to talk about the problem as *he* sees it. He often begins sentences with phrases such as "I think this is a good idea" or "My suggestion is to . . . ." Studies suggest that groups that reach consensus generally use more pronouns like *we, us,* and *our,* while groups that do not reach consensus use more pronouns like *I, me, my,* and *mine.*[97] Using group-oriented words can foster cohesiveness.

- *Avoid opinionated statements that indicate a closed mind:* Communication scholars consistently find that opinionated statements and low tolerance for dissenting points of view inhibit agreement. This is especially apparent when the opinionated person is the discussion leader. A group with a less opinionated leader is more likely to reach agreement. Remember that using facts and relying on information obtained by direct observation are probably the best ways to avoid making opinionated statements.

- *Clarify misunderstandings:* Although not all disagreements arise because conflicting parties fail to understand one another, misunderstanding another's meaning sometimes creates conflict and adversely affects group consensus. Dealing with misunderstanding is simple. Ask a group member to explain a particular word or statement that you do not understand. Constantly solicit feedback from your listeners. During periods of disagreement, consider repeating the previous speaker's point and ask if you've got it right before you state your position on an issue. This procedure can become time-consuming and stilted if overused, but it can help when misunderstandings about meanings arise. It may also be helpful for you to remember that meanings are conveyed through people, not words. Stated another way, the meaning of a word comes from a person's unique perspective, perception, and experience.

- *Emphasize areas of agreement:* When the group gets bogged down in conflict and disagreement, it may prove useful to stop and identify the issues and information on which group members *do* agree. One study found that groups whose members were able to keep refocusing the group on areas of agreement, particularly following episodes of disagreement, were more likely to reach consensus than groups that continued to accentuate the negative.[98] Another study found that one of the most important ways of helping a group reach consensus is to be genuinely supportive of others.[99]

How to Promote Honest Interaction and Dialogue   To help groups and teams avoid a false consensus (groupthink) and to share ideas in a climate of openness and honesty, consider these suggestions.

- *Do not change your mind too quickly just to avoid conflict:* Although you may have to compromise to reach agreement, beware of changing your mind too quickly just to reach consensus. Groupthink occurs when group members do not test and challenge the ideas of others. When agreement seems to come too fast and too easily, be suspicious. Make certain that you have explored other alternatives and that everyone accepts the solution for basically the same reasons. Of course, you should not create conflict just for the sake of conflict, but do not be upset if disagreements arise. Reaching consensus takes time and often requires compromise. Be patient.

- *Avoid easy techniques that reduce conflict:* You may be tempted to flip a coin or to take a simple majority vote when you cannot resolve a disagreement. Resist that temptation, especially early in your deliberation. If possible, avoid making a decision until the entire group can agree. Of course, at times, a majority vote is the only way to resolve a conflict. Just be certain that the group explores other alternatives before it makes a hasty decision to avoid conflict. When time permits, gaining consensus through communication is best.

- *Seek out differences of opinion:* Remember that disagreements may improve the quality of a group's decision. With a variety of opinions and information, a group has a better chance of finding a good solution. Also remember that complex problems seldom have just one solution. Perhaps more than one of the suggestions offered will work. Actively recruit opposing viewpoints if everyone seems to be agreeing without much discussion.[100] Or, appoint someone to play the role of devil's advocate. Of course, do not belabor the point if you think that group members genuinely agree after considerable discussion.

- *Involve everyone in the discussion; frequently contribute to the group:* Again, the more varied the suggestions, solutions, and information, the greater the chance that a group will reach quality solutions and achieve consensus. Encourage less-talkative members to contribute to the group. Several studies suggest that members will be more satisfied with a solution if they have had an opportunity to express their opinions and to offer suggestions.[101] Remember not to dominate the discussion. Good listening is important, too, and you may need to encourage others to speak out and assert themselves.

- *Use a variety of methods to reach agreement:* One researcher has found that groups are more likely to reach agreement if members try several approaches to resolve a deadlocked situation rather than using just one method of achieving consensus.[102] Consider (1) combining two or more ideas into one solution; (2) building, changing, or extending existing ideas; (3) using effective persuasion skills to convince others to agree; and (4) developing new ideas to move the discussion forward rather than just rehashing old ideas.

- *Expand the number of ideas and alternatives:* One reason a group may not agree is because none of the ideas or solutions being discussed are good ones. Each solution on the table may have flaws. If that is the case, the task should change from trying to reach agreement on the alternatives in front of the group to generating more alternatives.[103] Switching from a debate to brainstorming may help pry group members away from a foolish adherence to existing solutions. Consider using a structured way to set more ideas on the table when the group seems stuck.

Are there differences between the ways face-to-face groups reach consensus and the ways virtual groups that interact online do? As we noted earlier in the chapter, one research study found that virtual groups use more negative conflict management behaviors.[104]

Negative behaviors include taking a quick vote rather than discussing issues, suppressing differences of opinions, and assuming an "I-must-win-you-must-lose" approach to managing differences. Both online and in person, it's best to encourage honest conversation and dialogue and avoid squelching opposing viewpoints.

In summary, research suggests that groups that search for areas of agreement while critically testing ideas and reducing ambiguity are more likely to reach consensus than groups that don't do these things. Also, one research team found that groups that strive for unanimous agreement ultimately are more likely to at least reach consensus than groups that are seeking only minimal consensus.[105] As you strive for consensus, rather than just saying, "No, you're wrong," identify specific issues that need to be clarified. Groups that focus on disagreement about procedures rather than on substantive issues are less likely to reach consensus. Building consensus takes time and skill and is not necessarily the goal of the group, but if it can be achieved, consensus may result in a better quality decision.

REVIEW

▶ SUGGESTIONS FOR REACHING CONSENSUS

ORIENT THE GROUP TOWARD ITS GOAL

Effective Group Members

- Talk about the discussion process using metadiscussional phrases.
- Help keep the group focused on the goal.
- Display known facts for all members in the group to see.
- Suggest possible solutions throughout the group's deliberation.

Ineffective Group Members

- Do little to help clarify group discussion.
- Go off on tangents and do not stay focused on the agenda.
- Fail to provide summaries of issues or facts about which members agree or rely only on oral summaries.
- Wait until time is about to run out before suggesting solutions.

BE OTHER-ORIENTED: LISTEN TO THE IDEAS OF OTHERS

Effective Group Members

- Give their ideas to the group.
- Approach conflict as a problem to be solved rather than a win/lose situation.
- Use group-oriented pronouns to talk about the group.
- Avoid opinionated statements that are not based on facts or evidence.
- Clarify misunderstandings.
- Emphasize areas of agreement.

Ineffective Group Members

- Argue for an idea because it is their own.
- Assume that someone will win and someone will lose an argument.
- Talk about individual accomplishments rather than group accomplishments.
- Are closed-minded and inflexible.
- Do not clarify misunderstandings or check to see whether their message is understood.
- Ignore areas of agreement.

PROMOTE HONEST INTERACTION AND DIALOGUE

Effective Group Members

- Do not change their minds quickly just to avoid conflict.
- Avoid easy conflict-reducing techniques.
- Seek out differences of opinion.
- Try to involve everyone in the discussion and make frequent, meaningful contributions to the group.
- Use a variety of methods to reach agreement.
- Expand the number of ideas and alternatives using various techniques.

Ineffective Group Members

- Give in to the opinion of group members just to avoid conflict.
- Find easy ways to reduce the conflict, such as taking a quick vote without holding a discussion.
- Do not recruit a variety of viewpoints.
- Permit one person to monopolize the discussion or fail to draw out quiet group members.
- Use only one or two approaches to reach agreement.
- Seek a limited number of options or solutions.

► SUMMARY OF PRINCIPLES

Conflict can have both positive and negative effects on a group. Conflict occurs because people are different and because they have their own ways of doing things. These differences affect the way people perceive and approach problem solving.

Collaborative Conflict-Management Principles

- Separate the people from the problem.
- Focus on shared interests.
- Generate many options to solve problems.
- Base decisions on objective criteria.

Groupthink

The absence of conflict or a false sense of agreement is called groupthink. It occurs when group members are reluctant to voice their feelings and objections to issues. To help reduce the likelihood of groupthink, review the following suggestions:

- If you are the group leader, encourage critical, independent thinking.
- Be sensitive to status differences that may affect decision making.
- Invite someone from outside the group to evaluate the group's decision making.
- Assign a group member the role of devil's advocate.
- Ask members to subdivide into small groups to consider potential problems and suggested solutions.

Consensus

Consider applying the following suggestions to help reach consensus and to help manage the conflicts and disagreements that arise in groups.

- Keep the group oriented toward its goal.
- Be other-oriented: Listen to the ideas of others.
- Promote honest interaction and dialogue.

► GROUP PRACTICE

Agree-Disagree Statements about Conflict

Read each statement once, and mark whether you agree (A) or disagree (D) with it. Take five or six minutes to do this.

1. _____ Most people find an argument interesting and exciting.

2. _____ In most conflicts someone must win and someone must lose. That's the way conflict is.

3. _____ The best way to handle a conflict is simply to let everyone cool off.

4. _____ Most people get upset with a person who disagrees with them.

5. _____ Most hidden agendas are probably best kept hidden to ensure a positive social climate.

6. _____ If people spend enough time together, they will find something to disagree about and will eventually become upset with one another.

7. _____ Conflicts can be solved if people just take the time to listen to one another.

8. _____ Conflict hinders a group's work.

9. _____ If you disagree with someone in a group, it is usually better to keep quiet than to get the group off track with your personal difference of opinion.

10. _____ When a group cannot reach a decision, members should abide by the decision of the group leader if he or she is qualified and competent.

11. _____ To compromise is to take the easy way out of conflict.

12. _____ Some people produce more conflict and tension than others. These people should be restricted from decision-making groups.

After you have marked the statements, break up into small groups and try to agree or disagree unanimously with each statement. Try in particular to find reasons for differences of opinion. If your group cannot reach a unanimous opinion on a given statement, you may change the wording in the statement to promote consensus. Assign one group member to observe your group interactions. After your group has attempted to reach consensus, the observer should report how effectively the group used the guidelines suggested in this chapter.

Win as Much as You Can

This activity is designed to explore the effects of trust and conflict on communication.[106] You will be paired with a partner. There will be four partner teams working in a cluster.

Scoring

4 Xs: Lose $1 each
3 Xs: Win $1 each 1 Ys: Lose $3
2 Xs: Win $2 each 2 Ys: Lose $2 each
1 Xs: Win $3 3 Ys: Lose $1 each
4 Ys: Win $1 each

Directions: Your instructor will provide detailed instructions for playing this game. For ten successive rounds,

you and your partner will choose either an X or a Y. Your instructor will tell all partner teams to reveal their choices at the same time. Each round's payoff will depend on the decision made by others in your cluster. For example, according to the scoring chart, if all four partner teams choose X for round one of this game, each partner team loses $1. You are to confer with your partner on each round to make a joint decision. Before rounds 5, 8, and 10, your instructor will permit you to confer with the other pairs in your cluster; in these three rounds, what you win or lose will be multiplied by either 3, 5, or 10. Keep track of your choices and winnings on the score sheet below. When you finish the game, compare your cluster's results with those of others. Discuss the factors that affected your balances. There are three rules:

- Do not confer with the other members of your cluster unless you are given specific permission to do so. This applies to nonverbal and verbal communication.
- Each pair must agree on a single choice for each round.
- Make sure that the other members of your cluster do not know your pair's choice until you are instructed to reveal it.

Round	Time Allowed	Confer With	Choice	$ Won	$ Lost	$ Balance	
1	2 min.	Partner	——	——	——	——	
2	1 min.	Partner	——	——	——	——	
3	1 min.	Partner	——	——	——	——	
4	1 min.	Partner	——	——	——	——	
5	3 min.	Cluster					Bonus Round:
	1 min.	Partner	——	——	——	——	Pay × 3
6	1 min.	Partner	——	——	——	——	
7	1 min.	Partner	——	——	——	——	
8	3 min.	Cluster					
	1 min.	Partner	——	——	——	——	Pay × 5
9	1 min.	Partner	——	——	——	——	
10	3 min.	Cluster					
	1 min.	Partner	——	——	——	——	Pay × 10

▶ GROUP ASSESSMENT

Assessing Groupthink in Your Group

Complete the following groupthink assessment scale to determine whether a group you are part of avoids group-think. For each statement, circle a number between 1 (if your group *never* does what the statement describes) and 10 (if your group *always* does what the statement describes). The higher your score, the better your group does in avoiding groupthink; a perfect score is 60.

1. Members of our group encourage and reward other group members for evaluating evidence and using good reasoning skills.

   1   2   3   4   5   6   7   8   9   10

2. Members of our group periodically ask whether we are making accurate, high-quality decisions.

   1   2   3   4   5   6   7   8   9   10

3. Members of our group sometimes admit they made a mistake or acknowledge that they reached an inaccurate conclusion.

   1   2   3   4   5   6   7   8   9   10

4. Members of our group let other group members make up their minds without pressuring them to agree with what others think.

   1   2   3   4   5   6   7   8   9   10

5. Members of our group periodically check to make sure that decisions the group has made continue to be supported by other group members.

   1   2   3   4   5   6   7   8   9   10

6. Members of our group voice their honest opinions and do not just agree with what the group leader or dominant or most vocal group members suggest.

   1   2   3   4   5   6   7   8   9   10

Assessing Group Consensus Procedures

Groups need individual members who are skilled in helping the group reach consensus. Even if you are not the group leader you can have an important effect on helping a group reach agreement. Use the following assessment measure to take stock of your application of group consensus skills.

1 = Yes   2 = Sometimes Yes   3 = Uncertain
4 = Sometimes No   5 = No

1. I use metadiscussional statements (discussion about discussion) to help a group be more aware of its process and procedures.

   1   2   3   4   5

2. I remind the group what the goal or objective is when the group seems lost or off track.

   1   2   3   4   5

3. I offer solutions, suggestions, and proposals to help the group develop options.

   1   2   3   4   5

4. I consistently use group-oriented pronouns (we, us, our) rather than individual-oriented pronouns (I, me) to develop a sense of collaboration.

   1   2   3   4   5

5. I summarize, paraphrase, or help to clarify when the group members don't seem to understand one another.

   1   2   3   4   5

6. I look for areas of agreement among group members and verbalize the agreement to the entire group.

   1   2   3   4   5

7. I look for ways in which all group members can win and be successful rather than assuming someone must win and someone must lose.

   1   2   3   4   5

8. I try to involve all group members in the conversation, especially when the group seems bogged down and disagreement is high.

   1   2   3   4   5

9. I don't change my mind quickly just to avoid conflict, but I try to resolve issues when the group seems stuck.

   1   2   3   4   5

10. I help expand the number of ideas and options, especially when the group can't reach agreement.

    1   2   3   4   5

NOTES

1. E. Ross and A. Holland, *100 Great Businesses and the Minds Behind Them* (Naperville, IL: Sourcebooks, 2006) 105.

2. G. Kraus, "The Psychodynamics of Constructive Aggression in Small Groups," *Small Group Research* 28 (1997): 122–45.

3. S. M. Farmer and J. Roth, "Conflict-Handling Behavior in Work Groups: Effects of Group Structure, Decision Processes, and Time," *Small Group Research* 29 (1998): 669–713.

4. W. W. Wilmot and J. L. Hocker, *Interpersonal Conflict* (New York: McGraw-Hill, 2007) 8.

5. M. Burgoon, J. K. Heston, and J. McCroskey, *Small Group Communication: A Functional Approach* (New York: Holt, Rinehart & Winston, 1974) 76.

6. O. Dahlback, "A Conflict Theory of Group Risk Taking," *Small Group Research* 34 (2003): 251–89.

7. L. L. Greer, K. A. Jehn, and E. A. Mannix, "Conflict Transformation: A Longitudinal Investigation of the Relationships Between Different Types of Intragroup Conflict and the Moderating Role of Conflict Resolution," *Small Group Research* 39 (2008): 278–302.

8. B. A. Fisher, "Decision Emergence: Phases in Group Decision Making," *Speech Monographs* 37 (1970): 60.

9. K. A. Jehn and E. A. Mannix, "The Dynamic Nature of Conflict: A Longitudinal Study of Intragroup Conflict and Group Performance," *Academy of Management Journal* 44 (April 2001): 238–52.

10. J. Li and D. C. Hambrick, "Factional Groups: A New Vantage on Demographic Faultlines, Conflict, and Disintegration in Work Teams," *Academy of Management Journal* 48 (2005): 794–813; C. De Dreu and L. Weingart, "Task Versus Relationship Conflict, Team Performance, and Team Member Satisfaction," *Journal of Applied Psychology* 88, 4 (2003): 741–49.

11. V. D. Wall and J. L. Nolan, "Small Group Conflict: A Look at Equity, Satisfaction, and Styles of Conflict-Management," *Small Group Behavior* 18 (May 1987): 188–211.

12. M. Nussbaum, M. Singer, R. Rosas, M. Castillo, E. Flies, R. Lara, and R. Sommers, "Decision Support System for Conflict Diagnosis in Personnel Selection," *Information & Management* 36 (1999): 55–62.

13. Portions of the following discussion of misconceptions about conflict were adapted from R. J. Doolittle, *Orientations to Communication and Conflict* (Chicago: Science Research Associates, 1976) 7–9.

14. See F. E. Jandt, ed., *Conflict Resolution Through Communication* (New York: Harper & Row, 1973).

15. C. R. Franz and K. G. Jin, "The Structure of Group Conflict in a Collaborative Work Group During Information Systems Development," *Journal of Applied Communication Research* 23 (1995): 108–27.

16. U. Klocke, "How to Improve Decision Making in Small Groups: Effects of Dissent and Training Interventions," Small Group Research 38 (2007): 437–68; S. Schulz-Hardt, A. Mojzisch, F. C. Brodbeck, R. Kerschreiter, and D. Frey, "Group Decision Making in Hidden Profile Situations: Dissent as a Facilitator for Decision Quality," *Journal of Personality and Social Psychology* 91 (2006): 1080–93.

17. Doolittle, *Orientations to Communication*, 8.

18. G. R. Miller and M. Steinberg, *Between People: New Analysis of Interpersonal Communication* (Chicago: Science Research Associates, 1975) 264.

19. S. D. Johnson and C. Bechler, "Examining the Relationship Between Listening Effectiveness and Leadership Emergence: Perceptions, Behaviors, and Recall," *Small Group Research* 29 (1998): 452–71.

20. Miller and Steinberg, *Between People.*

21. J. Sell, M. J. Lovaglia, E. A. Mannix, C. D. Samuelson, and R. K. Wilson, "Investigating Conflict, Power, and Status Within and Among Groups," *Small Group Research* 35 (2004): 44–72.

22. D. J. Devine, "Effects of Cognitive Ability, Task Knowledge, Information Sharing, and Conflict on Group Decision-Making Effectiveness," *Small Group Research* 30 (1999): 608–34.

23. B. M. Gayle and R. W. Preiss, "Assessing Emotionality in Organizational Conflicts," *Management Communication Quarterly* 12 (1998): 280–302; A. Ostell, "Managing Dysfunctional Emotions in Organizations," *Journal of Management Studies* 33 (1996): 525–57.

24. K. Lovelace, "Maximizing Cross-Functional New Product Teams' Innovativeness and Constraint Adherence: A Conflict Communications Perspective," *Academy of Management Journal* 44 (2001): 179–94; M. A. Von Glinow, D. L. Shapiro, and J. M. Brett, "Can We Talk, and Should We? Managing Emotional Conflict in Multicultural Teams," *Academy of Management Review* 29 (2004): 578–92.

25. V. Schei and J. K. Rognes, "Small Group Negotiation: When Members Differ in Motivational Orientation," *Small Group Research* 36 (2005): 289–320.

26. S. Ting-Toomey, "Toward a Theory of Conflict and Culture," in W. Gudykunst, L. Stewart, and S. Ting-Toomey, eds., *Communication, Culture, and Organizational Processes* (Beverly Hills, CA: Sage, 1985).

27. S. Ting-Toomey, "A Face Negotiation Theory," in Y. Kim and W. Gudykunst, eds., *Theories in Intercultural Communication* (Newbury Park, CA: Sage, 1988).

28. Ting-Toomey, "Conflict and Culture."

29. K. W. Phillips and D. L. Loyd, "When Surface and Deep-Level Diversity Collide: The Effects on Dissenting Group Members," *Organizational Behavior and Human Decision Processes* 99 (2006): 143–60.

30. K. W. Phillips, G. B. Northcraft, and M. A. Neale, "Surface-Level Diversity and Decision-Making in Groups: When Does Deep-Level Similarity Help?" *Group Processes and Intergroup Relations* 9 (2006): 467–82.

31. See also an excellent review of conflict and culture research in W. B. Gudykunst, *Bridging Difference: Effective Intergroup Communication* (Newbury Park, CA: Sage, 1994).

32. Ting-Toomey, "A Face Negotiation Theory."

33. R. Rodriguez, "Challenging Demographic Reductionism: A Pilot Study Investigating Diversity in Group Composition," *Small Group Research* 26 (1998): 744–59.

34. See: J. M. Olsen, *The Process of Social Organization* (New York: Holt, Rinehart and Winston, 1978); D. K. Ivy and P. Backlund, *Genderspeak: Personal Effectiveness in Gender Communication* (Pearson/Allyn & Bacon, 2008) 257–61.

35. For an excellent review of conflict and gender, see M. Argyle, *The Psychology of Interpersonal Behavior* (London: Penguin Books, 1994).
36. R. Kilmann and K. Thomas, "Interpersonal Conflict-Handling Behavior as Reflections of Jungian Personality Dimensions," *Psychological Reports* 37 (1975): 971–80.
37. U. Becker-Beck, "Methods for Diagnosing Interaction Strategies: An Application to Group Interaction in Conflict Situations," *Small Group Research* 32 (2001): 259–82.
38. T. M. Brown and C. E. Miller, "Communication Networks in Task-Performing Groups: Effects of Task Complexity, Time Pressure, and Interpersonal Dominance," *Small Group Research* 31 (2000): 131–57.
39. B. Beersma, J. R. Hollenbeck, D. E. Conlon, S. E. Humphrey, H. Moon, and D. R. Ilgen, "Cutthroat Cooperation: The Effects of Team Role Decisions on Adaptation to Alternative Reward Structures," *Organizational Behavior and Human Decision Processes* 108 (2009): 131–42.
40. A. Sinclair, "The Effects of Justice and Cooperation on Team Effectiveness," *Small Group Research* 34 (2003): 74–100.
41. D. Romig, *Side-by-Side Leadership: Achieving Outstanding Results Together* (Austin, TX: Bard Press, 2001).
42. C. Kirchmeyer and A. Cohen, "Multicultural Groups," *Group & Organization Management* 17 (June 1992): 153–70; C. L. Wong, D. Tjosvold, and F. Lee, "Managing Conflict in a Diverse Work Force: A Chinese Perspective in North America," *Small Group Research* 23 (August 1992): 302–21.
43. D. Cramer, "Linking Conflict Management Behaviors and Relational Satisfaction: The Intervening Role of Conflict Outcome Satisfaction," *Journal of Social and Personal Relationships* 19 (2000): 425–32.
44. D. Weider-Hatfield and J. D. Hatfield, "Superiors' Conflict Management Strategies and Subordinate Outcomes," *Management Communication Quarterly* 10 (1996): 189–208; also see P. J. Carnevale and T. M. Probst, "Social Values and Social Conflict in Creative Problem Solving Categorization," *Journal of Personality and Social Psychology* 74 (1998): 1300–09.
45. R. Fisher and W. Ury, *Getting to Yes: Negotiating Agreement Without Giving In* (Boston: Houghton Mifflin, 1991).
46. See J. L. Hocker and W. W. Wilmot, *Interpersonal Conflict Management* (New York: McGraw-Hill, 2007); Fisher and Ury, *Getting to Yes*; R. Bolton, *People Skills: How to Assert Yourself, Listen to Others and Resolve Conflict* (New York: Simon & Schuster, 1979) 217; D. A. Romig and L. J. Romig, *Structured Teamwork Guide* (Austin, TX: Performance Resource, 1990); D. A. Romig, *Breakthrough Teamwork: Outstanding Results Using Structured Teamwork* (New York: Irwin, 1996).
47. J. Gottman, C. Notarius, J. Godso, and H. Markman, *A Couple's Guide to Communication* (Champaign, IL: Research Press, 1976).
48. Hocker and Wilmot, *Interpersonal Conflict Management*.
49. R. A. Meyers and D. E. Brashers, "Argument in Group Decision Making: Explicating a Process Model and Investigating the Argument-Outcome Link," *Communication Monographs* 65 (1998): 261–81.
50. J. B. Walther, "In Point of Practice, Computer-Mediated Communication and Virtual Groups: Applications to Interethnic Conflict," *Journal of Applied Communication Research* 37 (2009): 225–38.
51. Becker-Beck, "Methods for Diagnosing Interaction Strategies."
52. S. M. Miranda, "Avoidance of Groupthink: Meeting Management Using Group Support Systems," *Small Group Communication Research* 25 (February 1994): 105–36.
53. K. Thomas and W. Schmidt, "A Survey of Managerial Interests with Respect to Conflict," *Academy of Management Journal* 19 (1976): 315–18.
54. J. M. Juran, *Juran on Planning for Quality* (New York: Free Press, 1988).
55. J. M. Wellen and M. Neale, "Deviance, Self-Typicality, and Group Cohesion: The Corrosive Effects of the Bad Apples on the Barrel," *Small Group Research* 37 (2006): 165–86.
56. Boulton, *People Skills*, 217.
57. Gayle and Preiss, "Assessing Emotionality in Organizational Conflicts."
58. A. Ostell, "Managing Dysfunctional Emotionality in Organizations," *Journal of Management Studies* 33 (1996): 523–57.
59. O. B. Ayoko, V. J. Callan, and C. E. J Härtel, "The Influence of Team Emotional Intelligence Climate on Conflict and Team Members' Reactions to Conflict," *Small Group Research* 39 (2008): 121–49.
60. For an excellent review of causes of anger during conflict, see R. J. Turner, D. Russell, R. Glover, and P. Hutto, "The Social Antecedents of Anger Proneness in Young Adulthood," *Journal of Health and Social Behavior* 45 (2007): 68–83; W. R. Cupach, D. J. Canary, and B. H. Spitzberg, *Competence in Interpersonal Conflict* (Long Grove, IL: Waveland Press, 2010) 91–106.
61. M. Seo and L. F. Barrett, "Being Emotional During Decision Making—Good or Bad? An Empirical Investigation," *Academy of Management Journal* 50 (2007): 923–40.
62. A. M. Bippus and S. L. Young, "Owning Your Emotions: Reactions to Expressions of Self-versus Other-Attributed Positive and Negative Emotions," *Journal of Applied Communication Research* 33 (2005): 26–45.
63. Becker-Beck, "Methods for Diagnosing Interaction Strategies."
64. R. J. W. Cline, "Detecting Groupthink: Methods for Observing the Illusion of Unanimity," *Communication Quarterly* 38 (Spring 1990): 112–26; D. D. Henningsen, M. L. M. Henningsen, J. Eden, and M. G. Cruz, "Examining the Symptoms of Groupthink and Retrospective Sensemaking," *Small Group Research* 37 (2006) 36–64.
65. W. Safire, "On Language: Groupthink—A Collaborative C Search for Coinage," *New York Times Magazine* (August 6, 2004), p. 16.
66. D. D. Henningsen, M. L. M. Henningsen, J. Eden, and M. G. Cruz, "Examining the Symptoms of Groupthink and Retrospective Sensemaking," *Small Group Research* 37 (2006) 36–64.
67. I. L. Janis, *Victims of Groupthink* (Boston: Houghton Mifflin, 1973); D. C. Matz and W. Wood, "Cognitive Dissonance in Groups: The Consequences of Disagreement," *Journal of Personality and Social Psychology* 88 (2005): 22–37.
68. R. K. M. Haurwitz, "Faculty Doubted Bonfire's Stability," *Austin-American Statesman* (December 10, 1999), p. A1.52.
69. R. Y. Hirokawa, D. S. Gouran, and A. Martz, "Understanding the Sources of Faulty Group Decision Making: A Lesson from the

Challenger Disaster," *Small Group Behavior* 19 (November 1988): 411–33.

70. D. Jehl, "Panel Unanimous: 'Group Think' Backed Prewar Assumptions, Report Concludes," *New York Times* (July 10, 2004), p. I; also see: *The 9/11 Commission Report: Final Report of the National Commission on Terrorist Attacks upon the United States* (Washington, DC: National Commission on Terrorist Attacks, 2004).

71. J. F. Veiga, "The Frequency of Self-Limiting Behavior in Groups: A Measure and an Explanation," *Human Relations* 44 (1991): 877–95.

72. D. D. Henningsen, M. L. M. Henningsen, J. Eden, and M. G Cruz, "Examining the Symptoms of Groupthink and Retrospective Sensemaking," *Small Group Research* 37 (2006): 36–64.

73. M. D. Street, "Groupthink: An Examination of Theoretical Issues, Implications, and Future Research Suggestions," *Small Group Research* 28 (1997): 72–93; M. D. Street and W. P. Anthony, "A Conceptual Framework Establishing the Relationship Between Groupthink and Escalating Commitment Behavior," *Small Group Research* 28 (1997): 267–93; A. A. Mohaned and F. A. Wiebe, "Toward a Process Theory of Groupthink," *Small Group Research* 27 (1996): 416–30; K. Granstrom and D. Stiwne, "A Bipolar Model of Groupthink: An Expansion of Janis's Concept," *Small Group Research* 29 (1998): 32–56; W. Park, "A Comprehensive Empirical Investigation of the Relationships Among Variables in the Groupthink Model," *Journal of Organizational Behavior* 21 (2000): 873–87.

74. Adapted from I. L. Janis, "Groupthink," *Psychology Today* 5 (November 1971): 43–46, 74–76.

75. W. Park, "A Review of Research on Groupthink," *Journal of Behavioral Decision Making* 3 (1990): 229–45; Street, "Groupthink"; Street and Anthony, "A Conceptual Framework."

76. See R. Hotz and N. Miller, "Intergroup Competition, Attitudinal Projection, and Opinion Certainty: Capitalizing on Conflict," *Group Processes and Intergroup Relations* 41 (2001): 61–73.

77. Cline, "Detecting Groupthink."

78. See K. Andersen and T. Clevenger, Jr., "A Summary of Experimental Research in Ethos," *Speech Monographs* 30 (1963): 59–78.

79. C. B. Gibson and T. Saxton, "Thinking Outside the Black Box: Outcomes of Team Decisions with Third-Party Intervention," *Small Group Research* 36 (2005): 208–36.

80. For a discussion of the role of the central negative, see E. G. Bormann, *Discussion and Group Methods: Theory and Practice* (New York: Harper & Row, 1969).

81. M. A. Dorado, F. J. Medina, L. Munduate, I. F. J. Cisneros, and M. Euwema, "Computer-Mediated Negotiation of an Escalated Conflict," *Small Group Research* 33 (2002): 509–24.

82. A. Zornoza, P. Ripoll, and J. M. Peiro, "Conflict Management in Groups That Work in Two Different Communication Contexts: Face-to-Face and Computer-Mediated Communication," *Small Group Research* 33 (2002): 481–508.

83. J. P. Walsh and N. G. Maloney, "Collaboration Structure, Communication Media, and Problems in Scientific Work Teams," *Journal of Computer-Mediated Communication* 12 (2007): 712–32. Also see P. Bosch-Sijtsema, "The Impact of Individual Expectations and Expectation Conflicts on Virtu-

al Teams," *Group Organization Management* 32 (2007): 358–88.

84. M. Montoya-Weiss, A. P. Massey, and M. Song, "Getting It Together: Temporal Coordination and Conflict Management in Global Virtual Teams," *Academy of Management Journal* 44 (December 2001): 1251–62.

85. Miranda, "Avoidance of Groupthink."

86. Miranda, "Avoidance of Groupthink."

87. J. T. Polzer, C. B. Crisp, S. L. Jarvenpaa, and J. W. Kim, "Extending the Faultline Model to Geographically Dispersed Teams: How Colocated Subgroups Can Impair Group Functioning," *Academy of Management Journal* 49 (2006): 659–92.

88. For an excellent discussion of the definition of *consensus,* see M. A. Renz, "The Meaning of Consensus and Blocking for Cohousing Groups," *Small Group Research* 37 (2006): 351–76.

89. R. Y. Hirokawa, "Consensus Group Decision-Making, Quality of Decision and Group Satisfaction: An Attempt to Sort 'Fact' from 'Fiction,'" *Central States Speech Journal* 33 (Summer 1982): 407–15.

90. R. S. DeStephen and R. Y. Hirokawa, "Small Group Consensus: Stability of Group Support of the Decision, Task Process, and Group Relationships," *Small Group Behavior* 19 (May 1988): 227–39.

91. Portions of the following section on consensus were adapted from J. A. Kline, "Ten Techniques for Reaching Consensus in Small Groups," *Air Force Reserve Officer Training Corps Education Journal* 19 (Spring 1977): 19–21.

92. See D. S. Gouran, "Variables Related to Consensus in Group Discussions of Questions of Policy," *Speech Monographs* 36 (August 1969): 385–91; T. J. Knutson, "An Experimental Study of the Effects of Orientation Behavior on Small Group Consensus," *Speech Monographs* 39 (August 1972): 159–65; J. A. Kline, "Orientation and Group Consensus," *Central States Speech Journal* 23 (Spring 1972): 44–47.

93. Gouran, "Variables," 385-91; Knutson, "Experimental Study"; Kline, "Orientation."

94. A. Gurtner, F. Tschan, N. K. Semmer, and C. Nagele, "Getting Groups to Develop God Strategies: Effects of Reflexivity Interventions on Team Process, Team Performance, and Shared Mental Models," *Organizational Behavior and Human Decision Processes* 102 (2007): 127–42.

95. See Hirokawa, "Consensus Group Decision-Making"; R. Y. Hirokawa, "Discussion Procedures and Decision-Making Performance: A Test of the Functional Perspective," *Human Communication Research* 12 (Winter 1985): 203–24; R. Y. Hirokawa and D. R. Scheerhorn, "Communication in Faulty Group Decision-Making," in R. Y. Hirokawa and M. S. Poole, eds., *Communication and Group Decision-Making* (Beverly Hills, CA: Sage, 1986).

96. Hirokawa, "Consensus Group Decision-Making."

97. See J. A. Kline and J. L. Hullinger, "Redundancy, Self-Orientation, and Group Consensus," *Speech Monographs* 40 (March 1973): 72–74.

98. C. A. VanLear and E. A. Mabry, "Testing Contrasting Interaction Models for Discriminating Between Consensual and Dissentient Decision-Making Groups," *Small Group Research* 30 (1999): 29–58.

99. K. L. Sager and J. Gastill, "The Origins and Consequences of Consensus Decision Making: A Test of the Social Consensus Model," *Southern Communication Journal* 73 (March 2006): 1–24.

100. A. Van Hiel and V. Franssen, "Information Acquisition Bias During the Preparing of Group Discussion: A Comparison of Prospective Minority and Majority Members," *Small Group Research* 34 (2003): 557–74.

101. See H. W. Riecken, "The Effect of Talkativeness on Ability to Influence Group Solutions of Problems," *Sociometry* 21 (1958): 309–21.

102. R. C. Pace, "Communication Patterns in High and Low Consensus Discussion: A Descriptive Analysis," *Southern Speech Communication Journal* 53 (Winter 1988): 184–202.

103. VanLear and Mabry, "Testing Contrasting Interaction Models."

104. A. Zornoza, P. Ripoll, and J. M. Peiro, "Conflict Management in Groups That Work in Two Different Communication Contexts: Face-to-Face and Computer-Mediated Communication," *Small Group Research* 33 (2002): 481–508.

105. S. Mohammed and E. Ringseis, "Cognitive Diversity and Consensus in Group Decision Making: The Role of Inputs, Processes, and Outcomes," *Organizational Behavior and Human Decision Processes* 85 (July 2001): 31–35.

106. J. W. Pfeiffer and J. E. Jones, eds., *A Handbook of Structured Experiences for Human Relations Training*, vol. 2 (La Jolla, CA: University Associates, 1974) 62–67.

Sociology

Classical and

Neoclassical Perspectives

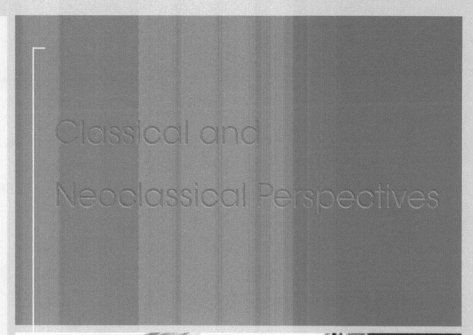

Classical and
Neoclassical Perspectives

Crime in the News

n May 2010, a lacrosse player at the University of Virginia allegedly killed his former girlfriend, Yeardley Love, also a lacrosse player, when he slammed her head against her bedroom wall during an argument. In the aftermath of Love's death, reports surfaced that the alleged assailant had allegedly attacked a male student a year earlier for kissing her and had also been put on probation for public intoxication and resisting arrest. The arresting officer in the latter incident said she needed to Taser the young man and that he said he would "kill everyone" at the police station. The officer added, "He was by far the most rude, most hateful and most combative college kid I ever dealt with."

Yeardley Love's death shocked the university and its quiet home town of Charlottesville. Befitting her last name, she was apparently loved by all who knew her. During her funeral service, Love's lacrosse coach recalled her fondly: "She was truly remarkable, not because she tried to be, but because she just was. It came easy for her to be great, to be kind-hearted, welcoming, encouraging and engaging to all who knew her. She was legitimately awesome."

Sources: Macur 2010; Nakamura, Swezey, and Vise 2010; Yanda, Johnson, and Vise 2010.

Why did this terrible crime happen? Why did this particular young man allegedly commit it? What can be done to prevent this type of crime and the many other types of crime that we read or hear about virtually every day?

A central task of criminology is to explain why crime occurs—yet very different explanations of crime exist. Your author once had a student who said the devil caused most crime. Her classmates snickered when they heard this. Undaunted, the student added that the way to reduce crime would be to exorcise the devil from the bodies it possessed. More snickers. I said I respected her religious beliefs, but noted that modern criminological theory does not blame the devil and does not think exorcism would help.

As this story illustrates, assumptions of what causes crime affect what we think should be done to reduce it. If we blame the devil, our crime-reduction efforts will center on removing the devil's influence. If we hold biological or psychological problems in individuals responsible, our efforts will focus on correcting these problems. If we hold poverty and inadequate parenting responsible, our efforts will center on reducing poverty and improving parenting skills. If we instead think criminals are simply depraved and that the criminal justice system is too lenient to keep them from committing crime, our efforts will focus on adding more police, increasing prison terms, and building more prisons. To develop the most effective approach, we must first know why crime occurs.

Contemporary theories of crime differ widely in their assumptions and emphases. In the social and behavioral sciences, sociology has contributed the most to understanding crime, with psychology and economics also making important contributions. Of the remaining sciences, biology has long been interested in crime. This chapter highlights neoclassical explanations, rooted in economic thinking, that emphasize the rationality of crime and criminals. After reading this chapter, you should have a good understanding of the reasons for crime that the various disciplines favor, of the strengths and weaknesses of the explanations they offer, and of the possible solutions to crime that these explanations suggest.

Understanding Theories of Crime

Theories of crime try to answer at least one of three questions: (1) Why are some individuals more likely than others to commit crime? (2) Why are some categories or kinds of people more likely than others to commit crime? (3) Why is crime more common in some locations than in other locations? Biological and psychological explanations tend to focus on the first question, whereas neoclassical and sociological explanations tend to focus on the last two questions.

These explanations also differ in other ways. Neoclassical explanations, as we shall soon see, assume that criminals act with free will, whereas the other explanations assume that people are influenced to commit crime by certain internal and external forces. To be more precise, biological and psychological explanations place the causes of crime inside the individual, whereas sociological explanations place these causes in the social environment outside the individual. Put another way, biology and psychology focus on the *micro*, or smaller, picture, and sociology focuses on the *macro*, or larger, picture. This distinction reflects long-standing differences in understanding human behavior. It does not mean that a macro approach is better than a micro approach, and neither does it mean the reverse. The approach you favor depends on whether you think it is more important to understand the smaller picture or the larger one.

Nevertheless, the approaches' different focuses do have different implications for efforts to reduce crime. If the fault for crime lies within the individual, then to reduce crime we must change the individual. If the fault instead lies in the social environment, then we must change this environment. And if neoclassical perspectives are correct, crime can be reduced by measures that convince potential criminals that they are more likely to be arrested and punished severely.

To help understand the distinction between the micro and macro orientations of biology/psychology and sociology respectively, let us leave criminology to consider two related eating disorders, anorexia (undereating or starvation) and bulimia (self-induced regurgitation after eating). What causes these disorders? Psychologists and medical researchers cite problems in the individuals with the disorders. Psychologists emphasize low self-esteem, feelings of inferiority, and lack of control, whereas medical researchers stress possible biochemical imbalances (Friedman and Stancke 2009). These individual-level explanations are valuable, and you may know someone with an eating disorder who was helped by a psychologist or a physician.

A sociological explanation takes a different stance. Recognizing that eating disorders disproportionately affect young women, sociologists say a cultural emphasis on slender female bodies, evidenced by Barbie dolls and photos in women's magazines, leads many women to think they are too heavy and to believe they need to diet. Inevitably, some women will diet to an extreme and perhaps not even eat or else force themselves to regurgitate (Darmon 2009). This type of explanation locates the roots of eating disorders more in society than in individual anorexics or bulimics. No matter how often psychologists and physicians successfully treat such women, other women will always be taking their place as long as the emphasis on female thinness continues. If so, efforts to cure eating disorders may help individual women, but ultimately will do relatively little to reduce the eating disorder problem.

Returning to criminology, if the roots of crime are biological and psychological problems inside individuals, then to reduce crime we need to correct these problems. If the roots of crime instead lie more in criminogenic features of the social environment, then new criminals will always be emerging and the crime problem will continue unless we address these features.

Actress Jamie-Lynn Sigler, who played the daughter in *The Sopranos* struggled with an eating disorder that began during high school. Whereas psychologists attribute eating disorders to low self-esteem and other psychological problems, sociologists highlight the cultural emphasis on slender female bodies.

That said, it is also true that most people do not commit crime even if they experience a criminogenic social environment, just as most women do not have eating disorders despite the cultural emphasis on thinness. To understand why certain people do commit crime (or why certain women have eating disorders), individual-level explanations are necessary. To reiterate, whether you favor micro or macro explanations of crime (or of eating disorders) depends on whether you think it is more important to understand the smaller picture or the larger one.

It is time now to turn to the many theories of crime. The term *theories* can often make students' eyes glaze over. Perhaps yours just did. That is why this chapter began by stressing the need to understand *why* crime occurs if we want to reduce it. If you recognize this need, you also recognize the importance of theory. As you read about the various theories, think about what they imply for successful efforts to reduce crime.

From Theology to Science

Our excursion into the world of theory begins by reviewing the historical change from theology to science in the understanding of crime.

GOD AND DEMONS AS CAUSES OF CRIME AND DEVIANCE

Like many folk societies studied by anthropologists today, Western societies long ago had religious explanations for behavior that violated their norms. People in ancient times were thought to act deviantly for several reasons: (1) God was testing their faith, (2) God was punishing them, (3) God was using their behavior to warn others to follow divine rules, and (4) they were possessed by demons (McCaghy et al. 2008). In the Old Testament, the prophets communicated God's unhappiness to the ancient Hebrews with behavior that today we would call mad and even violent. Yet they, and Jesus after them in the temple, were regarded as divinely inspired. Ancient Greeks and Romans, who believed in multiple gods, had similar explanations for madness.

From ancient times through the Middle Ages, witches—people who supposedly had associated with or been possessed by the devil—were a special focus of attention. The Old Testament mentions witches several times, including the commandment in Exodus (22:18), "Thou shalt not suffer a witch to live." Witches also appear in ancient Greek and Roman literature. Biblical injunctions against witches took an ominous turn in Europe from the 1400s to the 1700s, when some 300,000 "witches," most of them women, were burned at the stake or otherwise executed. Perhaps the most famous witch-hunting victim was Joan of Arc, a military hero for France in its wars with England, whom the English burned at the stake in May 1431. Other witches put to death, often by the Roman Catholic Church that dominated continental Europe, were what today we would call healers, midwives, religious heretics, political protesters, and homosexuals. In short, anyone, and especially any woman, who violated church rules could have been branded a witch (Demos 2008).

As this brief summary suggests, religion was the dominant source of knowledge in the Western world through the Middle Ages. Religion was used to explain norm-violating behavior, but it was also used to explain natural, physical, and social phenomena too numerous to mention. Science was certainly not unknown in the West, but it played a secondary role to religion as people sought to understand the social and physical worlds around them. They widely believed that God controlled all human behavior and that the church's authority was to be accepted without question. Although they learned these basic beliefs from childhood as part of their normal socialization, it is also true that the persecution of alleged witches would have made people afraid to question the primacy of the church. Regardless of the reason, religion was the ruling force during the Middle Ages, and science was hardly even in contention.

Tens of thousands of women considered to be witches were executed in Europe during the 1400s to the 1700s.

THE AGE OF REASON

This fundamental fact of Western life through the Middle Ages began to change during the seventeenth and eighteenth centuries, when religious views began to give way to scientific explanations. This period marked the ripening in Europe of the Age of Reason, or the **Enlightenment,** which developed a new way of thinking about natural and social phenomena that eventually weakened religion's influence. Enlightenment philosophers included such famous figures as René Descartes (1596–1650), Thomas Hobbes (1588–1679), John Locke (1632–1704), and Jean-Jacques Rousseau (1712–1778), all of whom are still read today along with many others. As innumerable works have discussed (e.g., Israel 2010), these political philosophers influenced Western thought in many profound ways, and their ideas are reflected in the Declaration of Independence and other documents crucial to the founding of the United States.

The views of the Enlightenment philosophers differed in several important respects. For example, Rousseau thought that human nature was basically good, Hobbes thought that human nature was basically bad, and Locke thought that it was neither good nor bad as people were born with a "blank slate" and thereafter shaped by their experiences and social environments. Yet as Enlightenment philosophers, they shared certain fundamental assumptions that helped shape the classical school of criminology to be discussed shortly.

One of these assumptions was that God had left people to govern their own affairs through the exercise of free will and reason. In this Enlightenment view, people rationally calculate the rewards and risks of potential actions and adopt behavior promising the greatest pleasure and least pain. To ensure that people not act too emotionally, Enlightenment thinkers stressed the need to acquire an education to develop reasoning ability.

Another assumption centered on the idea of the *social contract*. According to Enlightenment thinkers, individuals as rational actors needed for various reasons to enter into a social contract called the *state*—to form and live in a society characterized by the familiar social institutions of government, education, and the economy. An Enlightenment philosopher's view of the social contract or state as a good thing or bad thing depended heavily on the view held of human nature. For example, because Hobbes thought human nature was so wicked that individuals would normally be perpetually at war without the constraints of society, he thought that the development and existence of the state was both good and necessary. In contrast, because Rousseau and Locke viewed human nature as basically good or neutral, respectively, they feared that the state could corrupt individuals and limit their freedom.

Although these and other Enlightenment views represented significant advances beyond the philosophy of the Middle Ages, this more "enlightened" way of thinking did not extend to the criminal justice system. Europeans suspected of crimes during the Age of Reason were often arrested on flimsy evidence and imprisoned without trial. Torture was commonly used in continental Europe to force people to confess to their alleged crime and to name anyone else involved. In England, the right to jury trials for felonies should have lessened the use of torture. However, English defendants convicted by juries risked losing their land and property to the king. Many defendants thus refused jury trials, only to suffer a form of torture known as *pressing* (finally abolished in 1772), in which a heavy weight was placed on the defendant's body. Some were crushed to death instantly, but others lasted a few days until they either confessed or died. If they managed to die without confessing, their families kept their land and property (Roth 2011).

Although torture was less common in England despite the use of pressing, the death penalty was often used, with more than 200 crimes, including theft, punishable by death. Common citizens could be found guilty of treason for plotting the death of the king, servants for plotting the death of their master, and women for plotting the death of their husband. Execution was a frequent punishment for such "treason," with the "traitors" sometimes disemboweled or dismembered before they were killed.

Justice was severe during this period, but it was also *arbitrary*, as different judges would hand out very different punishments for similar crimes. As Francis T. Cullen and Robert Agnew (2011:22) summarize this problem, "Laws in the 1700s were frequently vague and open to interpretation. Judges, who held great power, would often interpret these laws to suit their own purposes. So the punishment for a particular crime might vary widely, with some people receiving severe penalties and others not being punished at all. Poor people, who could not afford to bribe the judges, were at a special disadvantage."

THE CLASSICAL SCHOOL OF CRIMINOLOGY

Against this frightening backdrop of torture and arbitrary justice, Italian economist and political philosopher Cesare Beccaria (1738–1794) wrote a small, path-breaking book on crime, *Dei Delit ti e Delle Pene (On Crimes and Punishments)*, in 1764 (Beccaria 1819 [1764]). Essentially a plea for justice, Beccaria's treatise helped found what is now called the **classical school** of criminology, also called *utilitarianism* (see Table 1). Beccaria was appalled by the horrible conditions in the European criminal justice system at that time. Like other Enlightenment thinkers, he believed that people act rationally and with free will, calculating whether their behavior will cause them more pleasure or more pain; he thought this was true of criminals and noncriminals alike. Influenced by Hobbes, Beccaria also believed that the state needed to ensure that people's natural impulses would stay controlled.

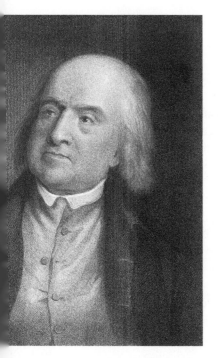

Jeremy Bentham was one of the founders of the classical school of criminology; he felt that the severity of legal punishment should be limited to what was necessary to deter crime.

For this to happen, he wrote, the criminal justice system needed to perform effectively and efficiently. But because people think and act rationally, they will be deterred by a certain degree of punishment, and harsher punishment beyond that is not needed. The criminal justice system thus needed only to be punitive enough to deter people from committing crime, and not more punitive than this level. This reasoning led Beccaria to condemn torture and other treatment of criminals as being much crueler than this more humane standard. He also opposed executions for most crimes and believed that judges should ordinarily hand out similar punishments for similar crimes. To use a contemporary term to describe this latter belief, Beccaria believed that *judicial discretion* should be reduced or eliminated.

As should be clear, Beccaria believed that the primary purpose of the criminal justice system was to deter criminal behavior rather than to avenge the harm that criminals do. He thought that legal punishment is most effective in deterring crime if it is *certain* and *swift*. The criminal justice system thus needs to be efficient in two respects. It needs to ensure that criminals believe they have a strong chance of being arrested and punished, and it needs to ensure that any arrest and punishment happen quickly. In focusing on certainty and swiftness, Beccaria explicitly minimized the importance of the severity of punishment, which he thought far less important than the certainty of punishment for deterring crime. As he put it, "The certainty of a small punishment will make a stronger impression, than the fear of one more severe, if attended with the hopes of escaping" (Beccaria 2006[1764]: 25).

Beccaria is widely regarded as the father of modern criminology, and his treatise is credited with leading to many reforms in the prisons and criminal courts (Bernard, Snipes, and Gerould 2009). However, some critics claim that this credit is at least partly undeserved (Newman and Marongiu 1994). They note that, although Beccaria has been lauded for opposing torture and the death penalty, his treatise actually contains many ambiguous passages about these punishments. Moreover, the criminal justice reforms with which he has been credited were actually already being implemented before he wrote his treatise (Newman and Marongiu 1994). Yet even these critics concede that Beccaria's views greatly influenced legal systems in Europe and affected the thinking of John

TABLE 1 **Classical and Neoclassical Theories in Brief**

THEORY	KEY FIGURE(S)	SYNOPSIS
Classical Theory (Utilitarianism)		
	Cesare Beccaria Jeremy Bentham	People act with free will and calculate whether their behavior will cause them more pleasure or more pain. Legal punishment needs to be severe enough only to deter individuals from committing crime, and not beyond that.
Neoclassical Theories		
Rational Choice Theory	Gary Becker Derek B. Cornish Ronald V. Clarke	Offenders commit crime because of the benefits it brings them. In deciding whether to commit crime, they weigh whether the potential benefits exceed the potential costs. Because offenders do not always have the time or ability to gather and analyze all relevant information relevant for their decision, their decision making is sometimes imperfect.
Deterrence Theory	—	Potential and actual legal punishment can deter crime. General deterrence refers to the deterrence of potential offenders because they fear arrest and/or punishment; specific deterrence refers to the deterrence of convicted offenders because they do not want to experience arrest and/or punishment once again.
Routine Activities Theory	Lawrence E. Cohen Marcus Felson	Crime and victimization are more likely when three factors are simultaneously present: (1) motivated offenders; (2) attractive targets; and (3) an absence of guardianship. Crime trends can be explained by changes in levels of attractive targets and of guardianship.

Adams, Benjamin Franklin, Thomas Jefferson, and the writers of the U.S. Constitution. And it is certainly true that Beccaria's classical belief that "offenders are rational individuals who choose to engage in crime" forms "the foundation of our legal system" today (Cullen and Agnew 2011: 23).

The other great figure of the classical school was English philosopher Jeremy Bentham (1748–1832). Like Beccaria, Bentham felt that people weigh whether their behavior is more apt to cause them pleasure or pain and that the law was far more severe than it needed to be to deter such rational individuals from behaving criminally. His writings inspired changes in the English criminal law in the early 1800s and helped shape the development of the first modern police force in London in 1829. They also influenced the creation of the modern prison. Before the time of Bentham, Beccaria, and other legal reformers, long-term incarceration did not exist; jails were intended only for short-term stays for suspects awaiting trial, torture, or execution. The development of the prison in the early 1800s thus represented a major and still controversial change in the punishment of criminals.

Although the classical school of criminology led to important reforms in the criminal justice system throughout Europe, critics then and now have said that its view of human behavior was too simplistic. Even though individuals sometimes weigh the costs and benefits of their actions, other times they act emotionally. Also, although people often do act to maximize pleasure and to reduce pain, they do not always agree on what is pleasurable. Classical reformers also assumed that the legal system treated all people the same and overlooked the possibility that race or ethnicity, social class, and gender might make a difference.

Review and Discuss

How were criminals treated during the Age of Reason? How may the classical school of criminology be considered a reaction to this treatment?

THE RISE OF POSITIVISM

Notice that we have said nothing about the classical school's views on the causes of crime, other than its belief that some people choose to commit crime when they decide as normal, rational actors that the benefits outweigh the risks. In his famous treatise, Beccaria did not really try to explain why some people are more likely than other people to commit crime, as he focused on the punishment of criminals rather than the reasons for their criminality. But he did acknowledge that a crime like theft results from "misery and despair" among people who are living "but a bare existence." This implied that poor people may reach a different decision than wealthier people in considering the potential risks and rewards of committing theft, and thus that poverty is a cause of this type of crime, but Beccaria did not develop this implication in his book. As Cullen and Agnew (2011: 23) note, then, the explanation of crime beyond the rational calculation of its risks and rewards does "not form a central part of classical theory."

As this observation suggests, classical scholars largely failed to recognize that forces both outside and inside individuals might affect their likelihood of breaking the law. This view was the central insight of a new way of thinking, **positivism,** which came to dominate the nineteenth century and derived from the great discoveries in the physical sciences of Galileo, Newton, and others. These discoveries indicated to social philosophers the potential of using science to understand not only the physical world but also the social world.

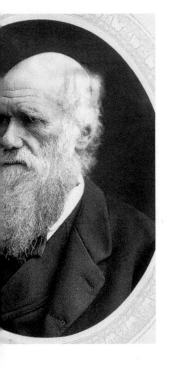

Charles Darwin's theory of evolution established the credibility of science for understanding human behavior and helped usher in scientific explanations of criminal behavior.

French social philosopher Auguste Comte (1798–1857) founded the positive school of philosophy with the publication of his six-volume *Cours de Philosophie Positive (Course in Positive Philosophy)* between 1830 and 1842. Comte argued that human behavior is determined by forces beyond the individual's control. Biologists and psychologists generally locate these forces inside the individual, whereas sociologists find them outside the individual. Research in biology, psychology, and sociology that attempts to explain what causes crime is all positivist in its orientation, even though these disciplines' perspectives differ in many other ways.

The rise of science as a mode of inquiry was cemented in 1859 with the publication of Charles Darwin's *Origin of Species*, in which he outlined his theory of evolution, and in 1871 with the publication of his book on human evolution, *Descent of Man.* The idea that science could explain the origin and development of the human species was revolutionary. It spawned great controversy at the time of Darwin's publications and is still attacked today by people who accept the biblical story of creation. However, Darwin's theory eventually dominated the study of evolution and also established the credibility of science for understanding human behavior and other social and physical phenomena.

Since the time of Comte and Darwin, positivism has guided the study of crime and other human behaviors. Although positivist research has greatly increased our understanding of the origins of crime, critics charge it with several shortcomings (Bernard, Snipes, and Gerould 2009). First, positivism accepts the state's definition of crime by ignoring the possibility that society's ruling groups define what is criminal. Positivism thus accepts the legitimacy of a social system that may contain serious injustices. Second, in arguing that external and internal forces affect individual criminal behavior, positivism sometimes paints an overly deterministic model of human behavior that denies free will altogether. Third, positivism assumes that criminals are different from the rest of us not only in their behavior, but also in the biological, psychological, and social factors determining their behavior. Noncriminals are thus normal, and criminals are abnormal and even inferior. As self-report studies indicate, however, the line between criminals and noncriminals might be very thin, with "noncriminals" very capable of breaking the law. Despite these criticisms, positivism remains the dominant approach in criminology. This is true for virtually all biologists and psychologists who study crime, but also true, despite notable exceptions, for most sociologists.

Neoclassical Perspectives

We now turn to neoclassical explanations of crime. They are called *neoclassical* because they all ultimately rest on the classical view that criminals are normal, rational individuals who choose to commit crime after calculating the potential risks and rewards of doing so. The three neoclassical explanations we discuss all share this fundamental assumption, even if they differ in other respects. They should thus be viewed as "close cousins" with certain different emphases that ultimately all manifest the classical view just described. As such, they are often said to have revived classical theory.

RATIONAL CHOICE THEORY

Contemporary **rational choice theory** assumes that potential offenders choose whether to commit crime after carefully calculating the possible rewards and risks. An individual commits crime after deciding that the rewards outweigh the risks and does not commit crime after deciding that the risks outweigh the rewards.

As was just stated, the roots of rational choice theory lie in the classical school, but its modern inspiration comes from economic models of rational decision making and more generally from a growing emphasis in sociology and other fields on the rationality of human behavior (McCarthy 2002). In criminology, the introduction of rational choice theory is widely credited to a very influential journal article published more than four decades ago by Gary S. Becker, a famed economist at the University of Chicago (Becker 1968). Becker wrote that choosing whether to commit crime is akin to choosing whether to buy almost any product that consumers purchase. Following what is now termed Becker's *expected utility model*, if individuals decide that the expected utility, or monetary value, of committing a crime exceeds the expected utility of not committing a crime, they decide as rational actors to commit it. Conversely, if they decide that the expected utility of not committing a crime exceeds the expected utility of committing it, they decide not to commit it. In making these decisions, they take into account several factors, including: (1) their possible opportunities for earning money from legitimate occupations; (2) the amount of legitimate money they might earn; (3) the amount of money they might gain from committing crime; (4) the possibility of being arrested for committing crime; and (5) the possibility of being punished if arrested.

In addition to taking into account all these factors, Becker added, people committing crime resemble consumers in at least one other respect. Consumers use whatever information they have to decide how to spend their money. Sometimes they make good decisions, and sometimes they make bad decisions, but whatever decisions they do make are based on a calculation of the relative benefits and costs of the decision. Criminals are no different. They decide whether to commit crime based on whatever information they have; sometimes they make good decisions from their perspective (i.e., they commit a financially beneficial crime and get away with it), and sometimes they make bad decisions (i.e., they get caught).

In likening decisions to commit crime to decisions to purchase a product, Becker explicitly stated that sociological concepts like anomie and differential association are *unimportant* for these decisions. As two scholars have summarized Becker's view on this issue, "As an economic purist, he asserts provocatively that there is little reason for theorizing that treats offenders as if they have a special character that leads them to crime. Becker extends his logic to conclude that the most prominent theories of motivation in criminology are not needed; basic economics addresses their problem sufficiently. Criminal offenders are normal, reasoning economic actors responding to market forces" (Hochstetler and Bouffard 2010: 20–21). However, other economists recognize that concepts from sociology and the other social sciences improve their economic models of criminal behavior (O'Donoghue and Rabin 2001).

As might be expected, Becker's expected utility model of criminal behavior was initially popular but also controversial. Subsequent development of rational choice theory retained Becker's emphasis on the overall rationality of crime, but did not try to reduce decisions to commit crime to a simple matter of economics. Still, most work using a rational choice perspective takes motivation to commit crime as a "given"; that is, it assumes that there will always be people motivated to commit crime and that no special explanation is needed of why some people are more motivated than other people in this regard. Using this assumption of a general motivation to commit crime, the rational choice literature focuses instead on understanding how individuals reach decisions to commit crime and the circumstances that affect their decision making. In doing so, the literature focuses more on decisions to commit a particular crime at a particular time and in a particular place (*event decisions*) than on decisions to commit crime in the first place (*involvement decisions*). Sociological explanations may help understand the latter decisions, many rational choice theorists acknowledge, but rational choice explanations are needed to help understand decisions to commit a specific crime under specific circumstances.

These general assumptions and focus were developed and popularized by two very influential theorists in contemporary rational choice theory, Derek B. Cornish and Ronald V. Clarke (Clarke and Cornish 1985; Clarke and Cornish 2001; Cornish and Clarke 1986). As these authors note, criminology had previously neglected the actual decision-making processes of criminals. In contrast, their rational choice perspective focuses specifically on these processes, as it assumes that offenders choose to commit crime because of the benefits it brings them. Given this assumption, their rational choice perspective "explains the conditions needed for specific crimes to occur, not just why people become involved in crime. It makes little distinction between offenders and nonoffenders and emphasizes the role of crime opportunities in causation" (Clarke and Cornish 2001: 23).

In addition to these elements, Cornish and Clarke emphasized that potential offenders take into account other possible benefits of crime beyond monetary gain, including fun, excitement, and prestige. They also emphasized that offenders do not always have the time or ability

Contemporary rational choice theory assumes that potential offenders take into account other possible benefits of crime beyond monetary gain, including fun, excitement, and prestige.

to gather all information relevant to their decision, and neither do they always have the time and ability to analyze this information completely and accurately. To this extent, criminal offenders are acting with *limited* or *bounded* rationality, as their decision making is often imperfect. Nonetheless, offenders still make decisions that appear rational to them at the time they make them.

Like other rational choice theorists, Cornish and Clarke (2001) distinguish between involvement decisions and event decisions, mentioned just earlier, and focus more on the latter than on the former. Event decisions have at least five stages: (1) preparing to commit a crime; (2) selecting a target; (3) committing the crime; (4) escaping; and (5) aftermath of the crime. Involvement decisions have three stages: (1) committing crime for the first time (*initiation*); (2) continuing to commit crime (*habituation*); and (3) ceasing to commit crime (*desistance*). For a comprehensive understanding of crime, the factors affecting all these decisions must be fully understood.

In this regard, the rational choice perspective has made valuable contributions to understanding event decisions, which criminological theory had previously neglected. In explaining these decisions, the perspective emphasizes two related concepts: (1) *situational factors* (aspects of the immediate physical setting, such as street lighting and the presence or absence of surveillance cameras); and (2) the *opportunities* that exist, or fail to exist, for an offender to commit crime without fear of arrest or other negative consequences. According to Cornish and Clarke, this emphasis in turn leads the rational choice perspective to regard criminals as not very different from noncriminals, as it argues that even normally law-abiding people may turn to crime if the need and temptation are great enough and if the opportunity presents itself.

Evaluating Rational Choice Theory

Rational choice theory has made major contributions to the understanding of criminal behavior by focusing on offenders' decision making. Studies of active (i.e., not incarcerated) robbers, burglars, and other offenders find that they do indeed often plan their crimes by taking into account their chances of being caught and also their chances of being put in danger by victims who resist the crime (Cromwell 1994; McCarthy and Hagan 2005; Wright and Decker 1994; Wright and Decker 1998). Burglars make sure no one is home before they break into a house, and robbers make sure that no police or bystanders are around before they hold someone up (Bernasco and Block 2009; Bernasco and Luykx 2003). White-collar criminals in the world of corporations seem to plan their crimes very carefully (Piquero, Exum, and Simpson 2005). In all these ways, offenders act rationally and proceed only if they perceive that the potential benefits outweigh the potential risks, just as rational choice theory assumes.

The focus of rational choice theory on the criminal event, and especially on the situational factors and opportunities that affect decisions to commit crime, has also made a major contribution. It reminds us that criminals do make choices (Nagin 2007), that criminal behavior is more likely if opportunities for it exist, and that these opportunities must be addressed for crime to be reduced. This focus underlies the work on situational crime prevention that is discussed later in this chapter.

Despite these contributions, rational choice theory has been criticized for exaggerating the rationality of criminal offenders, who often do not think or act as deliberately as rational choice theory implies. Evidence of this problem comes from the studies of active burglars and robbers just mentioned (Shover and Copes 2010). Although, as was noted, many offenders plan their crimes to some degree and try to ensure that they do not get caught, many other offenders actually give very little thought, if any, to this prospect. As one scholar put it, they "simply do not think about the possible legal consequences of their criminal actions before committing crimes" (Tunnell 1990:680). Some offenders also have a fatalistic attitude and go ahead and commit a crime even if they think they might be arrested (Tunnell

International Focus

Mandatory Penalties in International Perspective

A hallmark of the "get tough" approach that has guided U.S. criminal justice policy since the 1970s is the use of mandatory penalties. These include additional prison time for crimes involving the use of guns; long, automatic prison terms for drug crimes and violent crimes; and additional prison time for repeat offenders. These penalties have been intended to deter potential criminal offenders and simply to keep those already convicted locked up for longer durations.

Despite these goals, a large body of research has found that mandatory penalties have had only a small impact, and probably no impact, on the crime rate. This small or nil impact partly reflects the several reasons discussed in the text for why the general deterrent impact of law is usually low or nonexistent. In addition to these reasons, mandatory penalties are not consistently applied. Recognizing that the prison system is already overcrowded, prosecutors often avoid mandatory penalties by charging defendants with lesser crimes. They also reduce the charges because defendants facing long, automatic prison terms have little incentive to forgo jury trials, which are long and expensive. As Samuel Walker (2011:163) notes, "An increase in the severity of the potential punishment creates pressure to avoid its actual application."

The conclusion that mandatory penalties in the United States do not work as intended would be reinforced if it were also found in other nations. However, no other Western nation has enacted mandatory penalties to the extent found in the United States. A few nations do have these penalties to

some degree, including Australia, Canada, England and Wales, and South Africa. The effects of mandatory penalties in these nations have been studied, and these studies find that prosecutors and judges find ways to circumvent the harsh penalties. They also find that harsher penalties, including mandatory penalties, do not reduce crime.

For example, the Sentencing Advisory Council in Australia's state of Victoria concluded, "Ultimately, current research in this area indicates that there is a very low likelihood that a mandatory sentencing regime will deliver on its [deterrent] aims." The Canadian Sentencing Commission similarly observed, "Evidence does not support the notion that variations in sanctions . . . affect the deterrent value of sentences. In other words, deterrence cannot be used with empirical justification, to guide the imposition of sentences." The National Research Institute of Policy in Finland concluded, "Can our long prison sentences be defended on the basis of a cost/benefit assessment of their general preventative effect? The answer of the criminological expertise was no."

These international assessments on mandatory penalties and general deterrence reinforce the conclusion from U.S. research that mandatory penalties and other harsher punishments have little or no general deterrent effect. This body of research in the United States and elsewhere leads deterrence expert Michael Tonry (2009:65) to observe, "There is no credible evidence that the enactment or implementation of such sentences has significant deterrent effects."

Sources: Tonry 2009; Walker 2011.

1996). Research on prisoners also finds that about half of all inmates were under the influence of alcohol and/or drugs at the time of their offense (Beck et al. 2000), making it difficult or impossible to think carefully about the possible consequences of their actions. Further, many crimes are obviously violent crimes, and these crimes often tend to be very emotional in nature. People committing them act from strong emotions, such as anger and jealousy, and thus are not able to carefully consider the consequences of their actions as they strike out against someone. For all these reasons, many offenders do not act in the rather careful, deliberate manner that rational choice theory assumes.

DETERRENCE THEORY

Because rational choice theory assumes that criminals weigh the risks of their actions, it implies that they can be deterred from committing crime if the potential risks seem too certain or too severe, as Beccaria argued in his famous treatise. To turn that around, theoretical belief in the law's deterrent impact is based on a rational choice view of potential criminals. As two scholars have observed, "What makes deterrence work is that human beings are both rational and self-interested beings. Persons make rational assessments of the expected costs and benefits of making numerous decisions—buying a house or car, changing jobs, committing a crime—and choose the line of behavior that is most beneficial (profitable) and least costly" (Paternoster and Bachman 2001:14). For obvious reasons, then, rational choice theory is closely aligned with **deterrence theory,** which assumes that potential and actual legal punishment can deter crime. In fact, the two theories are often considered synonymous (Matsueda, Kreager, and Huizinga 2006). Their assumptions underlie the "get tough" approach, involving harsher punishment and more prisons, that the United States has used since the 1970s to fight crime.

TYPES OF DETERRENCE

In addressing the deterrent effect of the law, scholars distinguish several types of deterrence. A first distinction is between absolute deterrence and marginal deterrence. **Absolute deterrence** refers to the effect of having some legal punishment (arrest, incarceration, and so forth) versus the effect of having no legal punishment. The law certainly has a very strong absolute deterrent effect; if the criminal justice system did not exist, crime would be much higher, or so most scholars believe. In the real world, of course, we usually do not have to worry about the criminal justice system disappearing short of a natural or human disaster. Thus, questions of deterrence are actually questions of **marginal deterrence,** which refers to the effect of increasing the severity, certainty, and/or swiftness of legal punishment.

A second distinction is between general and specific deterrence. *General deterrence* occurs when members of the public decide not to break the law because they fear legal punishment. To take a traffic example, we may obey the speed limit because we do not want to get a speeding ticket. **Specific deterrence** (also called *individual deterrence*) occurs when offenders *already punished* for lawbreaking decide not to commit *another* crime because they do not want to face legal consequences again. Remaining with our traffic example, if we have already received a speeding ticket or two and are close to losing our license, we may obey the speed limit because we do not want to suffer further consequences.

A final distinction is between objective and subjective deterrence. **Objective deterrence** refers to the impact of *actual* legal punishment, whereas **subjective deterrence** refers to the impact of people's *perceptions* of the likelihood and severity of legal punishment. Deterrence theory predicts that people are deterred from crime by actual legal punishment that is certain and severe and also by their own perceptions that legal punishment will be certain and severe.

Taking a Closer Look at Deterrence

In considering how much marginal deterrent impact the criminal law might have, it is important to keep in mind several considerations that affect the size of any impact that can be expected.

A first consideration concerns the *type of criminal offense.* Simply put, some types of crime might be more deterrable than other types of crime. A well-known distinction

Violence is expressive behavior. As such, it is relatively difficult to deter by the threat of arrest and punishment.

here is between **instrumental offenses,** those committed for material gain with some degree of planning, and **expressive offenses,** those committed for emotional reasons and with little or no planning. William Chambliss (1967), who popularized this distinction, thought that instrumental crimes are more deterrable than expressive crimes because they are relatively unemotional and planned. Because the people committing expressive crimes are by definition acting emotionally, they often do not take the time to think about the legal consequences of their actions. All things equal, then, marginal deterrence should be higher for instrumental crimes than for expressive crimes, and it might in fact be very low for these latter offenses.

A second consideration, according to Chambliss (1967), is whether offenders have high or low commitment to criminal behavior. Professional criminals such as "cat burglars" are very skilled and also very committed to their way of life; drug addicts are also very committed, because of their addiction, to using illegal drugs. In contrast, amateur criminals such as teenagers who take a car on a joy ride are less committed to criminal behavior. Chambliss said that offenders with higher commitment to their crime are less likely to be deterred by legal punishment.

A final consideration is whether a crime tends to occur in public, such as robbery, or in private, such as domestic violence and some illegal drug use. Public crimes, precisely because they are public and thus potentially more noticeable, are more deterrable by legal punishment, all things equal, than private crimes.

Putting all these considerations together, expressive crimes are less deterrable than instrumental crimes; high-commitment offenders are less deterrable than low-commitment offenders; and public crimes are more deterrable than private crimes. Efforts that try to increase marginal deterrence by making arrest more certain and/or by making punishment harsher are thus likely to have only a relatively small deterrent effect on expressive crimes, on crimes involving high-commitment offenders, and on private offenses. These relatively undeterrable crimes involve many violent and property offenses, and perhaps the bulk of these offenses.

This pessimistic appraisal of the expected size of any marginal deterrent effect becomes even more pessimistic when we recall the studies of active burglars and robbers, discussed earlier, that focus on their decision making. Although these individuals are committing instrumental offenses, recall that many of them do not really think about their chances of getting caught. Others do think about their chances of getting caught but plan their crimes so that they will not be arrested. Still others have a fatalistic attitude and commit a crime with the expectation of being arrested. All these offenders are relatively undeterrable by legal punishment. Also recall that up to half of all offenders are on drugs and/or alcohol at the time of their offense; they, too, are undeterrable by legal punishment. Many offenders, then, do not think or act in the way they must think or act for marginal deterrence to have a relatively large impact (Shover and Copes 2010).

Additional considerations add even further to this pessimistic appraisal (Walker 2011). First, arrest and imprisonment have become so common in the United States, especially among young males in large cities, that scholars think these legal sanctions have lost the stigma they used to have (Hirschfield 2008). Rather, these sanctions have become an expectation, and, if this is true, not a deterrent. Second, arrest and imprisonment have been found to increase the feelings of masculinity of urban youths: they become more "macho" and are more likely to reoffend for that reason (Rios 2009). Third, increased penalties and other deterrence-oriented criminal justice policies are not always implemented as legislators might have expected. For example, prosecutors might not charge an offender with the maximum charge because of prison overcrowding. If these deterrent policies are not fully implemented, then their deterrent impact cannot be expected to be very high.

Fourth, the chances of arrest and imprisonment are so low that it would be surprising if legal sanctions did have a high deterrent impact. Victims of violent and property crime report only about 40 percent of their victimizations to the police, and that police make an arrest in only about 20 percent of the crimes known to them. Putting these figures together yields a rough arrest rate of only 8 percent for all violent and property crime. Less than one-fifth of these arrests result in a felony conviction and imprisonment, resulting in a risk of imprisonment of less than 2 percent of all violent and property crime. On TV crime shows, the "perp" usually gets what is coming to him, but in the real world of crime, the perp actually has an incredibly low risk of arrest and punishment. This risk is so low that a strong deterrent effect of the law cannot be expected.

Research on Deterrence

All these considerations suggest that the size of the marginal deterrent effect of legal punishment is likely to be relatively small. Research on deterrence generally confirms this pessimistic expectation. Most research has focused on the **certainty** of punishment (the likelihood of being arrested) and on the **severity** of punishment (whether someone is incarcerated and, if so, for how long).

Early research found that states with high certainty rates, measured as the number of arrests divided by the number of known crimes, had lower crime rates, as deterrence theory would predict. Some early studies also found that states with more severe punishment again had lower crime rates (Gibbs 1968; Tittle 1969). Although these findings indicated a marginal deterrent effect, some scholars challenged this interpretation and instead argued that crime rates affect certainty and severity (Decker and Kohfeld 1985; Pontell 1984). In this way of thinking, called the **system capacity argument,** areas with high levels of crime have lower arrest rates for two reasons: their police are "extra" busy, and their police also realize that too many arrests would overburden the criminal justice system. For these reasons, areas with high crime rates end up with low certainty rates. Similarly, areas with high crime rates also have lower severity of punishment because their prisons are too full to handle their many offenders. Prosecutors and judges both realize this, and prosecutors seek reduced charges and judges impose shorter sentences.

More recent research on deterrence has been much more methodologically sophisticated than the early research. Suffice it to say here that the recent evidence generally finds that arrest and punishment (or, to be more precise, increases in the probability of being arrested and more severely punished) have only a weak general or specific deterrent effect on crime and delinquency, and perhaps no effect at all (Doob and Webster 2003; Pratt et al. 2006; Walker 2011). A recent review concluded that "there is little credible evidence that changes in sanctions affect crime rates" (Tonry 2008:279). To the extent that a deterrent effect does exist, it exists more for the certainty of punishment than for the severity of punishment.

For example, although deterrence theory predicts that higher imprisonment rates should produce lower crime rates, this pattern often does not occur: sometimes crime rates decline when imprisonment rates rise, as deterrence theory would predict, but sometimes crime rates decline only slightly, do not change at all, or even increase. During

☻ Crime and Controversy

Three Strikes Laws Strike Out

Beginning in the 1990s, several states enacted so-called "three strikes" laws in an effort to reduce the crime rate. These laws required life imprisonment or, at the least, a very long prison sentence for offenders convicted of their second or third felony. A major reason given for these laws was that they would send a message to potential offenders and thus deter them from committing their third felony, and perhaps even their first or second felony.

The introduction of these laws provided criminologists an opportunity to test their deterrent impact. Drawing on deterrence theory, they gathered and analyzed various kinds of data to test the hypothesis that three strikes laws would reduce the street crime rate.

A central conclusion that emerges from this body of research is that the three strikes laws have had no discernible deterrent effect on criminal behavior. During the 1990s, violent crime dropped throughout the nation, but it dropped at a greater rate in states that did *not* enact three strikes laws than in states that did enact them. Moreover, studies of specific states that enacted three strikes laws found that crime did not fall at a greater rate in those states after the laws came into effect. Some studies even find that homicides *increased* after three strikes laws were enacted, perhaps because offenders who are committing their third (or fourth, etc.) felony do not want to risk life imprisonment and thus decide to kill their victim to make it more difficult to arrest and convict them.

If three strikes laws have not reduced crime, they have increased the number of prison inmates serving life sentences or very long terms. Many of these inmates will stay in prison long after they would have "aged out" of crime, imposing a considerable financial cost not only from the cost of keeping them in prison, but also from the geriatric medical care many of them need. Three strikes laws thus provide important evidence against deterrence theory, and they also illustrate the financial costs that the "get tough" policy since the 1970s has incurred.

Sources: Ehlers, Schiraldi, and Ziedenberg 2004; Kovandzic, Sloan, and Vieraitis 2004; Marvell and Moody 2001; Walker 2011.

the late 1980s, U.S. imprisonment rates rose, but so did crime rates. Although crime rates finally declined after the early 1990s as imprisonment rates continued to rise, crime declined less in states with the greatest increase in imprisonment rates than in states with lower increases in imprisonment rates. Also, deterrence theory predicts that when penalties for certain crimes are made harsher, the rates of these crimes should decline, but once again this often does not happen (Walker 2011).

What about specific deterrence? Although it seems obvious that offenders who are arrested and imprisoned should reoffend less because of their punishment, evidence of this specific deterrent effect is mixed at best. There is even evidence of an opposite effect: that punishment *increases* the chances that offenders will break the law again (Nieuwbeerta, Nagin, and Blokland 2009; Pogarsky and Piquero 2003). A recent review of the literature on this issue concluded that "most studies of the impact of imprisonment on subsequent criminality find [either] no effect or a criminogenic [crime-causing] effect" (Nagin, Cullen, and Jonson 2009:121). The authors added that this conclusion "casts doubt on claims that imprisonment has strong specific deterrent effects" (p. 115).

As was suggested earlier, it should not be very surprising that deterrence research casts doubt on the size of general and specific deterrent effects. For deterrence to occur, criminals must calculate their behavior, as rational choice and deterrence theories assume they do. This assumption is critical for deterrence theory, because if criminals did not weigh the risks of their behavior, then the threat of arrest and punishment could not deter them. Yet, as we have seen, studies of active offenders do not provide much support for this assumption (Shover and Copes 2010). Although some crimes, such as corporate crime, involve careful planning and weighing of all risks, many other crimes typically do not involve such efforts, and many "street crime" offenders do not think and act in the ways that rational choice and deterrence theories assume. Most criminals are smart enough to avoid committing a crime in front of a police station or elsewhere where they might be detected, but in other places many apparently do not worry about being arrested and punished. For this reason, increases in the penalties for crimes do not seem to deter them.

Increases in penalties for crime do not seem to deter criminals, in part because they do not act in the ways that rational choice and deterrence theories assume.

Some research also documents the deterrent effect of internal punishment (e.g., guilt, shame, embarrassment, and conscience) and of informal sanctions such as the disapproval of friends and loved ones (Nagin and Pogarsky 2001). However, such evidence says nothing about the deterrent effect of *legal* punishment (Akers and Sellers 2009).

In sum, deterrence research suggests that the general and specific deterrent effect of legal sanctions is small or nonexistent. Certain policing strategies do seem to deter some types of crime, but strategies involving harsher punishment generally do not seem to deter crime. Although deterrence theory might sound appealing at first glance, then, deterrence is more of a dream than a reality in the real world of crime.

ROUTINE ACTIVITIES THEORY

A third and very influential neoclassical perspective is **routine activities theory** (also called *routine activity theory*) is an explanation of criminal victimization patterns. To briefly recall that discussion, routine activities theory assumes that crime is more likely when three factors are simultaneously present: (1) motivated offenders; (2) attractive targets; and (3) an absence of guardianship (such as police, bystanders, and even a dog). Because the theory also assumes that offenders are more likely to decide to commit crime when they have attractive targets and when there are no guardians, it reflects rational choice assumptions of criminal decision making and is considered a neoclassical theory.

Routine activities theory was introduced in 1979 by Lawrence E. Cohen and Marcus Felson (Cohen and Felson 1979) and elaborated in other works (e.g., Felson and Boba 2010). Cohen and Felson wrote that for crime to happen, offenders, targets, and the absence of guardians must all converge at the same time and in the same location. Because routine activities of everyday life affect the likelihood of this convergence, when people's routine activities change, crime rates change as well. Like rational choice theory, routine activities theory further assumes there will always be a supply of motivated offenders, and it does not try to explain why some people are more motivated than others to commit crime, nor why motivation to commit crime might change as other social changes occur. As Cohen and Felson maintain (1979: 604), "The convergence in time and space of suitable targets and the absence of capable guardians can lead to large increases in crime rates without any increase or change in the structural conditions that motivate individuals to engage in crime." As they imply, the theory instead focuses on changes in the supply of attractive targets and in the presence or absence of guardianship as key variables affecting changes in crime rates. Because these variables affect the opportunity for offenders to commit crime, or what Cohen and Felson (1979: 592) call the "criminal opportunity structure," routine activities theory is often considered an *opportunity theory* of crime.

Cohen and Felson reasoned that routine activities inside or near one's home result in less victimization than activities that occur away from home. When people are at home, they are safer from burglary, because they provide guardianship for their home, and they are also safer from robbery and other predatory crimes, because they are not out in public providing attractive targets for motivated offenders. Cohen and Felson also reasoned that as smaller and more expensive consumer items go on the market, people are more likely to have these items in their homes or on their persons when away from home, making them attractive targets for offenders. The authors then used these two sets of reasoning to help understand two important trends in crime and victimization: (1) differences in criminal victimization rates for various categories of people, such as young versus old; and (2) why U.S. crime rates increased during the 1960s even though poverty and unemployment fell and median income and education levels rose during that decade.

For example, they hypothesized that young people should have higher victimization rates than older people because they spend so much more time away from home, and that is exactly what data from national victimization surveys find. They also hypothesized that single-person households should suffer higher burglary rates than multiple-person households because they are have less guardianship (i.e., they are more likely to be empty at any one time or to have fewer people at home when someone is there), and that is also what victimization data find.

Turning to the 1960s crime rate increase, Cohen and Felson argued that this increase resulted from the simultaneous increase in suitable targets and decrease of guardianship during that decade. Regarding guardianship, for example, many more women began working outside the home during the 1960s, and many more residences were occupied by only one person. These two facts meant that many more homes began to be empty most of the day as people went to work. Not surprisingly, burglary rates increased dramatically during the 1960s. Regarding target availability, Cohen and Felson found that the sales of consumer goods increased greatly during the 1960s, as did the sale of smaller and more valuable goods (i.e., smaller televisions). These trends provided "more suitable property available for theft" (p. 599), and more such theft occurred.

Cohen and Felson concluded that that crime results in part from the activities that so many people ordinarily enjoy. As they put it, "It is ironic that the very factors which increase the opportunity to enjoy the benefits of life also may increase the opportunity for predatory violations. For example, automobiles provide freedom of movement to offend- ers as well as average citizens and offer vulnerable targets for theft. . . . Rather than assuming that predatory crime is simply an indicator of social breakdown, one might take it as a byproduct of freedom and prosperity as they manifest themselves in the routine activities of everyday life" (p. 605).

Evaluating Routine Activities Theory

In the more than three decades since its introduction, routine activities theory has proven very popular and has stimulated much research (Marcum 2010). It is popular be- cause it seems to explain important aspects of differences in crime rates among different categories of people and among different locations, and because it also seems to explain important aspects of changes in crime rates over time. For example, crime is ordinarily higher during the summer than other times of the year. Routine activities theory provides an explanation for this trend. Homes are more likely to be empty during the summer as people travel, and homes' windows are more likely to be open. These two facts make homes more vulnerable to burglary during the summer. During the summer, people are also more likely to be out in public, increasing their vulnerability to crimes like robbery and assault. To take another example, locations in cities with high numbers of bars and taverns have higher rates of robbery and assault (Roncek and Maier 1991). People visiting these establishments are attractive targets because they tend to carry relatively large sums of money or credit/debit cards, and because they lack personal guardianship once they become inebriated. As routine activities theory would predict, the presence of these establishments contributes to higher rates of crime and victimization.

The popularity of routine activities theory has increased as various works have added to the original insights of Cohen and Felson. Certain studies have deepened understanding of the factors that contribute to target availability and the absence of guardianship. For example, adolescents with strong bonds to their parents reduce their target availability because they are more likely to stay home and not venture out to places where they might encounter motivated offenders (Schreck and Fisher 2004). Other work has extended the theoretical scope of routine activities theory. Although the theory was originally developed to explain victimization, some scholars have used it to explain offending. In their way of thinking, individuals' routine activities can make it more or less likely that they will have the opportunity to offend. When they do have this opportunity, they are more likely to commit crime. For example, adolescents who spend more time away from home and who are not involved in youth activities at school or elsewhere have more opportunity to get in trouble, and so they do (Osgood and Anderson 2004; Osgood et al. 1996).

Situational crime prevention involves efforts in specific locations to reduce the opportunity for criminal behavior. Camera surveillance on city streets is an example of this type of crime prevention.

In one possible problem, routine activities theory has been criticized for ignoring the factors that motivate offenders to commit crime (Akers and Sellers 2009). In their original formulation, Cohen and Felson readily conceded this neglect but argued the importance of considering the factors on which they did focus: target suitability and the absence of guardianship.

Situational Crime Prevention

One of the major contributions of routine activities theory, along with rational choice theory, has been the stimulation of work on **situational crime prevention,** or efforts in specific locations that aim to "reduce exposure to motivated offenders, decrease target suitability, and increase capable guardianship" (Knepper 2009; Marcum 2010: 54; Welsh and Farrington 2009). These efforts try to reduce the opportunities for committing crime by accomplishing all three of these goals. Examples of these efforts include installing or increasing lighting and camera surveillance on city streets or in public parks, and providing and installing better security systems for motor vehicles, commercial buildings, and homes. Another example is *hot-spot policing,* which involves police patrol of high-crime areas (Braga and Bond 2008).

One concern regarding these efforts is that crime might simply be displaced to other locations and to other victims. However, a recent analysis of situational crime-prevention studies concluded that displacement is not a problem (Guerette and Bowers 2009). Sometimes it does occur, but just as often the opposite consequence (*diffusion of benefits*) happens, in which crime is reduced in nearby locations. Moreover, when displacement does occur, the additional crime elsewhere is lower than the crime that was displaced, resulting in a lower crime rate overall. The authors of this analysis concluded that their results "provide continued support for the view that crime does not simply relocate in the aftermath of situational interventions. Instead, crime displacement seems to be the exception rather than the rule, and it is sometimes more likely that diffusion of crime-control benefit will occur. The findings also indicate that when displacement does occur, on average, it tends to be less than the gains achieved by the situational intervention, which means that the initiatives remained worthwhile" (p. 1357).

Conclusion

Classical and neoclassical perspectives all assume that individuals commit crime when they decide that the potential gains outweigh the potential costs. They ultimately attribute crime to the choices offenders make about their own behavior, and they explicitly or implicitly state that increasing the risk of legal punishment should reduce crime. Crime policies based on these views aim to affect offending decisions by making punishment more certain and more severe. However, it is unclear whether the decision making of potential criminals follows the rational choice model, as well as whether increasing the certainty and severity of punishment can reduce crime rates significantly. Moreover, the world of classical and neoclassical perspectives is largely devoid of social inequality. To the extent that inequality helps generate criminality, these perspectives ignore significant sources of crime. At the same time, together they provide an important understanding of crime from the offender's perspective, and they have stimulated contemporary efforts in situational crime prevention that show promise in reducing crime.

Neoclassical perspectives are important for at least one other reason. Their emphasis on the rationality of criminals, belief in the deterrent power of law, and lack of emphasis on the social causes of crime are all reflected in the "get tough" approach that has guided U.S. criminal justice policy since the 1970s. Among other changes, this approach has involved mandatory incarceration and longer prison terms, which most criminologists probably think do little to reduce crime and cause many other problems (Clear 2010). Sound social policy must always be based on good theory, and the neoclassical perspectives are good theories in many ways. But the "get tough" approach is based on assumptions from these perspectives that do not stand up well upon closer inspection. Criminals often do not act as rationally as rational choice theory assumes, and deterrence does not work nearly as well as deterrence theory assumes. Moreover, the advocates of the "get tough" approach tend to minimize or deny the role played by poverty and other structural problems in criminal behavior. Cullen and Agnew (2006:460) say that this denial "ignores the rather substantial body of research showing that inequality and concentrated disadvantage are related to street crime."

Summary

1. To reduce crime most effectively, we must first understand why crime occurs. Biological and psychological explanations place the causes of crime inside the individual, whereas sociological explanations place the causes of crime in the social environment. To reduce crime, biology and psychology thus suggest the need to correct problems inside the individual, whereas sociology suggests the need to correct problems in the social environment.

2. Historically, deviance and crime were first attributed to angry gods and fiendish demons. The Age of Reason eventually led to more scientific explanations, especially those grounded in positivism, which attributes behavior to forces inside and outside the individual. The classical school of criminology arose with the work of writers such as Beccaria and Bentham, who believed that because people act to maximize pleasure and reduce pain, the legal system need only be sufficiently harsh to deter potential criminals from breaking the law.

3. Classical and neoclassical perspectives assume that potential criminals calculate whether lawbreaking will bring them more reward than risk and that increases in the certainty and severity of punishment will thus decrease their likelihood of engaging in crime. However, research finds that most criminals are not as calculating as rational choice theory assumes and that harsher and more certain legal punishment generally has only a weak or inconsistent effect on crime rates, or no effect at all.

Key Terms

absolute deterrence	expressive offenses	positivism	specific deterrence
certainty	general deterrence	rational choice theory	subjective deterrence
classical school	instrumental offenses	routine activities theory	system capacity argument
deterrence theory	marginal deterrence	severity	
Enlightenment	objective deterrence	situational crime prevention	

What Would You Do?

1. You are a policy advisor to a member of your state legislature. The legislature will soon be voting on a bill that would double the maximum prison term for anyone convicted of armed robbery. Your boss knows that you took a criminology course and has even seen this book proudly displayed on a bookcase in your office. She knows that the bill is very popular with the public, but wonders if it will really do much good and asks you to write a policy recommendation for her to read. What will you recommend to her? What will be the reasons for your recommendation?

2. You are a policy adviser to the mayor of a medium-sized city. A recent spurt of nighttime robberies has alarmed the city's residents and prompted the police to suspend vacation leave until the offenders can be arrested. Based on what you have read in this chapter, what would you advise the mayor to do to reduce the robbery problem in the city?

Index